BENJAMIN F. BART is professor of French and Director, Comparative Literature Program, University of Pittsburgh.

ROBERT FRANCIS COOK is a member of the Department of French at the University of Virginia.

The sources of *La Légende de Saint Julien l'Hospitalier*, one of Flaubert's finest literary works, have long been the subject of numerous conflicting theories. The implications of the controversy are broad and important, not only for Flaubert's work but also for our understanding of how writers generally use traditional material. Superficial resemblances have led critics to conclude that Flaubert relied heavily on a medieval tale of Saint Julian and that he borrowed details and specific phrases from his medieval predecessor. This book, by a world renowned specialist in Flaubert studies and a medieval philologist, demonstrates that the *Légende* is not medieval in structure or in spirit, and that its conception is distinctly modern; where Flaubert borrowed at all he used contemporary sources to recast the Julian legend in Romantic style. Bart and Cook establish definitely what the legendary sources were and show how Flaubert came into contact with them. Their extensive commentary compares the sources and the *Légende* in detail, explains the circumstances under which Flaubert used his materials, and analyses how they were woven into the texture of his own tale.

The book makes available source material scattered throughout obscure periodicals, reproduces accurately and dates correctly important segments of Flaubert's drafts and scenarios, and provides the first modern printed edition of the Alençon life of Saint Julian which Lecointre-Dupont adapted in 1838, thereby giving Flaubert indirect access to the old tale.

An Introductory chapter explores the broader question of the development of legends and how a particular legendary sequence, embodying powerful themes, was amplified and made explicit from the twelfth century to Flaubert's time.

BENJAMIN F. BART &

ROBERT FRANCIS COOK

The Legendary Sources of Flaubert's *Saint Julien*

University of Toronto Press

Toronto and Buffalo

© University of Toronto Press 1977
Toronto and Buffalo
Printed in Canada

Library of Congress Cataloging in Publication Data

Bart, Benjamin F
  The legendary sources of Flaubert's Saint Julien.
  (Romance series; 36)
  Bibliography: p.
  1. Flaubert, Gustave, 1821-1880. La légende de Saint
  Julien l'Hospitalier – Sources. I. Cook, Robert Francis,
  joint author. II. Title. III. Series: Romance series
  (Toronto) ; 36.
  PQ2246.L5B3   843'.8   77-7892
  ISBN 0-8020-5373-4

This book has been published during the
Sesquicentennial year of the University of Toronto

Je n'y comprends rien.
Comment a-t-il tiré ceci de cela?

Letter from Flaubert to Charpentier
16 February 1879

Contents

Preface

Over the past three-quarters of a century a considerable body of scholarship has examined the sources in legend upon which Flaubert drew to
write his account of the legend of *Saint Julien l'Hospitalier*. Scholars have
pointed most notably to the Julian window in Rouen Cathedral, the
Legenda aurea of Jacobus da Varagine, a study of stained-glass windows
written by Flaubert's friend Langlois, a nineteenth-century retelling of the
life of Julian based on a medieval manuscript at Alençon, and a further
medieval manuscript in the Bibliothèque Nationale, which also gives his
life. We shall examine the validity of each of these claims – almost all are
surely sound – but we shall also propose new approaches which, we believe,
reconcile many of the various discoveries and provide an integrated understanding of the long process of transformation which the legend underwent
during the medieval period and again in the nineteenth century.

'Comment a-t-il tiré ceci de cela?' Flaubert's question is the same one
which must be answered, openly or not, before any literary creation may
be fully understood. How is the *Légende de Saint Julien l'Hospitalier*, a
masterpiece of narrative craftsmanship and one of Flaubert's finest works,
related to the sequence of variegated forms of the story of Saint Julian,
whose history stretches further back into the Middle Ages than it is given
us to follow, yet had elements very close in time and place to Flaubert's
Tale itself? How much of the legendary material in Flaubert's *Légende* is
his own, and how much borrowed? How much of it is medieval, and how
much modern? In the hope of shedding genuine light on these obvious, but
still unanswered questions, we have made what is, to our knowledge, the
first attempt to write a complete study of all the scattered texts treated in
widely dispersed (and often fairly obscure) scholarly works, texts which
have never been fully discussed in relationship to each other before. We
shall limit ourselves, in this study, to the large issue of the legendary
sources and their influence on Flaubert's creation. Which of the versions

of the Julian legend were available to Flaubert, which did he know, and which can he be said, with certainty, to have actually used?

In the course of some three years' work on the versions of the Julian legend, we have found it useful to re-formulate, in our own terms and for our own purposes, one or two ideals of historical criticism which are older in fact than Flaubert's work itself, but which are, it seems, easily lost sight of in the heat of the source-chase. First, a source has had influence if the work of which it is a source could not have been the same without that influence. That much is patently obvious. A work is not the source of a second work if the author of the latter read the former, forgot it totally on both the conscious and the subconscious levels, and wrote exactly as he would have if he had never even read the first work. The notion that sources must thus be manifested in form leads to considerable reliance on internal or formal evidence: on resemblances and similarities between two books suspected to stand in a relationship involving influence. And, of course, internal evidence, similarity, is paradoxical. It is not only that it is vague or multivalent at times, to such a degree that it almost cries out for subjective evaluation. Sometimes it is also accidental, or the result of co-incidence; and such accidents of form may be neither detected, nor their existence disproven, by simple logic. This double ambiguity of internal evidence has led to situations in which each and every resemblance between two similar texts is explained as a borrowing, or dismissed as a coincidence, as the scholar's presuppositions in the matter of the text's history dictate. The paradox is real, and not so simple-minded as our statement may make it appear. To avoid falling into the trap along with certain of our predecessors, we have relied in the first instance exclusively upon external, historical evidence of Flaubert's contact with a given source before assuming any similarities to be meaningful (even though in one case we prefer to present the very striking internal evidence of Chapter Five before giving the external evidence in Chapter Six). On the other hand, when we reject totally a claimed source, it is on grounds of important extra-textual evidence and in the absence of any minimally acceptable internal evidence. Failing those criteria, we prefer not to judge: *Est quadam prodire tenus*, said Horace, *non datur ultra*. The very great importance some writers have wished to assign some sources, on rather uncertain evidence, seems justification enough for the risk we are taking of missing a source Flaubert cannot really be shown, beyond doubt, to have used.

Furthermore, the nature of coincidence and the rules of evidence have led us to consider a problem of definition never before treated in connection with the *Saint Julien l'Hospitalier*. The work appeared, after all, in a collection of short stories or at least of *contes*. But we think – and we find the omission of the point from previous criticism and scholarship is most serious – that the *Légende* really is the recounting of a *legend*, and that the difference between a novella or *conte* and a legend is an essential one. A legend is not free to develop in its own way, according to the requirements of its 'inner form,' or as the author comes upon suitable themes and materials for it. More exactly (and this is the burden of our first chapter), the legend undergoes that process gradually, and the development is the result of the collective, accretive work of several successive re-creators, all of whom respect almost entirely the structure already in place (for if they do not, the common legend they wish to exploit becomes unrecognizable). A legend is not a single and unique literary occurrence. The structure of the Julian story is at least partially fixed; that fact limits any author who takes it up, in important ways. Literature has done itself a disservice in this matter of nomenclature. For example, Victor Hugo strung a series of anecdotes into a loose sequence of his own invention and called it *Légende du Beau Pécopin et de la Belle Bauldour.* The terms *legend* and *legendary* are polysemic even within the discipline of literary criticism.

And yet Flaubert's *Légende* is one manifestation of a legend. If it is properly understood (and the proliferating texts of the twelfth and thirteenth centuries count for a great deal here), the legend is not just a story which is not true: short stories are that. But the author of the short story has certain freedoms which the re-creator of a legend does not have. By treating the *Saint Julien* in the same way that its medieval forbears (and indeed nearly all earlier medieval literature) must be treated, as subject to the power of tradition, we are able to concentrate on what Flaubert's achievement actually was. As scholars, critics, and historians, we can envisage no higher purpose.

Our route will be long and complex, for it must traverse at least three domains: the medieval creation of the Julian legend, its revival in new garb in the early nineteenth century, and only finally Flaubert's contribution to this long development, late in the century. It is our hope to have clarified both something of how traditional material evolves and something of what takes place when an individual creator elects to deal with it again at a much later time in the evolution of western culture.

Flaubert's *Légende de Saint Julien l'Hospitalier*, whose story line bears close relationships to the *Legenda aurea* and to a thirteenth-century French Prose Life of Julian, may be summarized as follows:

> The noble youth Julian, at whose birth mysterious prophecies seemed to portend for him both sainthood and a life of combat and secular glory, early showed equal fervour in performing his religious obligations and in hearing of great military exploits. His developing fascination with killing animals reached fulfilment when his father taught him

to hunt. Degenerating from his civilized state until 'he became like the animals,' he climaxed his slaughter in a first great hunt, during which no animal could resist his attack. At the end of the hunt, a stag he had fatally wounded pronounced a curse upon him: he would slay his parents. Thereupon, the stag died.

Fleeing his home to avoid the accomplishment of his fate, Julian achieved great military fame, which led to his winning the hand of an Emperor's daughter. He shunned hunting as connected with the curse, but eventually he was tempted into a second great hunt, in which none of his weapons were of any avail and hosts of animals crowded menacingly about him. Only dawn brought release. During his absence, however, his parents, who had long been seeking their lost son, came to his castle, were recognized and warmly received by his wife, and were honoured by being placed for the night in the bed of Julian and his wife. Returning to his castle, a frustrated and exasperated Julian found them there and, suspecting an adultery, slew them both in their sleep.

Fleeing again, Julian, alone, long sought a means of penance, until he established himself as a ferryman by a deserted river. There, awakening one stormy night to the call of a voice from the far side of the river, he crossed to ferry his caller back to the hospice, only to find a hideous leper awaiting him. Undaunted, Julian returned with him to his cabin, fed him, put him in his own bed, and finally lay with him to warm him with his own body. At this moment the leper transformed himself into the resplendent Christ and rose with Julian in his arms to heaven.

'Et voilà l'histoire de Saint Julien-l'Hospitalier telle à peu près qu'on la trouve sur un vitrail d'église dans mon pays.'

This book has been published with the help of a grant from the Humanities Research Council of Canada, using funds provided by the Canada Council, and with the help of grants from the University of Toronto and the Publications Fund of University of Toronto Press. We are grateful also for the opportunity to thank Douglas J. Daniels of Montana State University, who took time from a busy schedule to read and comment on this study in manuscript form. Our other debts are mentioned at appropriate places in the book.

The Saint Julian Window in Rouen Cathedral.

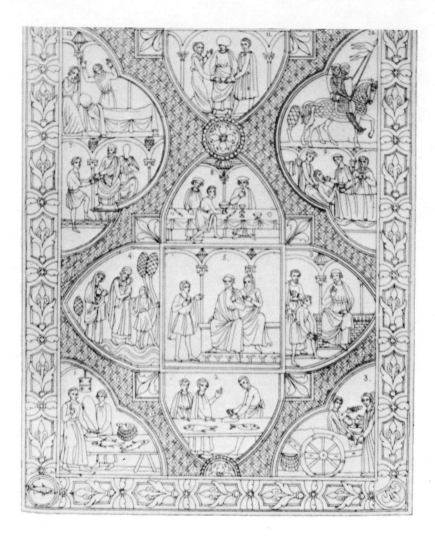

The Rouen Window. Detail: The donors; Julian's childhood; his marriage.

The Rouen Window. Detail: The arrival of Julian's parents; the parricide; the hospice; Christ's call is heard.

The Rouen Window. Detail: The couple's trial and their salvation;
Christ blessing.

The Legendary Sources of Flaubert's *Saint Julien*

CHAPTER ONE

The Genesis and Transmission of Legends: The Example of Saint Julian Hospitator

The creation of the medieval saints' Lives, a specifically Christian type of legend-making, may be seen as but one manifestation of mankind's age-old propensity for elaborating folklore. Of course legends are, as a general matter, both interesting to the literary scholar and frustrating to the historian, because they represent a nearly impenetrable mixture of traditions and inventions, of natural and un-natural. If we are to understand properly the nature and potentialities of the legendary sources available to Flaubert, however, and describe his use of these legends, we must first understand this legend-making process. Only a knowledge of what the legends are made of can elucidate the development of the Julian legend in the medieval period; and their history proves also to have bearing upon certain aspects of Flaubert's creative activity. The latter is our principal subject in this study; thus we have found it convenient to limit ourselves to a skeletal account, forbearing to pursue or even to define many of the questions that this chapter raises.[1]

---

1   We draw here principally upon: M. Oberziner, 'La Leggenda di S. Giuliano il parricida,' *Atti del Reale Istituto Veneto di scienza, lettere ed arti*, 93 (1933-34), Parte seconda, 253-309; and Baudouin de Gaiffier, 'La Légende de S. Julien L'Hospitalier,' *Analecta Bollandiana*, 63 (1945), 145-219. One may also consult two older, but still useful, studies: M. Schwob, 'Préface' to *La Légende de Saint Julien l'Hospitalier* (Paris: Ferroud, 1895), reprinted in *Spicilège* (Paris: Mercure de France, 1896), pp. 157-83; and G. Huet, 'Saint Julien L'Hospitalier,' *Mercure de France*, Tome 104, No. 385 (1 juillet 1913), 44-59. For a classic general study of the process of legend-making, see H. Delehaye, *Les Légendes hagiographiques*, 4th ed. (Brussels: Société des Bollandistes, 1955). Basic bibliography may be found in the *Encyclopedia Britannica*, s.v. *Hagiology*, and *The New Catholic Encyclopedia*, s.v. *Hagiography*. See also Vladimir Propp, trans. by Marguerite Derrida, Tzvetan Todorov, and Claude Kahn, *Morphologie du conte* (Paris: Poétique/Seuil, 1970).

A / THE HAGIOGRAPHICAL LEGEND
AS INSTRUCTION AND AS NARRATIVE

Two creative currents contributed Lives of saints to the stock preserved in the Western Christian tradition. An early, and largely pre-medieval current produced many Lives based on traditions having their origins with those who knew the martyrs and fathers themselves. The Middle Ages proper created for the most part another sort of saints' Lives – our subject here – which are not rooted in early Christian tradition even when they claim to be, but rather in what we would call folklore. They contain various motifs which they share with other Lives and with narratives of other types, and thus to modern eyes they seem clear examples of invention or fabrication, although neither their makers nor the medieval audience so perceived them. All this was true not only for saints such as Julian, who never existed, but also for historical persons, such as Elisabeth of Hungary. In the case of Julian, this ahistorical creative current extends from at least as early as the twelfth century to the end of the nineteenth century with Flaubert. It requires clarification if we are to understand what it represents in the hands of the latter.

For this purpose, we shall need to analyse as separate components aspects which normally occur as intertwined or even wholly integrated in actual medieval saints' Lives. We shall wish to distinguish among hagiography at one extreme, narrative fiction at the opposite extreme, and what we shall term 'hagiographical legend,' which lies between and encompasses aspects of both. The two extremes encroach upon the middle, of course, and our distinctions will be for purposes of analysis only: They are not meant to be general distinctions, but to explain why certain manipulations of the story matter occur.

The Life of a saint may be termed his 'story.' But, particularly in the early period of the development of such Lives, the dominant purpose was not precisely literary creation as we understand it today, but more instruction: to present didactically a Christian norm. Such a saint's Life did in fact take the form of a story, or successions of stories, each told in sequential form. Nevertheless, these 'stories' are not narrative fiction. As does any dogma or quasi-dogma, the account of a saint's life demands full acceptance on the part of the Christian believer, even when the account defies logic and normal causality; indeed, such miraculous aspects are of the essence in such Lives and constitute, in their didactic function, what we shall here term their hagiographical character. To buttress their claims to acceptance, such Lives are presented dogmatically as accepted truth, frequently with expressed or implied assertions of their descent from ancient tradition that is being handed down. As a concomitant, once certain hagiographical elements had been established for a given saint in a given tradition, they tended not to be altered.

Creative narrative fiction, on the other hand, has none of these characteristics: it cannot demand, but must rather seek, the reader's acceptance; its themes, subject, episodes, and techniques may perhaps be age-old, but it must present them in new garb; and, while a 'definitive edition' of a narrative is possible, no element of its make-up is unchangeable until that moment. On the contrary, the author of narrative fiction is always at liberty to change his story in the interests of giving his work more force, of pleasing his reader more, or of inducing more readily in the reader that willing suspension of disbelief he easily accords to narrative fiction, if it meets his minimal demands.[2]

It is, then, sometimes possible to separate narrative structure, which obeys its own impulses, from hagiography and its didacticism, which is attentive to the non-structural, external concerns it serves. For the purposes of our analysis, this distinction is central, since the hagiographical legend, such as the life of Julian, is an intermediate between hagiography and purer forms of narrative fiction, and owes some of its characteristics to each.[3] As we have described it, the hagiographical legend is a relatively late, typically medieval genre. In its developed form, it is *sui generis* and readily recognized as such, but it may be analyzed into its components. Some are hagiography, to be sure, but some tend toward what today would be found in narrative fiction, although the totality, the hagiographical legend, as we shall see, can never reach that latter stage. We shall need, then, to distinguish the hagiographical aspects and functions from those in which the canons of narrative fiction predominate.

2   We are assuming, with some modern specialists, that hagiography may thus be distinguished from pure narrative fiction by consideration of its intent. The first is above all normative and didactic; the second need not be. Our definitions and distinctions, elaborated for the purpose of this source study, do not correspond exactly to those in use elsewhere, notably Delehaye's, for he distinguishes truth and legend rather differently from the way we do; but our predecessors are not uniform either.
    'Hagiography' is widely used, as is 'hagiology,' in the literature of the discipline, to designate systematic study of saints' Lives; but we take the term in the equally common sense of the *creation* of orthodox Lives.
3   Our readers will have noticed that we are touching upon the old but incompletely understood notion of a literary intertwining of the hagiographical and the fictional modes of creation. We will later touch upon the possibilities of passage from the one mode to the other. While we are aware of the far-ranging implications these notions have for the study of medieval literature and aesthetics, we do not intend to treat any of them here, for we do not claim to know precisely how the medieval mind distinguished among dogma, experience and fiction.

The hagiographical legend presents itself, overtly or by implication, as stemming from tradition, which in some ways it obviously does; and yet it is not fixed at all points, and may be expanded by accretion. Nonetheless, the accretions, when they occur, must simultaneously meet the tests separately applied to hagiography and to narrative fiction: they must accord with commonly accepted tradition and they must induce suspension of disbelief and please the reader or listener. More than that: it is not only through an appearance of logical sequence that they induce the suspension of disbelief, but through reliance upon tradition itself, assumed to be coherent even though it may be made more so. It is this aspect which we shall examine first: the growth of the Julian legend in so far as it gains its appeal by embroidering upon successful narrative structures drawn in the first instance from tradition.[4]

A medieval saint's legend may arise – and in the case of Julian probably did arise – as an effort *ex post facto* to explain satisfactorily a special power or powers the saint was deemed, as a matter of faith, to possess.[5] The instructional function, then, the exposition of the power of the saint, is present before the 'story' is elaborated at all; and the desire to explain, and to furnish coherence, underlies the developing of Lives for those saints who, despite their popularity, either lacked a history, or had come to lack one. Thus the march of narrative toward its predetermined dénouement is what counts here, rather than the exposition of dogma.[6] The explanatory function, which gives rise to the story of a saint to whom one already prays, must be accomplished in the long run through the compelling logic of a narrative sequence, even though it be one whose end is already determined, in the nature of things, before the elaboration of the story begins.

Furthermore, modern readers might tend to think that providing such explanations is a function that the author may carry out in any way he

4 It is not necessary, in a structural study, to distinguish between religious or didactic tradition on the one hand, and folklore with its motifs on the other (see the preceding note): we are interested in the functions of tradition exclusively. Neither is it immediately necessary to distinguish between folkloric tradition in the broad sense, and the specific, ever-growing tradition associated with a given saint, and considered to be his life story.

5 We beg the reader's indulgence for a final assumption which will allow us to pass through the morass of philosophical and psychological attitudes into which we are led by consideration of the phenomenon of Faith explained. For the purposes of this chapter, we find it unnecessary to identify the impulse (be it doubt, or insecurity conscious or subconscious, or childlike curiosity, or delight in the representation of the natural world) which lies behind this amplification of theoretically autonomous beliefs.

6 This is particularly the case with legends, such as Julian's, which grew up at a time when the earlier, somewhat limiting ties between the Lives and the liturgy were weakening.

pleases; but that is not true of a saint's life that grows within the frame-work of hagiographical legend. It is in the nature of the hybrid genre with which we are dealing that the resulting narrative sequence must have a certain perceptible authority, and not simply arouse interest, in order to survive. Where the explanation of existing belief, and not the creation of new fiction, is a predominant function, only traditional episodes serve the purpose effectively. For most writers in the twelfth and thirteenth centuries, this meant that such explanatory episodes must come from what we call, for lack of a better term, folklore. We understand folklore to be (among other things) a traditional and recognized fund of explanations of the miraculous. Its motifs (natural, preternatural and supernatural) recur in very similar form in more than one context, and are used in analogous ways wherever they appear; they belong to an accepted system.[7] Folklore is called upon to fulfil an ordinary structural role – to furnish the beginning and middle which the ancient Aristotelian formula calls for. But in the medieval Lives, its most important function was to lend the weight of tradition to the explanatory matter.[8] Adherence to this requirement gave the needed authority to the explanation; but it also narrowed the scope of the creative imagination in significant fashion: it limited to some extent the choice of motifs, just as the presence of a pre-existing cult controlled the available fictional structures themselves, on a larger scale. The development of the Julian legend in the Middle Ages, some stages of which may be traced in preserved medieval versions, serves as a concrete illustration of these principles, just as they serve to explain it.

B / INSTRUCTION AND NARRATIVE
IN THE DEVELOPMENT OF THE JULIAN LEGEND

The earliest known references to Saint Julian occur only late in the twelfth century, and the genesis of his legend may be fully explained if we assume it was relatively new then. Hence we begin our account with this period, although it would be rash to state unequivocally that there is no continuity

---

7 The same impulses surrounded even natural events with explanatory folkloric material, especially when the events were startling or ill-understood: witness the various prophetic dreams attributed to important personages, and to William Rufus himself, on the night before that unfortunate king was killed. See C. Warren Hollister, 'The Strange Death of William Rufus,' *Speculum*, 48 (1973), esp. 640-2: 'In the Middle Ages every cataclysmic event was quickly entangled in a thicket of legend.'

8 Such a generic finds close parallels in other legends developed to explain the long-forgotten traditions which had given some saints their iconographical accompaniments.

of development between the known texts and analogous material from much earlier times.[9] In fact, there are excellent reasons to think the legend existed, in rather fully developed forms, some time before the earliest allusions to it in the written texts we have. For example, the *Legenda aurea* account (1250? 1270?) appears as the abbreviation of a traditional story of some complexity. Jacobus da Varagine is generally considered to be, not an original author, but a compiler of stories current in his day, and many details of his Julian story give every indication of being anterior to his formulation of the legend.[10] The same may be said of the earlier accounts of Bartholomew of Trent (1244? 1251?) and Vincent of Beauvais (1248?). Both the Rouen and Chartres windows – highly developed versions of the legend – are from the first half of the thirteenth century. And it is reasonable to suspect that the lengthy and detailed Old French Prose Life, one of the principal versions, also had oral or written sources not known to us.[11] Moreover, the Prose Life may possibly be older than the mid-thirteenth century date usually assumed for it. It is one of the very few prose legends in the vernacular to appear in isolation, outside of the collections of such Lives, or 'légendiers,' which date approximately from

9 Concerning the pre-history of the legend, of its themes and motifs, prior to the twelfth century, we refer the reader to Schwob and Huet (see Note 1, above), although their work is to some extent vitiated by failure to distinguish between common elements and borrowed ones, a weakness which has also marred scholarship on Flaubert's later use of these materials, as Chapter Three will make clear. Nevertheless, there are many real similarities between the Julian legend known in medieval Europe and various early Christian, classical, Near Eastern, and Eastern tales of great antiquity. But the relationship between medieval European literature and the ancient and Oriental material it sometimes resembles is not clearly understood (witness the confusion concerning the ultimate sources of the fabliaux or the beast epic). On the complexities of oral tradition see Delehaye's caveats, *Lég. hag.*, p. 70. In our Bibliography, pp. 182-84, Nos. 1-3, we give an abridged chronological summary, which the reader may wish to consult.

10 Here is only one striking example. Seemingly uncertain of the way in which Julian's wife learned his identity, Jacobus, who apparently is not at liberty to alter the given elements of the legend as he knew it, furnishes an explanatory conjecture instead: *intellexit quod viri sui parentes erant, ut puto, quia hoc a viro suo forte frequenter audierat*. See our Appendix A, page 101. The event is not shown, but surmised. This structural conundrum seems to have been a minor problem for Flaubert also, since it is not necessarily in character for Julian himself to tell her of his parents, yet she must be able to identify them in order to put them into her bed.

11 We prefer the title *Prose Life* to the widely used 'Prose Tale,' for the latter title may obscure the essential distinction between free narrative and hagiographical legend. The Prose Life is said by some to be a prosification of the roughly contemporary Verse Life of Julian; it probably is not (see our Appendix B), but if it is, then what we say here applies to the Verse Life rather than the Prose.

the middle of the century, and which normally represent groups of translations from existing Latin Lives. No such Latin life is known for Julian,
which fact tends to support the notion that his Old French Life is an independent creation older than the *légendiers*, and thus, of course, probably
older than Jacobus.[12]

But ultimately, limited as we are by the accidents of preservation and
transmission, we may describe only the logical sequence of those versions
which happen to have survived and to have been rediscovered. Even their
relative dating is obscure – most of them seem, accidentally, to be almost
contemporary with each other – for a late text or representation may be
the résumé of a very early one, or may show its influence.[13] But even with
that important caveat in mind, the dynamic of elaboration – the logical
sequence of the materials, rather than their chronological sequence – may
be discerned in very general terms.

The late twelfth-century texts mention the cult of Saint Julian Hospitator and make clear that already then one prayed to him for lodging at
night when on a journey and far from home.[14] The succeeding fifty to one
hundred years witnessed the greatest development of this legend. Thus, by
the end of the twelfth century or the beginning of the next, Julian Hospi-

---

12 See Paul Meyer, 'Légendes hagiographiques en français,' in *Histoire littéraire de
   la France*, 33 (1906), 388, and cf. 335.
13 Thus, Bartholomew of Trent, who wrote an epitome of Julian's life (*Liber epilogorum in gestis sanctorum*, see *New Catholic Encyclopedia*, II, 134) does not
   mention the prescient stag or other talking animal which occurs in most versions
   of the Life, and from whose warning to Julian Flaubert drew such a strong scene.
   Did Bartholomew know the stag tradition, but reject it? Or did it already exist,
   but unknown to him? Or is it posterior to his epitome? See his text in Gaiffier,
   pp. 168-9.
14 Gaiffier, pp. 164-8. We may add that 'l'ostel Saint Julien' was already a common
   locution used to describe comfortable lodgings by the end of the twelfth century.
   Along with the materials of English origin known to Gaiffier, there are numerous
   references to Julian as the patron of hospitality in continental texts from the late
   twelfth century, such as Chrétien's *Perceval*, or from the turn of the twelfth to
   the thirteenth centuries, such as the *Roman de Guillaume de Dôle*. A reference in
   Jaufré (late twelfth century?) seems to indicate Julian was known in the South at
   that time as well, although it is not entirely clear: Jaufré's host greets him in
   Julian's name upon rising in the morning, but it may be a *pro forma* invocation of
   the type which any saint's name might fit. (See *Jaufré*, ed. Clovis Brunel [Paris:
   S.A.T.F., 1943], 11. 4599-605.) Additional references to Julian from the twelfth
   to the fifteenth centuries are listed in L.-F. Flutre, *Table des noms propres ... dans
   les romans du Moyen Age* (Poitiers: C.E.S.C.M., 1962), p. 115, and E. Langlois,
   Table des noms propres ... dans les chansons de geste (Paris: Bouillon, 1904), p.
   386; there are surely others. Those we have been able to see are simply passing
   references to Julian's role as patron of travellers. We thank our colleague, Barbara
   Nelson Sargent, for drawing our attention to the *Perceval* text.

tator had annexed some of the vast folklore of the host-guest relationship, thanks to the existence of the cult which gave him his name. He had a small hospice in which, during his lifetime, he lodged travellers in an out-of-the-way place. In addition, he had annexed the ancient folkloric role of the ferryman, a theme at least as old as Charon, and thus had near his hospice a ferry, with which he aided his guests and other travellers to cross an otherwise impassable river.

The likely motivations for the inclusion of these elements are different. The ferrying probably obeys the didactic or hagiographic imperative, which is again present a little later in the century in the elaborating of the Christopher legend. It gives the story of Saint Julian greater interest and attractiveness, and his cult greater prestige and authority. The hospice motif, on the other hand, probably marks an effort to furnish an explanation, intended to satisfy curiosity concerning the saint's relationship with travellers and his power to aid them.[15]

The presence of the hospice was enough by itself to explain the popular prayer for lodging. Thus, in one of the very oldest known versions, Julian and his wife simply go off of their own volition (*sponte*) to carry out this ancient service to mankind.[16] But although this action could be explained as the result of divine inspiration of the couple's will, it does not seem to have been enough to satisfy the narrative urge: paradoxically, something led the writers and the public of the age to seek a better understanding of the prayer for lodging which, presumably, one and all addressed to Julian with sincere hope of success. Hence further elements were forthcoming.

Let us recall that the period we are dealing with did not share our critical attitudes toward all that purports to be history. The life of the medieval Julian was not history or biography in any modern sense, but rather an abstraction, an image, a manifestation of eternal and revealed truth. To improve the image, to make it longer for example, to make it correspond still further with what was known of the eternal fact of sainthood, was precisely not tampering or even creation, but rather making concrete and immanent the transcendant truth everyone agreed was there all along.[17]

15 The distinction holds true whatever the real chronology of the accretions. Both of Julian's tasks would occur naturally to medieval people, and it seems possible that they were usually associated, as being both indispensable for travel. We may also be fairly sure these are indeed accretions rather than the elements of an old fixed tradition, for no Julian tale is known from the Dark Ages or from the early passionals.

16 Gaiffier, p. 165, note 1.

17 A structural parallel with some nineteenth-century modes of creation can be made: we shall consider some of them when we come to examine Flaubert and his immediate predecessors.

Further elaboration was therefore still possible. It may be well, however, to repeat that our interest here is exclusively logical and in no important sense chronological. We have treated Julian's roles as ferryman and hospitator as the 'first' additions because they happen to appear in a very early text and because it is not unlikely that they were in fact the first. But this apparent chronological priority is irrelevant to our thesis and serves us only as a mode of presentation. If other episodes were put into place first, the logical mechanism we are displaying would have operated, we believe, in exactly the same way: that is, further episodes (e.g., what we now call the 'first' episodes) would have been called for and would have been forthcoming. We shall take it henceforth that our 'chronological' presentation is in no sense to be understood as necessary. What is necessary is the logical framework, into which other data may be fitted, if and when the record becomes more complete.

We posit, then, a short tale involving Julian as ferryman and as hospitator; and we have suggested why elaboration was in order. But, in addition to the earlier requirement that such new elements come, likewise, from the common fund of folklore, they had also to concord with Julian's role as ferryman and hospitator, which comfortable tradition by then insisted upon. Unless all new data met these criteria, the legend would indeed become an invention and hence without authority: not recognizable, and thus not credible.

We shall treat several elements which were added to the Julian story; but a crucial linked pair of episodes, the parricide and the ferrying of the leper, must be discussed first. It is significant that the short version we discussed above had the couple go to the river bank spontaneously: that writer found no need whatsoever to explain the desire of the couple to go there. But there are also versions which have the couple establish the ferry for a plausible reason: because Julian committed the horrible crime of parricide. These versions also recount his ferrying a leper to attain salvation: these seem to us to evidence the explanatory urge at work. It was possible to feel a need for a reason which would explain Julian's presence at the side of a river so distant from other humans that no other ferryman already provided this service commercially. And also, the account needed to be fleshed out with an episode explaining more fully the origin of Julian's particular power to intercede for a night's lodging for the believer. Of course he takes the leper into his hospice, even into his bed, and we are not surprised to learn that in the oldest versions the leper is already supernatural: Julian is entertaining an angel unawares.

The two complementary episodes are variations on standard motifs and both were put into place, we think, to explain more adequately what the original story was intended to teach.[18] But they do not themselves have primarily a teaching function. They are a further response to the narrative or explanatory impulse: in the addition of the parricide and the sacrifice, the demands and the possibilities inherent in fictional creation are beginning to make themselves felt by the side of the initial hagiographical intent. Moreover – the record proves it – they were successful additions and hence were widely retained, although versions were to arise and subsist which lack one or the other of them, and other relatively late versions, unknown to us, may always have lacked both. Once again, some of the additions we describe may have been made in an order other than the one we tentatively ascribe to them. Nevertheless, the varying uses of the motifs tend to bear out our assumption that we are dealing to a significant extent with a core tale plus later accretions, some logical in mode, and some rather hagiological: the expanding legend, whatever its precise course, is following the tendencies we have outlined above.

In order to analyse the development of hagiographical legend, we earlier separated narrative from hagiography as constituents of the form. It is obvious that at the (logical) stage in the development of the legend which we are now discussing – represented by a tale in which Julian's necessary presence at his hospice must be explained by the addition of other narrative elements – the logic of narrative is beginning to assume the role of prime mover. For the parricide, originally introduced to explain something else, now seems to require explanation in its turn. The age sought it in the same ancient fund of folklore from which the parallel to Charon had been drawn. Two traditions developed, which we shall examine successively. In the first, the parricide will be foretold, and Julian will follow approximately in the steps of Oedipus: forewarned but foredoomed, he will seek to avoid the crime and, in seeking to avoid it, will incur it. This tradition – found, not invented – provides the essential thread of the principal versions of the story as we know it, and lends itself to many sorts of elaboration, still within folklore. There are, for example, many possibilities for the prediction, and it never really attained the status of a fixed element. Julian may learn his fate from a Magus, or from an old man, or simply from a *quidam*. A 'certain stag' may forewarn him, but not the stag we know, for it has *quasi faciem hominis* (or, as the French Verse Life has it, *samblant*

---

18 For example, the episode of the leper in the bed, a leper who is Christ or who is understood as representing Christ, is an important part of the legend of Saint Elisabeth of Hungary, who lived in the thirteenth century; see Delehaye, *Lég. hag.*, 85, S. Baring-Gould, *The Lives of the Saints*, 2d rev. ed. (Edinburgh: John Grant, 1914), November, vol. XIV, pp. 415 ff., esp. 424-25 and the note; and cf. Francesco Negri Arnoldi in *Bibliotheca Sanctorum*, IV (Rome: Istituto Giov. XXIII della Pontif. Univ. Lateranense, s.d. [1964]), cols. 1122-23.

et face d'omme avoit); finally, there is the preternatural stag familiar to all readers of Flaubert, a stag which has the gifts of speech and of prophecy. And the prediction may be made before Julian's birth, or while he is young, or after he is a grown man who has left his parents' home and married.[19] The remarkable variation among possible predictions occurs in a part of the tale which is not fixed by prior tradition, and which is, so to speak, fair game for the literary mind. Yet every one of the variants is a motif lying well within the domain of folklore and requiring, in the version in which it occurs, only minor adjustments in the story line.[20]

Wide divergences between forms of the legend are obviously to be expected. The prediction itself may not appear, for there are other different traditional ways in which Julian may be forewarned, particularly by the premonitory dream, which may give rise to a second tradition. The dream may come to Julian's parents, and they may or may not tell him about it. Or it may come to Julian himself, but long after he has left his parents (with the accompanying, structurally permissible shifts in the story line). In addition, the dream notion is richer and more suggestive than the simple mechanics of premonition admit of, and it may intrude upon the tradition in other ways. Examples exist in which the dream comes to the fully-grown Julian, who is married and, at the moment, away from home. This situation itself may in turn give rise to a variety of explanations, e.g., that he is away hunting, or, alternatively, fighting. It can then be a dream inspired, not by God, but by the devil; and it will arouse in Julian suspicions and jealousy concerning his wife. He will return home hurriedly, find his parents in the conjugal bed, and commit his murder. This, too, provides an adequate and acceptable explanation for the parricide, and the remainder of the story may then flow from it.[21]

---

19 Gaiffier, pp. 169 and 202; Oberziner, pp. 287 and 290.
20 For similar crystallizations see Arthur Dickson, *Valentine and Orson: A Study in Late Medieval Romance* (New York: Columbia University Press, 1929); Larry S. Crist, 'The Legendary Crucifixion of Jehan Tristan,' *Romania*, 86 (1965), esp. 296-8; and L.-F. Flutre, 'La Partie d'échecs de *Dieudonné de Hongrie*,' in *Mélanges offerts à Rita Lejeune* (Gembloux: Duculot, 1969), II, 757-68. This is, on a small scale, the process by which the epic cycles are being expanded during the same period: within a fairly constant framework of generally accepted episodes, intermediate narrative material drawn from the common stock of pseudo-historical elements may be inserted at will, assuming the minimum amount of care which permits the whole fabric to hang together. For an example, see 'Les Textes en vers,' in R.F. Cook and L.S. Crist, *Le Deuxième Cycle de la Croisade* (Geneva: Droz, 1972), esp. pp. 30-35.
21 The parallels with generative and transformational grammar are suggestive, but we cannot evaluate them here. For various forms of the dream, see Oberziner, p. 283; also our Appendix B, paragraph 2, and Appendix C, p. 168. For jealousy as a

The other component of the parricide, too – how the parents came to be in Julian's bed – may be felt to require similar clarification. Written versions, when they give any reason at all, agree broadly that the parents are looking for Julian specifically, and the logic of this version of the narrative approaches irony. But there is some confusion in the case of other versions, such as the Rouen and Chartres windows, in which Julian appears not to have been lost in the first place.

And finally, the parricide exerts logical or analogical influence on distant parts of the sequence. It is probably not until the thirteenth century that it becomes obvious that Julian, although called a martyr, is not precisely one in the Life as it is being developed for him: the sacrifice he makes in the leper scene does not involve his dying in witness to his faith. The thirteenth-century Prose Life appends an account of the death of Julian and his wife at the hands of a marauder who has come to the hospice to rob the couple of supposed treasures. This episode is further evidence of the explanatory urge, but imperfect in a way, for Julian's death is not willed there either, even though it may come to be identified there as an image of his parents' assassination.[22]

In sum, there are many turns the Julian legend, or any legend of its period, may take. Any of the folkloric motifs mentioned, and many more, may be present in any one version, since they are all common property available for nearly any purpose. Further, the legend does not have a fixed form in the sense that parts of today's Breviary do, for it is subject to an entirely different manifestation of the power of tradition. And its composition is not linear, since in its most common form, it is put together from demonstrably independent and no doubt discrete elements. Yet the security of the known, the recognizable, is still paramount, a *sine qua non*. The

motive, see Oberziner, pp. 283, 287, 291, 306, and our Appendix C, p. 168. For hunting or war as a reason for Julian's absence, see Oberziner, pp. 277, 283, 287, 288, 291, 306; also our Appendix B, paragraphs 44 and 49, Appendix C, p. 168, and Appendix E, p. 175.

22 Readers familiar with medieval literary history will have long since recognized, in what we call 'the explanatory urge,' the same desire for understanding which gives epic heroes their *enfances* – 'il faut savoir d'où viennent les héros' – developments which may run to many thousands of lines divided among several *chansons de geste*, and which finally acquire a reputation and logical life of their own. The most striking example of this is perhaps William of Orange, central figure of a great part of the *cycle de Guillaume*. Early tradition, for reasons now unknown to us, had attached to him the epithet *al corb nés*, 'William Hooknose.' The reading *al cort nés*, 'shortnose,' is apparently an error, yet it is the one which the redactor of the *Couronnement de Louis* goes to great length to justify: William is called thus because his nose was damaged by a Saracen during a battle. See Jean Frappier, *Les Chansons de geste du cycle de Guillaume d'Orange*, I (Paris: S.E.D.E.S., 1955), p. 91.

fund from which variants may be drawn is the finite repertory of folkloric tradition; additions to the legend, and elements which replace others, must come from there if they are to provide the essential, acceptable structures to explain the mysterious and divine powers of the saint as intercessor.

To the twentieth-century reader, it might appear to have been possible to add such explanatory episodes or remarks *ad libitum* in ever-expanding versions of the legend; but in practice the Julian legend, like many others, reached what appears to be a state of structural equilibrium, a richness of episode, and consequently a length, beyond which it never went. From the mid-thirteenth century to the fifteenth century in France, for example, certain saints' legends in prose are copied over and over again, in numerous legendaries; but these particular texts, like the Latin one of Jacobus da Varagine, are not expanded, nor are they rewritten.[23] To be sure, outside France, in widely separated localities, the development of 'new' Julian legends went right on, retracing – as indeed they must have – the same steps we have described, although their nucleus was formed from other folkloric elements. But the two or three best-known French versions were never displaced in France, by these or any other versions of Julian's life. Perhaps that fact is, in part, testimony to the relative adequacy of structure they had achieved: legend as successful balance between hagiography and narrative fiction.

C / ELABORATION OF DETAIL
IN THE HAGIOGRAPHICAL LEGEND AND IN THE NOVELLA

Up to now we have been examining accretions on the level of theme and structure, which were drawn from folklore. The role of ferryman, the receiving of guests, a parricide that may be predicted by a prophetic animal, the premonitory dream, are all ancient themes here incarnated in episodes charged with occult power and stating or suggesting the intrusion of the supernatural or preternatural into the life of the saint. We turn now from the folkloric and often supernatural to the addition of completely natural elements. Given the function we have assigned to tradition in the creation of these legends, it is to be expected that the additions from the realm of everyday experience will concern almost exclusively matters of detail. They are, of course, entirely within the domain of narrative fiction also, except for an occasional pious overtone. Once the central structures

---

23 Instead, they finally go underground, to resurface only in the *Acta Sanctorum* or in the work of a Flaubert. Their disappearance from circulation is not due so much to the creation of late 'canonical' collections such as the *Legenda aurea* as to an apparent slacking of creative interest.

have been elaborated and the tale has become architectonically stable, the miraculous has been explained, and new explanations based in folklore are not required (although some were in fact added in versions very different from the ones we are describing). On the other hand, however, nothing hinders the elaboration of additional *natural* elements. But they will be just that: elaborations upon given supernatural or traditionalized data from folklore, which are, themselves, relatively fixed.

For example, a number of the events in Julian's life may be given precise, real location: his birthplace, the places where he married and where he later established his ferry, where he was buried and where his relics may still be found and worshipped.[24] The author of the thirteenth-century Prose Life of Julian obeys the urge to add explanatory detail of the most common sort when he describes Julian's natural – and not folkloric – difficulties in finding lodging during his first exile. (Unlike Flaubert's Julian, he has now become a beggar.) This analogy between the saint's situation and that of the believer who calls on him for aid gives useful reinforcement to an aspect of the cult, exactly as had the introduction of the hospice and leper motifs. But the prose redactor is here exploiting a bit of structure which he did not himself put into place (the exile), and he does not alter the fabric of the tale to make his new details central to it. He is, rather, acting logically in reference to fixed data; nevertheless, he draws upon the sort of material readily available also to the author of narrative fiction.[25]

Much the same is true of the descriptions of how the medieval Julian's appearance changes, an outward sign of inward transformation, during his various travails. The possibilities for such additions from the normal, natural world are clearly very large, for the only requirement is that the new material may be reasonably grafted onto the traditional elements. Yet this development never led, and never could lead, the hagiographical legend to adopt the status of a novella. The novella does not merely allow variations in matters of natural detail: since its structure itself may be changed endlessly, such details may always be added to it, at least until it reaches its 'definitive version.' Short narrative fiction attracts a writer eager to invent, whereas the hagiographical legend invites elaboration of something already in place, to which congenial elements may be added. There is a sense in which the new writer (or teller) of a legend does not own the

---

24 Gaiffier, pp. 178-84.

25 We are aware of the critical tendency to explain this characteristic of the literature of the thirteenth century by reference to social change and specifically to the appearance of a *bourgeois mentality* on the scene; neither the medievalist (Cook) nor the *Flaubertiste* (Bart) feels he is qualified to discuss the phenomenon here. The history of the Julian legend, at least, may be explained without any reference to it.

legend; if he changes unduly what tradition has already agreed upon, the result will no longer be that legend, but rather another and unrecognizable one. The development of the Christopher legend, also an account of a ferryman and also elaborated in the thirteenth century, is again a case in point. Legends are often stated to be anonymous; we prefer to describe them as collective or accretive.

It is clear, from what precedes, that the elaborations of a given writer who recasts the legend in a given time will tend to be in part the same as those of many other writers in other ages and even in other countries. Flaubert himself, writing centuries later, will be as free as were his predecessors to add relevant and possible details to what was handed down to him. But he will also be as limited as they, in that his additions must have the stamp of credibility in relation to the fixed structural data. He could and did add a childhood to the Julian story, filled, as it should be, with details, some natural and some preternatural; and he was at liberty to develop new details of Julian's career as knight. He could even emphasize Julian's psychological motivation. But, on pain of losing what was essential about Julian's life (his hagiology) or what held the Life together (his narrative story), Flaubert could not negate the thematic and structural core of the legend as he knew it: the forewarning, the parricide, the ferry and the hospice, the transporting of the guest over the river, and the final salvation and sainthood. In all of these, and in the details which depend on them, he was as bound as were his predecessors or as any one else will be, who may later elect to tell the Julian story as hagiographical legend.

CHAPTER TWO

Flaubert and the Medieval Tradition

The concepts we have proposed concerning the nature and development of hagiographical legends suggest two lines of inquiry which should be pursued before we address ourselves directly to the question of Flaubert's use of legendary sources. The first is to determine why Flaubert, a highly successful author of narrative fiction, should have turned to the hagiographical legend; the second is to establish the canons to be observed in identifying his use of the traditional materials the past transmitted to him.

The reasons or urges behind Flaubert's turning to the hagiographical legend in 1875 are not far to seek and have been amply investigated elsewhere: we may therefore treat them only summarily here.[1] In 1875 Flaubert's entire personal life was definitively shattered by the financial collapse of Ernest Commanville, husband of Flaubert's beloved niece Caroline, whom he had brought up from infancy. Unsure of where his food or lodging would come from (one recalls Julian's initial function), bereft of almost all his older friends – for a succession of their deaths had marked the immediately preceding years – and exhausted beyond endurance by his trials, he had come to doubt even his power to write and had laid aside his long, unfinished work, *Bouvard et Pécuchet*. The past welled up about him during his melancholy and plagued his dreams at night. In deep despair, he turned to ancient lore and wisdom to guide him. He was to find guidance in the saints, as he wrote of Saint Julian, a project of many years' standing; of the saint-like Félicité; and of Saint John the Baptist, who join to make up his *Trois Contes*.[2]

---

1 A fuller statement may be found in Bart, *Flaubert* (Syracuse, N.Y.: Syracuse University Press, 1967), pp. 645-54 and 670-86. Elsewhere in this same study (see the index), the reader will find discussions of Flaubert's interest in the legend at other periods of his life.

2 'Après saint Antoine, saint Julien; et ensuite saint Jean-Baptiste; je ne sors pas des saints,' wrote Flaubert in June 1876 (*Correspondance*, [Paris: Conard, 1926-33], VII, 309).

Julian's was the first of the three Tales he wrote, and is the only one that need concern us. Moreover, our concern here is exclusively with the form of the Tale as it evolved in 1875, for whatever legendary sources may have been involved in Flaubert's earlier thinking about Julian's story, none appear to have produced anything more than a brief Plan (1856), which we shall discuss in due course. Why, then, might Flaubert have been attracted once again to this legend, specifically at this moment of great stress in his life? We cannot be sure, but certain aspects of the Tale as he told it suggest a natural and plausible motivation, for behind the traditional givens of the legend, Flaubert divined his own story. In the first two parts, Julian's role – though Flaubert need never have realized it consciously – may be seen as representing that of Flaubert's niece Caroline, who had ruined and destroyed him without meaning to do so, as Julian had killed his parents. This is echoed in the original opening sentence of the story: 'Jamais il n'y eut de meilleurs parents – ni d'enfant mieux élevé que le petit Julien.'[3] In the Third Part, Julian assumed Flaubert's own role, as the saint sought release from a catastrophe for which his own share of responsibility was not clear. He found it in a total acceptance of the human condition and in the peace and joy of the pantheistic vision of the ending. The elements of the legend of Julian thus appealed to Flaubert, as man, because they could readily be made to bear the symbolic burden of his own anguish; to these mythic structures Flaubert, as author, rapidly found he could easily add the sort of natural detail which it delighted him to write. The hagiographical legend agreed with his psychological and aesthetic needs.[4]

The matter of the canons to be observed in assigning, as direct sources for Flaubert, certain prior accounts of the life of Julian is far more complex and must be explored in close detail before we turn to the sources themselves. For certain negative guides must first be established.

In describing the way some medieval legends developed and were made coherent, we have gone far toward describing how Flaubert, or his nineteenth-century predecessors, or any other writer, is likely to deal with his sources when treating traditional legendary material. Failure to understand these fundamental canons in the development of a legend, and its relationship to the freer types of literary creation, has produced much unnecessary confusion in scholarship concerning Flaubert's use of legendary sources in his *Saint Julien*. Episodes, and details within them, do appear in Flaubert's Tale and also in one or another of the medieval versions. But not all of them may properly be used to identify a 'source' for Flaubert. Insignificant ones – and

3   B.N., N.A.F. 23663, fol. 492r.

4   This is not the place to treat these matters more fully. For a discussion of other aspects of Flaubert and his use of the legend of Julian to fulfil them, see Bart, 'Psyche into Myth: Humanity and Animality in Flaubert's *Saint Julien*,' *Kentucky Romance Quarterly*, 20 (1973), 317-42.

some of this character have been adduced – we shall have to reject: they are inadequate to support a claim for a source. But even significant recurring episodes and structures must be closely examined. Since folklore, despite all its fertility, depends at its roots upon the human psyche, it will tend therefore to reduplicate itself; for it may draw, if it is to be successful, only upon those elements of psyche which are universal or nearly so, those conceptually akin, for instance, to such things as Jungian archetypes, or to Freudian images and complexes, or to the structures of Lévi-Strauss or of Chomsky.

And, *a fortiori*, significant recurring details, too, must be carefully scrutinized before being admitted as evidence for the use of a source, since such details will always be no more than embroideries upon a tradition, their colour and texture depending upon the basic tale, and hence tending to recur from one teller to the next without any need at all for direct transmission. We have already seen, at the end of Chapter One, that Flaubert is limited by the traditional, coherent nature of the legend he is recreating; the coherence of that tradition will necessarily have suggested to him, by its very nature, pathetic, or mysterious, or simply interesting details which it had already suggested to other writers also.

To make our point clearer, we offer the following examples of similarities which we have deliberately drawn exclusively from Italian versions of the legend known in France only long after Flaubert's death. In some of these forms of the legend, a *zingara* predicts Julian's fate to his parents (recall the 'Bohéme' in Flaubert, who performs a similar function). Or *un vecchio* (recall the 'vieillard'). In another the highly intelligent young Julian makes himself a small gun (the better to kill his prey), as Flaubert's Julian will find a hollow reed through which to shoot dried peas at birds. Or Julian may hear bells sound mysteriously and a cock crowing both at the time of his first killing (in this case, thieves) and again when he kills his parents, a motif which parallels the belling of the great stag in Flaubert. The list of these coincidences is long and should be cautionary, for none of these episodes or details could Flaubert possibly have known.[5] Such recurrences are inevitable, for the *Légende de Saint Julien* is not a short story but the legend its title claims it is. In a very fundamental sense, it represents the mixture of tradition and accretion of natural detail which we have discerned in the medieval versions of the saint's life.

5 Oberziner, pp. 287-88. It might also be remarked at this point that Flaubert's text is often closer to the little-known Old French Verse Life than to the works more commonly claimed to be his sources. In the Verse Life (probably written before 1267), Julian kills the prophesying stag, lives the violent life of a knight, and is visited in his hut not by an angel but by Jesus Christ. This point is usually overlooked. 'Jo sui cil qui riens n'oblie; Nule cose ne m'est coverte.' A. Tobler, 'Zur Legende vom hl. Julianus,' *Archiv*, 102 (1899), lines 4778-79; see also lines 101-02, 2342-44, 4300-08. The stag is killed in lines 215-78, and Julian joins the Hospitalers – a motif of course inspired by the second possible meaning of the French *hospitalier* – in lines 1044-73.

An opposite situation arises when we know, from extra-textual evidence, that Flaubert read a given version of the legend. When an element from such a version reappears in Flaubert's Tale, we shall take it that he borrowed it from that earlier source. But even then we shall have to make the reservation that an author adopts or adapts only what temperament or prior experience has prepared him to accept. There are three versions of the legend which documentary evidence shows Flaubert read: the *Legenda aurea*, his friend Langlois's account of the Julian window at Rouen, and a Spanish version Flaubert stumbled upon in a book he used to learn about hunting. In addition, we shall examine the claims for a fourth version, a nineteenth-century retelling of the thirteenth-century Prose Life. There is some very suggestive documentary evidence to indicate Flaubert must have had occasion to see this adaptation; and we can validate the claims made for it with what we find to be convincing and numerous recurrences of material from it in Flaubert; hence we shall consider it a source. A fifth major source has been adduced: a medieval manuscript giving the same Prose Life in Old French. A number of recurring details have been claimed, and a great deal has been made of presumed structural and tonal parallels between the medieval work and Flaubert's. All of these we shall examine with the care they deserve: our conclusion will be negative.

The Spanish version may be treated briefly at once. Flaubert found a markedly Romanticized retelling of it in Joseph LaVallée's *Chasse à tir*, whose fifth edition appeared in 1873. Flaubert's notes, made as he prepared the early parts of the *Légende*, with their detailed references to medieval hunting practice, mention LaVallée by name: he must thus have been aware of this version of the tale. Yet curiously enough, the variant text seems to have reached LaVallée by oral transmission; it does not derive from the *Legenda aurea*, which it contradicts. And it does not raise the major issues of influence raised by the other works we have just mentioned. As a result, we have preferred to reproduce LaVallée's version in Appendix E, and to present all material relevant to it there. This does not mean that we dismiss its possible importance in the evolution of the Tale (on the contrary: see our Notes to Appendix E) but rather that it does not fit the tight filiation to be discussed in the next four chapters.

But there is a further phenomenon to be taken into account in tracing Flaubert's sources in legend. First, several different explanations of Julian's

All three events represent important, even decisive differences between the *Légende de Saint Julien* and, say, the Old French Prose Life (as shall be shown in Chapters Three and Seven). Yet no one has ever made the claim that the Verse Life is one of the sources of the *Légende*, and we doubt such a claim could be made seriously, since the Verse Life contains several other important episodes not found in any other version including Flaubert's (e.g., the whole story of Julian's Breton host Gervais), and Flaubert's agreements with it against other versions can be otherwise accounted for. The Verse Life is in any case an enigma, since it contradicts itself (see Appendix B).

powers as intercessor were proposed, as we have seen, almost from the very beginning. As these traditions moved down through time and were retold in later generations, each teller in the series often no doubt took his immediate predecessor or predecessors as a compendium of prior material upon which to draw. Moreover, each, at his pleasure, drew further upon the common fund of folkloric material available to all and, equally, upon the fund of material details of daily life relevant to the folkloric story. When the various major traditions reached their state of equilibrium, or what we might term their 'canonical form,' perhaps by the middle of the thirteenth century, the process appeared to have come to an end. But when the nineteenth century revived interest in the Middle Ages, surprisingly, the process we have described had a rebirth. This time, however, the storehouse of acceptable themes and motifs from which to draw additional elements was no longer so much folklore as instead the new storehouse of Romanticism. Flaubert's predecessors in the nineteenth century began the process anew, and his own version is but the most recent successful example (there are, in fact, ill-starred descendents of it!), whose place in this development it must be our task to elucidate in due course.

As previous scholars have not seen this genesis through successive accretions to a cluster of related tales about Julian, earlier studies of Flaubert's sources have substituted what we may think of as 'short circuits,' linking Flaubert directly – rather than through an intermediary – to one or another prior element in the belief that such an earlier story must necessarily have furnished Flaubert with anything his *Légende* and the earlier story may have in common. This has had serious consequences, for it replaces the real genesis with a factitious, direct influence upon Flaubert of medieval elements 'as they were.' Knowing the real genesis allows us, instead, to understand the far more complex, but far more natural, evolution which leads to Flaubert.

Although Flaubert could – and, to some extent, did – make direct contact with medieval accounts and representations of the Julian legend, these are not alone or even principally what appear to have moved him, at profound levels, to write his story. Rather, it was nineteenth-century retellings of the legend which stimulated him. More than that: what he seems to have taken as *bona fide* medieval elements in these nineteenth-century accounts of Julian, those places which most moved him, were *Romantic accretions* to a medieval legend which, itself, had grown by similar accretions (*mutatis mutandis*) in the medieval period, and to which Flaubert would in turn make his own accretions by an analogous process.

With hindsight, we may well ask: How could it be otherwise? As *Salammbô* is a Romantic's concept of Carthage, so Flaubert's *Saint Julien* is a Romantic's concept of the Middle Ages. 'Scientistic history' may indeed have been a reigning doctrine in Flaubert's day, but it never was and never could be, in itself, the well-spring for literary creation. That lies elsewhere.

CHAPTER THREE

The Early Manuscript Accounts of Julian's Life

We may begin with the medieval origins of the Julian legend, whose earliest known forms arose, we recall, during the late twelfth and the thirteenth centuries. This age produced a series of legends about saints named Julian, to be added to the company of a not inconsiderable number of earlier saints of that name already in the Calendar. Among all of these, we shall have occasion to refer to only a few: Saint Julian of Le Mans, Saint Julian of Antioch, Saint Julian of Brioude, Saint Julian *le Pauvre*, and, of course, Saint Julian Hospitator. The enormously complex interrelationships among these originally separate saints have been studied at some length, but need concern us here only insofar as some of our texts refer to Saint Julian Hospitator by one of these other names (a confusion already common in the Middle Ages), or insofar as it will be necessary to point to specific confusions with the *vitae* of other saints of the same name in the elaboration of the Hospitator's legend.[1]

A whole congeries of lives of Julian Hospitator have been identified within the medieval period, and their transmission and variants have been studied to some extent. To study all the versions of his story would lead us far afield indeed. But our concern is Flaubert's sources: we shall therefore limit ourselves, for the present, to the two traditions which may categorically be stated to have played a role in the *Légende*'s development or composition. One of these is in Latin, the other in Old French, and they show important differences from each other; but within each of these two traditions the known texts show no crucial variations from one to another, at least for our purposes in this study.

The medieval Latin tradition is represented by the standard *vita* which the Bollandists borrowed from Saint Antoninus of Florence for inclusion in the *Acta Sanctorum*. It had already appeared, in essentially the same

---

1   For some of these confusions, see Gaiffier, pp. 184-91.

form, in Vincent of Beauvais, the *Legenda aurea*, the *Gesta Romanorum*, and elsewhere. The form most readily available to Flaubert was that of the *Legenda aurea* (Cap. XXX, 4), of which he owned a French translation.[2] Here, as in all the original Latin versions, the life of Julian is recounted in rapid, straightforward fashion, requiring only some five hundred words. Descriptive adjectives are rare, and those aspects which the nineteenth century was later to deem 'picturesque' in medieval texts are almost entirely absent. No details of Julian's childhood appear, nor is there any information on Julian's several periods of wandering in foreign countries; these travels and Julian's childhood, it will be recalled, Flaubert recounted at some length in his Tale. Toward the end of the *vita*, an angel brings word to Julian and his wife that God has accepted their penance (in Flaubert, Christ himself brings the message, a difference which is, as we shall see, extremely important).

The Old French life of Julian which interests us here is the prose version (although a related verse form exists), for it is the most widespread, appearing in numerous *légendiers*. The texts of all these manuscripts are as uniform as the well-known conditions of medieval manuscript transmission allow.[3] The Old French Prose Life often occupies ten or twelve leaves, recto and verso, and is thus far more developed than the Latin version. The Old French form contains considerable detail, some dialogue, quite a few stereotyped episodes which are not in the Latin version, and even some equally stereotyped delineation of Julian's psychology. To our knowledge, and despite the claims of some scholars, it has not been finally ascertained whether the Old French life represents an expansion of the Latin one (by the usual series of attached motifs: prophetic dreams, pilgrimages, wife-winning, parallel structural developments, and the like) or is a version of the source from which the Latin form was distilled; additionally, of course, both versions may well derive from a common, presently unrecovered source or sources. The relationship between the Prose Life and Flaubert's Tale is the subject of Chapters 5, 6, and 7.

A number of aspects of the Old French versions, principally the prose one, are essential to our problem. First, these versions give some slight,

---

2 For the Latin text and the French translation, see Appendix A. Flaubert may have owned a Latin edition of the *Legenda aurea* (there is no known record concerning it), but we may be sure he owned a copy of the French translation by Brunet, 2 vols. (Paris: 1843). See Sergio Cigada, 'La "Leggenda aurea" di Jacopo da Varagine e le "Tentation de Saint Antoine" di Flaubert,' *Contributi del Seminario di Filologia moderna*, I, 278-95, in *Pubblicazioni dell'Università cattolica di Sacro Cuore*, Nuova Serie, Vol. LXXII (Milan: Società editrice 'Vita e Pensiero,' n.d.).

3 For a list of these manuscripts, see Appendix B.

stereotyped information on Julian's early childhood: he was 'gracieux' and good-looking, blond, and well built; and he enjoyed hunting, a trait which is to be related to his later murder of his parents. Second, there is an uncommonly long development in these manuscripts concerning the whole latter part of Julian's life. Notably, it is Julian's wife (his companion in most of the medieval versions), and not Julian, who hears and heeds the call of the leper; she is to lie with him, for only her flesh can warm him; and it is to her that the angel's voice speaks from outside the hut (we will discuss in a moment the syntactically irregular *est* for *a*):

> li mesiaus [*leper*] ki fu defors li dist: 'Feme, ne pleure mie. Jhesu Cris vers cui nule cose n'est couverte, por ta grant merite et por la foi de ton signor vos est pardonés [*sic* for *a pardoné*] li pechiés de l'omecide ke vos feistes; si vos doing .i. don pardurable: quiconques sera soufraiteus d'ostel, si die sa patre nostre por vos et por cels ke vostre sire [*husband*] ocist, et il ne faudra pas a bon ostel.' (B.N. Fr. 6447, fol. 218c; Appendix B, para. 79)

After the leper's disappearance, the Prose Life is terminated by a brief postlude in which Julian and his wife receive martyrdom at the hands of a robber who (in a typologically significant gesture) kills them both in bed with one blow of a sword, much as Julian had killed his parents previously.[4] Neither of these elements, the presence of the wife or the martyrdom, is reflected in Flaubert's story; both are, nevertheless, of considerable importance to the medieval French Prose Life.

In addition, and of greater immediate importance to our argument, there is a rather involved question of a scribal slip, or a tendency to scribal error, related to the *est-a* confusion in the passage just quoted – a rather superficial misreading, but a widespread one, which eventually resulted in a radical change in the ending of the Life in the Old French versions. We may most easily begin with the Latin text, which we tend to believe represents the older tradition here. The leper has disappeared from the cabin: 'Post paululum ille ... hospiti suo dixit: Juliane, dominus misit me ad te, mandans tibi, quod tuam poenitentiam acceptavit et ambo post modicum in domino quiescitis.' The Latin versions are thus perfectly clear in their intent, and Antoninus will even go so far as to interpolate: 'erat enim angelus domini.' There is at least the strong suggestion that this was the intent of the original author of the Old French Prose Life as well, for some of

---

1 ⟨illegible⟩ maniere cor son pere et sa mere ocist, car uns lettres les ocist ambes deus a .i. colp.'

ıhu crıſ

Idealized rendering of the standard abbreviation *ihucriſ* 'Jhesu Cris'; for the letter forms of *ihu* see A. Cappelli, *Dizionario di Abbreviature latine ed italiane* (Milan: Hoepli, 1967), p. 176.

ılıu crıſ

Visual effect of a slight change in spacing: *ilui*.

ı ſuı crıſ

The intermediate reading 'i[e] ſui.'

the texts duplicate the sense of the Latin. Thus, in one manuscript the angel addresses Julian's wife:

> ... ne plorer mie. Jhesu Criz quu [*sic* for *qui*, a graphy of the dative *cui*] nulle chose n'est couverte ... vos a pardonné lou pechié de l'omicide que vos feistes. (B.N. Fr. 13496, fol. 12a)

It will be helpful to note that here *Jhesu Criz* is the subject of the verb *a pardonné*; and *lou pechié* is in the objective case. The implication is that Christ is not present, and that *vos a pardonné lou pechié* is the statement made by the intermediary angel.[5]

But utter confusion now enters. In one of several possible ways and in what was to become the major manuscript tradition for the Old French form of the Julian legend, this entirely clear and syntactically correct statement became confused. 'Jhesu Cris' (subject to abbreviation as on modern altar cloths, for it is a holy name, one of the *nomina sacra*) was often written as either 'ihu cris' or 'iesu cris.' Either form may lend itself to misreading or misunderstanding, particularly in the mind of a scribe already predisposed to expect the presence of Christ himself at the scene of the miracle, as in innumerable other legends. In 'ihu,' the manuscript would show a short vertical stroke for the 'i,' a second and longer vertical stroke for the upright element (*haste* or ascender) of the 'h,' and then three successive vertical strokes for the remainder of the 'h' and for the 'u.' The three latter strokes may be evenly spaced or irregularly spaced; the oval or 'bowl' of the 'h' may well be quite close to the next stroke. If, for whatever reason, the vertical stroke of the 'h' contained the slightest clockwise curve, or if (as is more likely) through inadvertence it were incorrectly seen (quite literally) as having such a curve, then it would be read as old-

---

5 The entire matter is both complex and obscure. Thus, for example, one of the first authors to give a brief but complete life of Julian is Bartholomew of Trent (in 1244-51; see Gaiffier, pp. 168-70 and our Chapter 1, Note 13), and his text is quite ambiguous concerning the nature of the nocturnal visitor: 'Post paululum hic, qui leprosus aparuerat, splendidus scandit ad aethera dicens hospiti [Julian is alone in this version] : "Dimissa sunt peccata, me cito sequeris."' Before the end of the twelfth century (thus very early in the development of the life as we know it), the author of the *Speculum laicorum* knew a version in which Julian is visited by an angel, not by Christ (see Gaiffier, p. 164). We strongly suspect that the Latin version and those Old French ones consistent with it are in fact representative of an older form of the legend, the one known to the redactor of the Prose Life, and that, so far as the manuscripts are concerned at least, the presence of Christ is a later version. In any case, should the opposite hypothesis be the correct one, it will not affect our central issue, which is that of Flaubert's sources, although it would be of interest for the study of the Julian legend itself.

fashioned long *s*, and what was really 'Ihu' could – and would – be misread as though it were 'J [e] sui' = 'I am'; the following word, 'Cris,' then makes sense, although the rest of the sentence will not.[6]

However it may have come about, a new tradition appeared in the manuscripts, making the 'guest' assert that he is Christ. The rest of the text is now altered to conform to this, so that it reads: 'Feme, ne pleure mie. Je suis Jhu cris cui nule cose [n'est] couverte. Pour ta grant merite ... vos est pardonnés li pechiés del homecide que vos feistes' = 'I am Jesus Christ. ... The sin is pardoned you....'[7] *Li pechiés* is now in the subjective case, as is *pardonnés* which is now conjugated with *être*; and *est* has been substituted for *a* to conform to the sense. This new statement (which does not affect the rest of the action) became part of the Old French tradition, which can now often be clearly distinguished from the Latin versions through the presence of Christ at the end: It is the version represented in the Julian window at Rouen, and it is this tradition which Flaubert will follow (at one remove) when he, too, has the leper become Christ.[8] We may recall that neither Jacobus da Varagine nor the scribes or authors of the various known Old French versions claimed to be the first to write of the legend. There was presumably an oral tradition behind them, and there were also some Latin and possibly Old French manuscript versions as well, which would have permitted the error to arise in these latter.

Thus the thirteenth century developed two major and distinguishable written traditions for Julian, the Latin *vita*, and the Old French Prose Life, in addition to innumerable lesser ones whose fate it was to die aborning or never to enjoy more than localized success. The major Latin tradition survived in the *Acta Sanctorum*, and when the Romantic period interested itself in the Middle Ages, it of course rapidly rediscovered the other major tradition, the Prose Life. Hence these were two medieval forms that Flaubert would almost necessarily come to know.

6 Alternatively (and we are unable to determine which hypothesis is correct), 'iesu' may readily be converted to 'je sui' through inadvertence, and the same reading results. This is not the place to treat this matter in greater detail. Medievalists interested in the matter will find B.N. Fr. 1546, fol. 221 recto gives precisely the reading we suggest: 'ie sui crist.'

7 B.N. Fr. 23112, fol. 166 recto and Fr. 185, fol. 110 recto.

8 Further complications play a role, but we can do no more than acknowledge them here, as they are not germane to our argument. Very briefly, versions exist, notably B.N. Fr. 17229 and Fr. 6447 (quoted above), which show 'Ihu crist,' but without syntactic relationship to anything in the remainder of the sentence, for the other changes which we discuss also appear; that is, *li pechiés* also appears as the subject of the verb *est pardonnés*. Inadvertence on the part of the scribe is perfectly clear here, at any rate, for there is no way to make sense of the sentence as it stands. We think this reading is transitional between the original and the fully accepted error with accompanying adjustments.

CHAPTER FOUR

The Julian Window at Rouen and Langlois's *Essai ... sur la peinture sur verre* (1832)

We have described how the Julian story grew by accretions. Our thesis is further illustrated by the examination of another of the medieval forms of the legend, represented by the Julian windows at Rouen and at Chartres. Flaubert himself points us toward the Rouen window, for he closes his Tale with the single-sentence paragraph (which we quote from his plan of 1856, even clearer than the later published form): 'et voilà la légende de St. Julien L'Hospitalier telle qu'elle est racontée sur les vitraux de la cathédrale de ma ville natale.'[1] But he also wrote to his publisher, Georges Charpentier, in connection with an *édition de luxe* of the Tale:

> Je désirais mettre à la suite de *Saint Julien* le vitrail de la cathédrale de Rouen. Il s'agissait de colorier la planche qui se trouve dans le livre de Langlois, rien de plus. Et cette illustration me plaisait *précisément* parce que ce n'était pas une illustration, mais un *document* historique. En comparant l'image au texte on se serait dit: 'Je n'y comprends rien. Comment a-t-il tiré ceci de cela?'[2]

---

1 B.N., N.A.F. 23663, fol. 490r. Cf. also: 'une légende qui se trouve peinte sur les vitraux de la cathédrale de Rouen' (G. Flaubert, *Correspondance: Supplément* [Paris: Conard, 1954], III, 212-13, letter of 3 October 1875). We believe these – in conjunction with Ockham's razor – dispose of the claims made for a Saint Hubert window at Caudebec as the source of the Tale. This hypothesis is aired and discussed by A.W. Raitt, 'The Composition of Flaubert's *Saint Julien l'Hospitalier,*' *French Studies,* 19 (1965), 358-72, and Colin Duckworth, editor, Flaubert, *Trois Contes,* 3d. ed. (London: Harrap, 1969).
2 *Correspondance,* VIII, 207. The Goncourt Brothers also report a conversation of similar tenor:
    FLAUBERT – Eh bien, Charpentier, faites-vous mon *Saint Julien?*
    CHARPENTIER – Mais oui ... Vous tenez toujours à ce vitrail de la cathédrale de Rouen, qui – c'est vous qui le dites – n'a aucun rapport avec votre livre?
    FLAUBERT – Oui, parfaitement, et c'est bien à cause de cela.

As a first step in the study of the sources of the Tale, we shall attempt here to respond to Flaubert's hypothetical question. How are the window and the text related?

Flaubert could, and presumably did, look at the Julian window whenever it pleased him to do so. But he did not look with unprejudiced eyes, for he was guided by an old family friend in Rouen, Eustache-Hyacinthe Langlois. Langlois (referred to in the letter to Charpentier, quoted above) was the author of an *Essai historique et descriptif sur la peinture sur verre ancienne et moderne* ..., which contains a long discussion of the Julian window at Rouen and a line-drawing of it by Langlois's daughter (our Plate 1): Flaubert owned this work.[3] The window itself is difficult to read because of its location in the north deambulatory, where strong light usually falls on it from the inside. Hence it is reasonable to suppose that the issue of convenience made this drawing and the accompanying explanations by Langlois Flaubert's real sources, far more than the window itself. Comparisons we shall make shortly will bear out this supposition.

Even in a good light, much of the window is enigmatic.[4] To Langlois, it was so puzzling that he skipped many panels, gave casual summaries of many more, and misinterpreted others. Moreover, he felt justified in adding what he no doubt deemed charming flights of fantasy to those aspects he did understand: we are in the 1830's, well before notions of scientific history became current. Still, Langlois's frequent bewilderment is easy to understand, for the window derives directly from neither the Latin versions nor the Old French ones, but rather in several of its parts from a version of the Julian legend which is represented in no written source known today.

We find no case where Flaubert appears to have gone directly to the window and to have taken it as meaning anything other than what Langlois proposed. Hence we shall examine the window in large measure as Langlois reports it and his daughter's drawing reproduces it. We shall also

---

ZOLA – Mais au moins, permettez à Charpentier d'introduire dans le texte quelques dessins ... Moreau vous fera une Salomé.

FLAUBERT -- Jamais ... Vous ne me connaissez pas, j'ai l'entêtement d'un Normand, que je suis.

– Mais, lui crie-t-on, avec votre vitrail seul, la publication n'a aucune chance de succès! Vous en vendrez vingt exemplaires ... Puis, pourquoi vous butez-vous à une chose que vous-même reconnaissez être absurde?

FLAUBERT, *avec un geste à la Frédérick Lemaître* - C'est absolument pour épater le bourgeois!

(*Journal des Goncourt*, Robert Ricatte, editor [Monaco: Imprimerie Nationale de Monaco, 1956], XII, 29). We think this latter remark to be no more than a *boutade*, as does Ricatte.

3   Rouen: Edouard Frère, 1832. See also Flaubert, *Correspondance*, VII, 262.

4   In Appendix C we propose an elucidation of most of it.

occasionally turn to the Julian window at Chartres for clarification. While the two windows are by no means identical, they are closely related and serve readily to complement each other.[5] In our analysis, we shall refer to the numbering in the panels in Mlle Langlois's drawing (although it is arbitrary and hence does not always follow the sequence of the story). The drawing represents the window as it was in Flaubert's day, albeit somewhat tendentiously.[6]

Panels 1-3 are the customary representations of the donors and need not detain us. Panels 4 through 8 clearly relate episodes from Julian's youth, before the moment when the other medieval sources begin their accounts: elements of accretion, then, which were not transmitted to the two major written forms of the legend. Panel 9 shows Julian's lord receiving the last sacraments. The next three panels are numbered in reverse, 12-11-10. In Panel 12, the lord is discovered to be dead. Panel 11 is a marriage scene. In it Julian is marrying the widow of his dead lord, as he does in the version of the Prose Life, but not in that of the *Legenda aurea*. In Panel 10, two knights in armour ride away, Julian and a companion going off to defend the new bride, an episode similar to what is reported in the Prose Life.

Until the death of Julian's lord (Panels 9 and 12), we are being told a story of which we today know nothing; if we can interpret these latter and Panels 11 and 10, it is only by reference to the Prose Life. Far more important, we are being shown nothing of the central prediction of the legend as we know it in either of the two major forms (or in Flaubert): Julian's hunt and the miraculous curse by the stag. The lack of this episode, missing both here and at Chartres, indicates that in this version the Oedipus theme has not, or has not yet, been annexed.

5 See Appendix C.
6 To avoid confusion, we note that at some time since then, when the window was taken down for cleaning or safekeeping, two panels were interchanged. Numbers 7 and 18 in Mlle Langlois's drawing are, today, reversed; her order is correct. Precise dating of the window seems unattainable, but the years 1220-40, approximately, have been proposed and seem not unreasonable; the dates might even be a little later. See Jean Lafond in Armand Loisel, *La Cathédrale de Rouen*, 'Petites Monographies des grands édifices de la France' (Paris: Laurens, s.d. [1913]), p. 112, and a further study of all the thirteenth-century windows in Rouen Cathedral by Bart, currently in preparation. For the purposes of this study the most useful discussion of the Chartres Julian window is in an older work by Y. Delaporte, *Les Vitraux de la cathédrale de Chartres*, 4 vols. (Chartres: Houvet, 1926). The relevant text is I, 350-6; the plates are II, CXXXII-CXXXV. The dating of the Chartres windows is at present the subject of considerable controversy. We do not feel qualified to take a position, beyond agreeing that the Julian window there probably dates from the first half of the thirteenth century. The close relationship of the two windows is apparent at a glance, from their style and arrangement. See Appendix C.

What was Langlois to do with these panels? He could, of course, have confessed that he really had no idea what was before him; but this is a level of scholarly virtue not always attained even in today's writing concerning either the Rouen or the Chartres window. Langlois's tone, instead, is confident: 'Ce saint, sur les lieux de la naissance et de la mort duquel les légendaires ont gardé le silence ...'[7] This opening remark has caused a great deal of unnecessary woe to modern scholars who were ill-equipped to verify it and all too ready, therefore, to take it at face value. 'Légendaires' no doubt meant to Langlois exclusively the *Legenda aurea* and its other Latin analogues. But the modern scholar knows that Old French versions also exist, and he can misunderstand Langlois to be including them as well.

This was to have far-reaching consequences for Flaubert studies. Thus Huet (to pick only one among many), in his otherwise excellent study, cites Langlois's remark and one of his footnotes as evidence for the conclusion that Langlois had read the Old French versions and could thus have been an intermediary for Flaubert's knowledge of them.[8] As the conclusion is not warranted by these facts, but has been integral to many later source studies on the *Saint Julien*, we must pause to examine in some detail this formulation of the argument.

Langlois's footnote, which refers to a speech he has just quoted in the text, reads: 'Ce dialogue pathétique est traduit presque mot pour mot des légendaires' (Appendix D, p. 171). In fact (and Huet could have determined this), the 'dialogue pathétique' is 'translated' – we would say 'adapted' – from one of the Latin versions of the *vita*, although not 'mot pour mot':

Legenda aurea	*Langlois*
... heu miser quid faciam? Quia dulcissimos meos parentes occidi; ecce impletum est verbum cervi, quod dum vitare volui, miserrimus ademplevi. Jam vale soror dulcissima, quia de caetero non quiescam, donec sciam, quod Deus poenitentiam meam acceperit. Cui illa: absit, dulcissime frater, ut te deseram et sine me abeas, sed quae fui tecum particeps gaudii, ero particeps et doloris.	Dieu tout puissant, s'écrie-t-il, mes affreux destins sont donc accomplis! Adieu, ma chère soeur, ajoute-t-il en embrassant tendrement son épouse après l'avoir instruite de son malheur, adieu, vivez heureuse, oubliez un misérable qui va dans le fond d'un désert s'imposer une pénitence dont il ne pourra proportionner la rigueur à l'énormité de son crime, mais qui, peut-être, lui en obtiendra le pardon de la miséri-

7 We reproduce the text of Langlois in Appendix D, to which our page indications refer. This quotation is p. 170.
8 Cf. Huet, page 45, footnote 4.

> corde infinie. Ah! mon frère, répond
> la châtelaine fondant en larmes,
> pouvez-vous méconnaître à ce point
> le cœur de votre épouse, pouvez-
> vous la croire capable de vous aban-
> donner lâchement sous le poids de
> vox maux? Oh! non, non, jamais!
> Eh bien, renoncez au monde, partez
> si vous le voulez; mais, après avoir
> partagé vos plaisirs, je m'attache à
> vos pas pour partager vos peines.

Langlois's text is an expansion, by a Romantic, of the Latin. None of his interpolations find their source in the Old French versions.[9]

Confusion is, unfortunately, worse confounded, for Langlois could, in fact, have consulted any of the considerable number of *légendiers* in the Bibliothèque Nationale, all briefly listed in various eighteenth- and early nineteenth-century manuscript catalogues which are still available there for readers' use. Such handwritten catalogues were kept at the Bibliothèque Nationale Manuscript Room from very early times.[10]

But if we now return to Langlois's statement on Julian's birthplace, we shall be able to determine categorically that he did not consult any *légendiers*, for he wrote, it will be recalled: 'Ce saint, sur les lieux de la naissance et de la mort duquel les légendaires ont gardé le silence ...' If indeed he had consulted the *légendiers*, or French *légendaires*, he would have known that, as with Homer, the problem is not to determine where Julian was born, but rather in which of the many places claimed for him he was actually to be deemed to have been born. For the *légendiers* place his birth all the way from Italy to the Languedoc and north to Anjou, Maine, and the Low Countries! Notably, the common Prose Life specifically places his birth at Le Mans and his death by the 'river Gardon.'[11]

---

9 That the Old French Prose Life is not Langois's source here will be clear to anyone comparing the text we quote with B.N. Fr. 6447, fols. 216-17, or Appendix
  B, paras. 54-58. The nearest thing to 'particeps gaudii/doloris' is Julian's speech:
  'nos ferons ensamble le bien et le mal ke Dex vos et nos donra' (fol. 217; para. 58).
10 The more important ones are listed in H. Omont, *Bibliothèque Nationale: Catalogue général des Mss. français. Nouvelles Acquisitions françaises*, vol. II (Paris:
  Ernest Leroux, 1900), 336-66. For example, B.N. Fr. 6447 and 17229 had belonged to the 'Ancien Supplément français' and would thus surely be mentioned,
  albeit perhaps briefly, in catalogue of the collection (now Ms. Nos. 5 121 51) or in the
  so-called 'Catalogue vert' (now Ms. Nos. 5560-93 of the Nouvelles Acquisitions
  françaises).
11 See Gaiffier, pp. 178-84.

Langlois continues: 'Ce saint ... sortait de parens illustres ...' This much he learned from the *Legenda aurea*: 'Julianus praedictus juvenis ac nobilis.' Of the enigmatic Panels 4 through 6, he writes: '[parens illustres] qui l'élevèrent dans les exercices convenables à sa condition relevée ...' The window shows no such thing. Langlois was right, insofar as the Old French versions do add some few details; but that he did not know. His vague statement, however, was to leave the way free for Flaubert to describe, in any way he chose, a medieval childhood and its surroundings. He elected to do so with a mixture of folklore and natural detail, as his medieval predecessors had.

Langlois dealt next with the stag episode. The reader will recall that the window specifically does not display it. But consider Jacobus da Varagine: 'quadam die venationi insisteret et quendam cervum repertum insequeretur, subito cervus versum eum divino nutu se vertit eique dixit: tu me insequeris, qui patris et matris tuae occisor eris?' And Langlois: 'aimant, dans sa jeunesse, passionément la chasse, un jour qu'il poursuivait un cerf qu'il était près d'atteindre et de mettre à mort, l'animal, se tournant vers son persécuteur, lui cria d'une voix terrible: *Tu me poursuis, toi qui tueras ton père et ta mère.*' The juxtaposition of the two versions shows Langlois's method: his text is, as before, a typically Romantic expansion of the *Legenda aurea.* He had little choice, as he had no idea what these early panels meant; hence he had to tell the story following the only version he knew, the *Legenda aurea.* But the problem is greater here than it had been in the case of the childhood: what to do about the fact that the window does not show the stag episode? Langlois discussed the matter as best he could in a footnote: 'La représentation de cette miraculeuse aventure que, dans un siècle sinon plus ami du merveilleux, au moins plus croyant que le nôtre, le peintre-verrier n'a très-probablement pas omise, devait faire partie des vitraux historiés de quelque fenêtre voisine, avec lesquels elle aura disparu'! Hence, in his text Langlois has followed, not the window, but the Latin version of the story, and he has even gone to some lengths to justify his recourse to a text which in fact is not related to the window he is supposed to be describing. Delaporte, perhaps the best student of the Rouen and Chartres Julian windows, of course qualifies Langlois's suggestion that the stag episode occurred in some other window as 'tout à fait invraisemblable.'[12]

The *Legenda aurea* nevertheless remained Langlois's guide. Jacobus da Varagine described Julian's reaction to the prophecy thus: 'Quod ille audiens vehementer extimuit et, ne sibi forte contingeret, quod a cervo audierat, relictis omnibus clam discessit, ad regionem valde remotam pervenit ibique cuidam principi adhaesit et tam strenue ubique et in bello et

12 Page 356, footnote 1.

in pace se habuit, quod princeps eum militem fecit. ...' In Langlois this becomes: 'Frappé d'horreur, et voulant éviter l'accomplissement de cette
épouvantable prophétie, le chasseur, à l'instant même, se bannit pour jamais
du manoir paternel, et se retire en secret dans une contrée lointaine vers un
certain prince (fig. 7). ...' The reader will have recognized the same Romantic aura infusing the translation.

To return to the window, Panels 9 and 12 show the lord receiving the
last sacraments and then dead and lamented by Julian and the widow.
These panels puzzled Langlois, further evidence that he did not know the
Old French form of the legend, in which the lord whom Julian serves is
ambushed by his enemies and dies shortly of his wounds. Langlois omits
these panels, too, perhaps in part because they put the succeeding panel
(No. 11) in a context he could not accept; for here Julian is being married,
and fairly obviously, to the widow.[13] Unfortunately for Langlois, the
Legenda aurea does not kill off the count but rather has him marry Julian
to another man's widow: 'et quandam castellanam viduam in conjugem ei
tradidit.' Langlois again rejects the version of his window in favor of the
Latin tradition: '[un certain prince] ... qui, bientôt appréciant ses grandes
qualités, lui confie le commandement de sa gendarmerie (fig. 10) et lui fait
obtenir la main d'une jeune veuve châtelaine de la plus haute extraction
(fig. 11).' In addition to knowing this tradition, Flaubert was also to come
into contact with an adaptation of the Prose Life (where Julian marries the
widow of his lord) before he actually wrote the relevant passages of his
Tale. However, as he had long intended to have Julian win as his wife the
daughter of a powerful lord, king, or emperor, he retained his original
structure, wittingly abandoning the source he claims, 'les vitraux de la
cathédrale de ma ville natale.'[14]

Panel 13, the next in order, is again enigmatic; hence Langlois omits it.
So does Flaubert. Panels 14 through 21 tell the story essentially as the
Legenda aurea gives it. Langlois had no difficulty with these and reported,
with Romantic embellishments, the journey of Julian's father and mother
in search of their 'fils bien-aimé' and his wife's reception of 'ces vénérables

13 It is even more obvious at Chartres.
14 See below, p. 58. For Flaubert's second plan, including the wife-winning, see
   B.N., N.A.F. 23633, fol. 493 recto. Though he did not know it, Flaubert was
   following ancient precedents in this marriage. Oberziner reports a version in which
   Julian marries the daughter of a rich man. And the later Saint Orso, whose *vita* is
   patterned on that of Saint Julian, marries the daughter of the King of Dalmatia.
   See Oberziner, pp. 287 and 306.
      The use of 'vitraux' rather than 'vitrail' may possibly arise from Flaubert's in-
   clusion of the stag episode, which Langlois imagined as finding its place in a neighboring window.

voyageurs.' The *Legenda aurea*, however, said nothing of the fatigue of the journey undertaken by Julian's parents, whereas the window (and therefore Mlle Langlois's drawing) shows it very clearly (her No. 14). Both pilgrims have strong staffs, and Julian's mother actually leans upon hers with both hands, which Langlois indicates only by noting that they had 'beaucoup de peines et de fatigues.' It was Mlle Langlois's drawing of the panel, then, and not her father's text which Flaubert was recalling when he noted in his drafts: 'Deux vieux appuyés sur des bâtons viennent demander l'hospitalité.'[15] It is further testimony to the well-known acuteness of Flaubert's visual memory that he included this indication in his plan of 1875, written in Brittany and without access to either Langlois or the window!

Then, Langlois continued, 'ramené par sa fatale étoile,' Julian finds ('O douleur, ô cruelle méprise!') the couple in his wife's bed, murders them with his 'funeste épée,' meets his 'chaste et douce épouse' ... and they have the dialogue we reported earlier (p. 32). They depart, come to a river, and establish 'un petit hôpital'; Julian becomes a ferryman. All of this, except for the wife's accompanying Julian, Flaubert will utilize.[16]

'Dans le fort d'un rigoureux hiver et vers le milieu de la nuit [*media nocte ... et gelu grave*],' Langlois wrote, Julian and his wife (Panel 24) suddenly heard a traveller (Panel 22) calling to them. This latter panel caused Langlois serious difficulties, which were to have important consequences for Flaubert: the figure wears the cruciform nimbus! The person who established the program for the window in the thirteenth century must have had access to a version of the Julian story which was, in this part at

---

15 B.N., N.A.F. 23633, fol. 493 recto.
16 Much has been made in certain quarters (e.g., Dr Duckworth in his edition of the *Saint Julien*, pp. 58-9) of Flaubert's decision to have Julian leave alone. Why did Flaubert have Julian refuse her company? Reasons have been offered, e.g., Flaubert's misogyny. We think the question may be more usefully phrased: Why did Flaubert decide not to have Julian's wife accompany him? In this case, it would be possible to reply that at least two medieval versions have Julian leave alone (see Oberziner, pp. 287 and 292) and that Bartholomew of Trent's Epitome (before 1252?) makes no mention of the wife. For the latter, one would assume Julian was alone, were it not for the final statement: 'ipse in Domino cum uxore quievit,' which may mean that she was with him (Gaiffier, p. 169). There is, therefore, precedent for Flaubert: it is possible so to conceive the story. Without wishing to reject hypotheses based on Flaubert's alleged distaste for women, we tend rather to see the decision as arising more probably from considerations of form, particularly of simplicity. Already in his plan for the story of 1856, Flaubert so conceived it: 'alla [*sic:* i.e., *singular*] s'établir au bord d'un grand fleuve' (fol. 490 recto). In his short *Conte* Flaubert found time to develop a psychology for Julian; to motivate his wife as fully would have required time devoted to her and could have seemed to Flaubert no more than a distraction of the reader's interest from Julian.

any rate, parallel to an Old French text or an oral tale in which Christ appears. Langlois handled his problem by first terming the figure only 'le pauvre étranger'; he then provided his elucidation in a footnote. Heretofore, when the window departed obviously from the *Legenda aurea*, he had rejected the former in favour of the latter. This time, however, he gave his preference to the window and explained that the figure was indeed Christ. We find at least two motives he may have had. First, since the cruciform nimbus was an iconographical symbol entirely familiar to his readers and since it recurs several times, he could not ignore its meaning, as he had ignored the earlier implication that Julian married the lord's widow. Second, and more important, we think, to bring Christ into the ending of the Tale was far more dramatic than to retain the angel of the Latin version. Langlois was here correct in sensing that Christ's presence was appropriately medieval; how he handled the material is another matter, as we shall see.

In a footnote Langlois drew attention to a fourteenth century seal showing Julian and the leper, also with a cruciform nimbus. The scene represented in the seal, he wrote, 'est beaucoup plus d'accord avec notre vitrail que Vincent de Beauvais et quelques hagiographes qui, d'après cet écrivain, peut-être, substituent, dans cette aventure nocturne, un ange à Jésus-Christ.'[17] Flaubert will follow Langlois in accepting this version of the legend, and presumably for the very reasons which induced Langlois to do so: the cruciform nimbus and the suitability of Christ's presence. Those scholars who have found the selection of Christ rather than an angel to be further evidence that Flaubert knew the Old French versions of the legend are ignoring this documented and much simpler source for this episode in his Tale.[18]

Langlois was now freed, and properly so, from his absolute dependence upon the *Legenda aurea*. A glance at the relevant panel in the window – or, even more, at Mlle Langlois's slightly exaggerated drawing of it (Panel 23) – shows clouds above the river on either side of Julian's head. Perhaps this was what now led Langlois to introduce a theme dear to his period, a storm: 'Dans cet instant une effroyable tempête semblait confondre les élémens, et les vents furieux bouleversaient les flots du fleuve qui rugissait au sein des plus noires ténèbres.'[19] Julian dressed and, guided by the torch

17 See Appendix D, footnote 5. As we have ourselves allowed earlier, it is perhaps possible that the Old French tradition is indeed the older and that the Latin is a deviation from it; but we have also urged our reasons for preferring to adopt the reverse of Langlois's positions.

18 E.g., Duckworth, *Trois Contes* (1969), p. 60.

19 The *Legenda aurea* gives no indication of a storm; it does occur in the far more detailed Prose Life.

his wife held for him on shore, traversed the angry waters to ferry the traveller back across the river.

Langlois now made a second Romantic addition to what his window depicted. In point of fact, nothing in the window suggests that the figure has leprosy! What small amount of his flesh appears has no spots; moreover, none of the later scenes with the leper in the cabin are shown. We doubt that leprosy was a part of this version. But Langlois had no such doubts and assumed the stranger was leprous, as he is in the written versions. We are, of course, in the period of the grotesque allied to the sublime; hence Langlois portrays the figure thus: 'L'inconnu, hideux rebut de la nature et de la société, est couvert d'une lèpre vive qui révolte horriblement l'odorat et la vue ...' (p. 172). The *Legenda aurea* had been content to describe him as merely 'sic infirmus et quasi leprosus.'[20]

Returning briefly to the *Legenda aurea* – though not to the window – Langlois next explained that Julian and his wife now found themselves unable adequately to warm the leper: he was about to die. But then Langlois departed from his text again, this time to bring out the sublime:

O sainte, ô ingénieuse pitié! Que font les deux époux? S'aveuglant sur le terrible danger auquel ils s'exposent, ils étendent au milieu d'eux, dans leur propre lit, leur affreux hôte ... [He continues the story, in similar tone, to the moment of the transformation of the leper] ... Généreux martyrs de la charité, quel beau jour va luire sur vos têtes! Déjà ses premiers rayons pénètrent dans votre sainte et secourable demeure, et, vous éveillant l'un et l'autre, vous cherchez, saisis d'étonnement et de crainte, à reconnaître le misérable malade dans l'être surnaturel qui, resplendissant de lumière et de majesté [*Leg. aur.*: 'splendidus scandet ad aethera'] , se montre à vos yeux éblouis. Mortels bienfaisans, n'en doutez point, vous le voyez encore cet objet de votre héroïque pitié, mais dans Jésus lui-même, dont la voix vous console, dont la main vous bénit (fig. 27).

After a few more lines in this tone, Langlois skips Panels 28, 29, and 30, and concludes his account by noting that shortly thereafter Julian and his wife 'furent chercher dans [le] sein [de Jésus-Christ] le bonheur dont ses paroles leur avaient donné l'assurance (fig. 31).'[21]

20 One recollects Hannon in *Salammbô*. It is entertaining to find Téodor de Wyzéwa, well into our century, succumbing to the same romantic temptation and rendering the Latin as 'qui était rongé de lèpre et répugnant à voir'! (*La Légende dorée* [Paris: Albin Michel, 1929], p. 118.)

21 Langlois was unable to handle the three devil scenes which intervene (Panels 28-30) between the apparition of Christ and the rising of the souls of Julian and his wife to heaven. Incorrectly, he dismisses them as belonging to another legend. Flaubert could make no use of them whatsoever.

Before setting Langlois aside, we should draw attention to the mechanics, albeit not the excellence, of his style.[22] His written source was in simple Latin; he had therefore no direct model to tempt him into using the sort of medieval vocabulary which was already delighting a Hugo. On the other hand, he was writing at the height of Romanticism and felt no need to inhibit his flights of emotionalism; hence he had no hesitation over departing from his text for that or similar purposes. In a word, he told a medieval tale in contemporary, nineteenth-century language, adding elements of the Hugolian grotesque-sublime to achieve a Romantic ending. Flaubert would follow his path, while, of course, restraining the emotionalism.

Langlois could scarcely have imagined that the young friend, Gustave Flaubert, whom he enjoyed escorting about the environs of Rouen to look at medieval monuments under his guidance,[23] would one day write the ending of his own *Saint Julien* under precisely this inspiration. For, as we shall later show, Langlois's intensifications and additions to the *Legenda aurea* concerning the storm, the leper, and the transfiguration of Christ are at the origins of the tremendous finale of Flaubert's *Conte*.

---

22 Huet speaks of 'le travail de l'honnête Langlois, exécuté dans le pire style Louis-Philippe' (p. 59).
23 See Raitt for an excellent discussion.

CHAPTER FIVE

Langlois and Lecointre-Dupont: Flaubert's Direct Sources

WE MUST consider a further nineteenth-century retelling of the medieval Julian legend. As if to underscore the complexity of the creative process, this one shows the direct influence of Langlois, and, in turn, it also influenced Flaubert.

To allow a clear presentation of this striking filiation, we shall reserve until the next chapter our presentation of the extra-textual evidence which shows when and how Flaubert came to read and to know this retelling. The Bibliothèque Municipale of Alençon possesses a manuscript volume (No. 27) containing, *inter alia*, one of the fifteen or so copies known today of the standard Old French prose version of the Julian legend. It had lain there quietly for at least one hundred years, when in the 1830's it came or was brought to the attention of a minor scholar, G.-F.-G. Lecointre-Dupont, who elected to publish an account of it.[1] We reproduce both texts in Appendix B, to which our paragraph and page citations will refer. It was the first time in three hundred years, at least to our knowledge, that anyone had looked closely at any of the Old French versions. Hence we may excuse Lecointre-Dupont for believing his version unique, although he might have learned of another manuscript of the Prose Life from the rather hasty remarks of Pierre-François Ginguené in the *Histoire littéraire de la France*.[2] However, as it turns out, Lecointre-Dupont was as little concerned to follow his manuscript as Langlois had been to respect his window. Lecointre-Dupont could not plead that he did not understand what was before him; but he also knew Langlois's work and even mentioned it in a

1 'La Légende de Saint-Julien le Pauvre, d'après un manuscrit de la Bibliothèque d'Alençon,' *Mémoires de la Société des Antiquaires de l'Ouest*, année 1838 (published at Poitiers, 1839), pp. 190-210; also published separately as a brochure of 24 pages (Poitiers: Saurin, 1839), with line drawings crudely derived from Langlois.
2 XV (1820), 483-4.

footnote (p. 153). He found in it a model and a warrant for the alterations he made in his own account of the Julian legend.

Lecointre-Dupont begins his story with a pleasant introduction, which states what he felt to be the canons of the author of his manuscript. The passage may stand as adequate evidence for Lecointre-Dupont's ignorance of the nature of medieval literature and its audience, for he sees them as Langlois saw the window, through a Romantic's eyes. The point will be of considerable importance when we come to evaluating the uses Flaubert made of this account:

> Les exercices ascétiques, les pénitences et les macérations des saints, leur charité ardente, leur abnégation héroïque, n'auraient point captivé seuls un auditoire vain et léger [celui du manoir féodal], qui ne respirait que batailles, amour, blasons, tournois et aventures; aussi la vérité historique ne présidait pas toujours à ces contes dévots, et la pieuse fraude du narrateur, pour donner quelque attrait aux utiles vérités qu'il voulait faire entendre, imaginait en l'honneur des saints une haute généalogie, de périlleux voyages, de brillants faits d'armes au milieu des combats ou de grands coups d'épée à l'encontre des diables, et mille fictions merveilleuses ... (p. 141).

The phrase *la pieuse fraude du narrateur* is singularly apt, for Lecointre-Dupont was about to continue the tradition by adding similar embellishments of his own, much as Langlois had done: we are witnessing the displacement of folklore by Romanticism as the storehouse from which to draw.

Lecointre-Dupont refers to 'Vincent de Beauvais, Jacques de Voragine, Thomas Friard,[3] les Bollandistes et nombre d'autres écrivains moins connus.' As with Langlois's *légendaires*, the phrase 'nombre d'autres écrivains' is largely for effect. Lecointre-Dupont states that he himself will draw upon 'un frère prêcheur, qui en savait sur [le] compte [de Julien] beaucoup plus long que les hagiographes que j'ai cités, en donnant sa vie dans un manuscrit ... de la bibliothèque d'Alençon ...' (p. 141).

We should note at once that the *frère prêcheur* (probably Friar Laurent, author of the *Somme le roi*) is not the author of the account of Julian's life at all: he only happens to be mentioned in another part of the Alençon manuscript, and in another connection entirely. More importantly, it will be well to examine in detail a few early lines from Lecointre-Dupont to

---

3 Author of a translation into French of Pedro Ribadeneira's *Flos sanctorum: Les Fleurs des Vies des saincts* .... (Rouen: Jean de la Mare, 1645-46); the *vita* appears in both versions on February 12.

determine exactly what kind of *fraude pieuse* he is prepared to carry out to make his text more agreeable to French readers at the height of Romanticism:

Alençon Ms. 27, Appendix B paragraph 3	*Lecointre-Dupont, Appendix B page 142*
Li enfes crut, et fu mult biax, et mult blons, et bien tailliez, et bien plesanz et mult gracieus a touz ceus qui le veoient. Et la contesse sa mere l'ama tant qu'ele mist tout son cuer en lui amer. ... Et quant li enfes ot passé .vii. anz, si fu mult granz de son aage, et mult ama deduit de chiens et d'oisiax sor totes choses; et deduit de bois ama il tant, qu'a grant paine s'en pooit il .i. jor tenir, ne ja ne li anoiast.	... les grâces et la force se développaient en lui; de blonds cheveux ombrageaient son front; sa taille était élancée: on admirait sa mâle beauté, son maintien gracieux; et sa mère l'aimait tant qu'elle mit tout son cœur à l'aimer, ... Après qu'il eut atteint sept ans, il fut, comme on est à cet âge, amateur passionné de déduits de chasse, de chiens et d'oiseaux. Rien ne lui plaisait tant que courir les forêts; et, passait-il un jour loin des bois, l'ennui déjà le prenait.

Lecointre-Dupont understands the general story line of his manuscript quite adequately, although he always renders it in a Romantic vein: what was simple and direct is transformed into more flowered language, and medieval phrasings become Romantic. In addition, however, he does make a considerable number of errors of detail. Thus, in the present instance he has mistranslated the false cognates *anoiast* and *ja*; the syntax of the original is a bit unusual, but it most probably means 'he loved the pleasures of the forest so much that he could abstain from them a single day only with difficulty, and it disturbed him greatly to do so.' Moreover, toward the start of the passage, *bien tailliez*, 'of sturdy build,' cannot be rendered as 'sa taille était élancée': the Romantic cliché, stimulated by *tailliez*, has imposed itself on Lecointre-Dupont.

This is all Lecointre-Dupont (or his manuscript) has to say on Julian's childhood. Argument from these scant lines has attempted to assert that Flaubert must have known them in order to conceive of telling Julian's childhood over several pages in his *Conte*. We have suggested, instead, that we find Langlois's vagueness on the matter was what set Flaubert off.

Lecointre-Dupont follows his manuscript reasonably closely – or with only departures from it which do not need to concern us here – through the slaying of the stag and the animal's cursing of Julian, and through a very long development on Julian's wanderings, which we may conveniently omit for the moment. In his early pages Lecointre-Dupont appears to be deliberately scrupulous when he departs importantly from his source. Thus, when he gives Julian's wife the name 'Basilisse,' he footnotes his text at once:

> Le manuscrit d'Alençon ne donne point le nom de la femme de saint Julien; mais comme il paraît avoir emprunté quelques particularités à la vie de saint Julien l'Hospitalier, martyr d'Antioche, pour les donner à saint Julien le Pauvre, j'ai cru pouvoir, sans plus de scrupule, donner aussi à ce dernier la femme du premier.[4]

When, immediately thereafter, he gives a description of the lady, he follows more or less the text of Alençon 27, which he quotes in the remainder of his footnote as warrant of his fidelity.

Only toward the end of his account does Lecointre-Dupont begin to depart seriously from his manuscript; and here he does so without acknowledgment or – at best – with an inadequate one. His motivation is the same as Langlois's: he is nearing the end of his tale and wishes to give it that tone which he and his readers associated with the picturesque Middle Ages. Just as Viollet-le-Duc and Abadie felt no hesitation over rebuilding Romanesque or Gothic churches to make them more 'correctly medieval,' so Lecointre-Dupont no doubt felt sure he was presenting a model truer to nature: it is only very recently that the flaw in this reasoning has become more important than is its attractiveness to the restorer. Moreover, to Lecointre-Dupont the impetus to improve on his text was the greater because he had the example of Langlois before him. Hence, in the episodes of the storm, the leper, and the final transfiguration, he abandoned his manuscript, which – for the most part – had almost as little on these matters as did the *Legenda aurea.*

The storm presents a special problem, both because Flaubert made it very important and because the Old French Prose Life, too, gives it considerable if different emphasis. The *Legenda aurea*, on the other hand, had made no mention of it: 'dum ... gelu grave esset.' Instead, it placed all its

---

4 P. 147. Lecointre-Dupont is here presumably following the lead of Langlois (See Appendix D, p. 173, footnote 6), who suggests a study of the life of Saint Julian of Antioch in the *Acta Sanctorum* to complete an understanding of the enigmatic panels in the Rouen window. While this is a false lead, the confusion of the two Julians was frequent in the Middle Ages and – though Lecointre-Dupont obviously did not know it – there are medieval manuscripts (mostly late) which also thus invalidly give Basilissa to Saint Julian Hospitator for wife. The tradition never totally disappeared and was given wide currency once again in the eighteenth century. See Oberziner, esp. pp. 265-7, and Gaiffier, esp. pp. 157 and 184-5.

emphasis upon the care Julian and his wife gave to their guest, 'qui sic infirmus et quasi leprosus apparuerat.' The Prose Life is quite other and, if the version known to the Rouen *vitrier* was similar to it, then Langlois's intuition that the clouds in his Panel are significant was indeed correct. The Prose Life, at any rate, reads: '... .i. jor leva .i. orage si grant et mult orrible, qui dura le jor et la nuit. ...' Julian's wife is deeply unhappy that the storm is keeping away travellers, whom she might otherwise serve. He is unable to console her, and eventually they lie down to go to sleep. 'Mes por tot l'or du monde ne dormist la dame, ainz se plaint de la pluie et du tens oscur qui li ont tolu ses ostes.' It is then she who first hears the voice: 'si en fu mult liée. ...' She wakens Julian, who protests that he cannot go out to ferry the travellers: 'Car l'eue est mult roide et parfonde, et li venz est si forz que la nef seroit mult tost emplie d'eue. Par jor i auroi[e] ge assez a fere.' She then says she will go herself, if he will not; 'lors se conmança a vestir,' whereupon he accedes to her desire. Julian then goes out and does have great difficulty in reaching the far bank: 'Juliens ... entra en la nef, puis s'enpaint enmi l'eue, si nage outre a grant painne, et ot grant paor ainz qu'il fust outre passez; mes il ot tot jorz en remembrance la passion Jhesucrist qui le conforta. Quant Juliens fu a la rive, si sailli hors de la nef. ...'[5]

Three points are of central importance here to the medieval author: Julian's wife plays an important role in insisting that her husband ferry the unknown traveller, and she even offers to go herself. And Julian, too, has a difficult task to perform in crossing the dangerous river. Finally, he is able to succeed in his obligation by recalling Christ's Passion. Both partners have to undergo trials, both are triumphant, and both will be saved. All of this Lecointre-Dupont reported, and Flaubert made his own use of all of it except for the role of the wife.

Lecointre-Dupont's rendering of the storm could have been based upon his manuscript: it was not to be so, for he preferred to embellish further the already Romantically embellished account of Langlois. Moreover, he preferred to generalize slightly Julian's precise focus upon Christ's Passion as his manuscript gave it to him (italics ours):

Langlois, page 172

Dans cet instant, une effroyable tempête semblait confondre les élémens, et les vents furieux bouleversaient *les flots* du fleuve *qui rugis-*

Lecointre-Dupont, page 150

... les sourds grondements de la foudre, et *les mugissements des flots*, et *les combats des vents* ...

L'orage augmentait sans cesse, la

---

5 See Appendix B, paras. 69-74.

sait au sein des plus *noires* ténèbres. ... [Julien] s'élance dans la barque, et, *luttant avec succès* contre les vents et les vagues ... il accueille ... le pauvre étranger.

nuit était *sans étoiles*; gonflé par les pluies, le torrent se précipitait en épais bouillons avec un bruit effrayant qui allait se répétant de cascade en cascade et d'écho en écho tout le long du rivage. ... Julien pousse sa nacelle au large, les vents le rejettent à la rive; *il lutte et il avance*; le courant l'entraîne, et la tempête couvre sa barque de flots et d'éclairs. *Il ne perd point courage; il prie Dieu de lui donner de sauver le malheureux qui l'appelle; fort de sa charité, il méprise les dangers, et redoublant d'efforts, il atteint enfin la rive opposée.*

Flaubert elected to make Julian's first crossing of the river miraculously easy, but otherwise he drew heavily on the storm scene, whose filiation we have sought to establish – a scene born, perhaps, in the mind of the Rouen *vitrier* or his programmer, developed by Langlois, and given its full Romantic elaboration by Lecointre-Dupont. Flaubert's text reveals its origins (italics again ours):

... *le mugissement des flots* ... Un *ouragan furieux* emplissait la nuit. *Les ténèbres étaient profondes*, et çà et là déchirées par la blancheur des vagues qui bondissaient. ... A chaque coup d'aviron, *le ressac des flots* la soulevait par l'avant. L'eau, plus *noire* que de l'encre, *courait avec furie des deux côtés du bordage.* Elle creusait des abîmes, elle faisait des montagnes, et la chaloupe sautait dessus, puis redescendait dans des profondeurs où elle tournoyait, ballottée par le vent.

Julien penchait son corps, dépliait les bras, et s'arc-boutant des pieds se renversait, avec une torsion de sa taille, pour avoir plus de force. La grêle cinglait ses mains, la pluie coulait dans son dos, la violence de l'air l'étouffait, il s'arrêta. Alors le bateau fut emporté à la dérive. Mais comprenant qu'il s'agissait d'une chose considérable, d'un ordre auquel il ne fallait pas désobéir, il reprit ses avirons; et le claquement des tolets coupait *la clameur de la tempête.*[6]

6   Flaubert, *Trois Contes* (Paris: Conard, 1928), pp. 120-22. All our references will be to this edition. Our citations, however, will be transcriptions from the autograph manuscript in the Bibliothèque Nationale (N.A.F. 23663). The differences are few in number.

In both the scenes which influenced Flaubert, he thought he was following a medieval account; but in reality he was being moved almost exclusively by additions to the medieval sources written only in the nineteenth century and in a Romantic vein. These, and not the medieval elements, were what he most responded to in his sources. We trust that, upon
reflection, the reader will join us in finding this entirely natural. Flaubert,
like the rest of us, took from 'the past' what he expected to find there.
Such, we believe, is the general nature of what is often termed 'influence.'
That some of what Flaubert found attractive in Langlois and Lecointre-
Dupont was in no wise genuine medieval past but rather his own Romantic
past, he could not know, and he therefore the more eagerly adopted it.[7]

A similar process seems to us also in evidence in the description of the
leper, which follows almost at once in Lecointre-Dupont. Langlois had
himself enlarged upon the very reticent text of the *Legenda aurea* ('sic infirmus et quasi leprosus'), it will be recalled: 'L'inconnu, hideux rebut de
la nature et de la société, est couvert d'une lèpre vive qui révolte horriblement l'odorat et la vue. ...' (p. 172). Lecointre-Dupont phrased this as
'la *hideuse* figure d'un lèpre à demi-mort'; his manuscript had reported
only 'uns povres mesiax mult meseaisiez et mult foibles' (para. 74). Flaubert, however, went considerably further: 'une lèpre *hideuse* le recouvrait.
... Ses épaules, sa poitrine, ses bras maigres disparaissaient sous des plaques
de pustules écailleuses.'

A few lines further on, however, in the Alençon manuscript, its anonymous scribe or author provided the sort of suggestion Lecointre-Dupont
enjoyed, and he eagerly seized upon it. We give in parallel columns the
Alençon passage, Lecointre-Dupont's expansion of it, and Flaubert's subsequent reworking of the text:

Alençon 27 *paragraph 74*	*Lecointre-Dupont* *page 151*	*Flaubert* *pages 123-4*
... prenez moy par les cuises, si me levez	Julien le prit sur ses bras, l'appuya contre	... ses ulcères coulaient. ... 'C'est comme de la

---

7 We are aware that Flaubert's description also owes much to other readings of his
and to his personal experiences of storms and of boating.

It is also possible that Flaubert knew that these additions were indeed Romantic
accretions to the legend and that he borrowed them nevertheless. While solid disproof of this possibility seems to us impossible – and hence we allow that it may
be true – still it seems to us so unlike Flaubert's scrupulousness as to be improbable. Moreover, within our knowledge, we are the first readers in one hundred and
fifty years to have come upon the fact that these are not *bona fide* medieval elements. Was Flaubert, predisposed by his Romantic temperament to accept them
as valid, likely to have discovered their spurious quality, to have suppressed his
discovery, and then to have utilized the materials? It is possible, but we doubt it.

contre vostre piz. ...
Juliens ... le leva con-
tremont son piz, et li
mesiax mist son
front contre le sien,
si qu'il alena adés en
la bouche Julien. ...

sa poitrine, et le front
rongé d'ulcères du
lépreux retomba sur le
front de son hôte, et
le sang livide du pauvre
roula sur les joues et
sur la bouche de Julien,
qui le souffrit avec
joie.

glace dans mes os!'[8] ...
Julien s'étala dessus
complètement, bouche
contre bouche, poitrine
sur poitrine.

The derivation is clear enough; but it conceals another problem, present throughout our study, and which may perhaps be most fruitfully raised at this point. While it is true that, here as elsewhere, Flaubert drew on written sources, it is also, and very frequently, true that his past lived experiences also fused insensibly with his present experience of reading a text. Moreover sometimes, as here, the lived experience (seeing lepers during his trip through the Near East) was one he had already used in earlier works (e.g., Hannon in *Salammbô*) and the experience of that writing of such a scene also enters. Finally, passages such as this one gain their immense power by drawing on far more than they overtly portray: here a barely concealed sexuality colours the scene. Hence many past experiences other than the one or ones overtly involved may also enter the creative stream: Flaubert's mistresses, and especially Louise Colet, are obvious examples. All these experiences, awakened by the episode and the vocabulary of Lecointre-Dupont and Langlois, interact in the course of the creative process to become the new experience, a fictional one, here lent to Julian. Our purpose, however, is exclusively the limited one of elucidating the role of legendary sources in this creative process; hence we do no more than remind our reader that they are but one of many experiences upon which Flaubert drew, here and throughout, to write his Tale.[9]

Lecointre-Dupont, to return to him, faced new problems as he approached the very end of his account. Commentators on his work have not paid sufficient attention to his scrupulous statement (p. 141) that his manuscript is incomplete. It breaks off, though he does not say so, just after the leper has asked to lie with Julian's wife so that she may warm him. She has indicated her willingness to do this for Christ's sake, and

8   Flaubert's 'C'est comme de la glace dans mes os!' is from Langlois, a few lines after our previous quotation: 'les membres glacés de ce malheureux.' It appears a little later in Lecointre-Dupont.

9   We forego discussing the other sources the more readily in this instance because the problem has been treated very fully and at the same time sensitively in a remarkable article by Sergio Cigada, 'L'Episodio del lebbroso in *Saint Julien l'Hospitalier* di Flaubert,' *Aevum*, 31 (1957), pp. 465-91.

Julian begins his reply: 'Dame, fet il, je n'osaie pour vous; mes quant ...'
Comparison with other manuscripts (e.g., B.N. Fr. 17229) shows that one
more leaf would have completed the *vita* (although Lecointre-Dupont
could not have surmised this). A division of volumes must once have followed the life of Julian in the Alençon manuscript, in such fashion that his
vita became the last in this volume.[10] Thus the key features of the medieval
ending, the wife's sacrifice and the couple's death (paralleling the original
murder by Julian), are missing; nor was there any way for Lecointre-
Dupont to know whether the leper was to become an angel, as in the
Legenda aurea, or Christ, as in Langlois.

What was Lecointre-Dupont to do? As he had earlier abandoned the Old
French Prose Life by choice in search of the picturesque, he must now
necessarily abandon it again, and this time the rupture is total: there is no
evidence Lecointre-Dupont ever learned how the medieval Life really ends.
To terminate the story where his manuscript left off was as unsuited to his
purpose and natural bent as it would have been for Langlois to cease describing the Rouen window when it departed from the *Legenda aurea* in its
later panels.

There were further problems, at least for a man of Lecointre-Dupont's
tastes. For in the final surviving leaf of the Alençon text (as in all the corresponding moments in other versions) the leper tests the Christian charity of
his hosts rather more strongly than Lecointre-Dupont was willing to report.
The leper is not merely cold; he does not merely wish the warmth of a human body in his bed. Julian's would have done for that, as it does in several
other versions. The leper is quite specific that he wants Julian's wife alone
and, although the text is ambiguous, it is highly likely that he wants her
carnally: 'Dame, fet il, il me covenist char de fame por moi eschaufer'; or,
as he tells Julian: 'por lui sé ge ça venuz' (fol. 5b: 'I came here on account
of her').[11] When the leper is later transformed into an angel, his declaration
to Julian's wife shows he means her holy conduct has motivated his visit –
'por ta grant merite,' he tells her, 'vos est pardonés li pechiés de l'omecide' – but Lecointre-Dupont did not have any way of finding that out,
since the statement occurs in the lost section of his manuscript; he must
surely have put the worst possible interpretation on the matter.[12]

---

10 Moreover, at some point when this volume was bound, or rebound, the present
   last leaf of the Julian *vita* was incorrectly bound as folio 5, when it should have
   been folio 183. Lecointre-Dupont was aware of this.
11 See Appendix B, para. 77, and compare the explicit sexual references made in the
   Old French verse life, lines 4692-4718.
12 Proof that Lecointre-Dupont knew no other manuscript, if such proof be needed,
   is to be found in his attempt to attribute Julian's life to the *frère prêcheur*, author
   of another work fortuitously bound in with the *Julien* in Alençon 27 and in no
   other Ms. See Appendix B and p. 41, above.

Lacking any ending at all and facing material he was not prepared even to paraphrase, Lecointre-Dupont turned instead to the source he had already been covertly following, Langlois. That the stained-glass window and the completed – but lost – version of the Prose Life both had Christ rather than an angel has confused some scholars into believing that Lecointre-Dupont did indeed seek out another Old French version. A comparison of his text with that of Langlois will show that there is no need to make any such hypothesis. He is continuing to embroider upon Langlois, just as he did in the preceding material (again, we italicize for clarity):

Langlois, pages 172-73

il va mourir .... [sic]. O *sainte*, ô ingénieuse *pitié*! Que font les deux époux? S'aveuglant sur le terrible *danger* auquel ils s'exposent, ils *étendent au milieu d'eux, dans leur propre lit*, leur *affreux* hôte, et se *pressent* à ses côtés pour lui communiquer *leur chaleur naturelle*; enfin ils le voient avec transport revenir à la vie, et bientôt *le sommeil* et la paix planent *sur la couche vénérable*. Généreux martyrs de la charité, *quel beau jour* va luire sur vos têtes! Déjà *ses premiers rayons* pénètrent dans votre sainte et secourable demeure, et, vous éveillant l'un et l'autre, vous cherchez, saisis d'étonnement et de crainte, à reconnaître le misérable malade dans l'être surnaturel qui, *resplendissant de lumière et de majesté*, se montre à vos yeux éblouis. Mortels bienfaisans, n'en doutez point, vous le voyez encore cet objet de votre *héroïque pitié*, mais dans Jésus lui-même, dont la voix vous console, dont la main *vous bénit* (fig. 27).

Lecointre-Dupont, page 151

Il va donc mourir? ..... [sic] Non, La courageuse *charité* de ses hôtes n'a point encore été poussée à son comble; ils n'ont point encore assez bravé pour Dieu *le danger* de la plus *affreuse* existence. ... Maintenant *les saints époux étendent entre eux, dans leur lit, le corps glacé* du pauvre, leurs membres couvrent ses plaies *hideuses, pressent* ses chairs en lambeaux, et enfin, ranimée par *leur chaleur*, la vie recommence à circuler peu à peu dans les veines du lépreux.

Tenant ainsi le lepreux réchauffé, et heureux du succès de leur *héroïque dévouement*, Julien et Basilisse avaient cédé à la *fatigue de la nuit et s'étaient endormis* tous les deux. ... Tout à coup les sons d'un concert angélique remplissent la chambre où reposent les saints époux, les parfums du ciel mille fois plus délicieux que le lis et la rose embaument l'air qu'ils respirent, et *une douce clarté* répandue autour de leur lit éclaire un dôme d'un azur diaphane. Le Lépreux avait disparu; mais, *rayonnant de lumière et de gloire*, le Sauveur des hommes s'élevait *majestueusement* vers les cieux et *bénissait ses hôtes*. ...

Lecointre-Dupont's final sentence draws the elements we have italicized from the corresponding elements in Langlois, of course. More precisely, however, Lecointre-Dupont also turned to Mlle Langlois's drawing of the window, for Langlois had somewhat abridged here. The drawing shows Christ seated with Julian and his wife and then (after the three devil-panels Langlois omitted) the souls of the saintly couple represented as infants in a starry mandorla being raised directly from their bed to heaven by two angels,[13] and finally Christ seated, holding the orb in one hand and blessing with the other.

Langlois had next paraphrased the *Legenda aurea*: Lecointre-Dupont did, too, but transcribed it as though it were a quotation from his manuscript; he then directly described a panel from the window: 'Selon d'autres hagiographes [*read*: le vitrail de Rouen], ils s'endormirent doucement dans le Seigneur, et leurs âmes, portées sur les ailes des chérubins, dans un cercle d'étoiles, s'envolèrent au bienheureux séjour que leur hôte leur avait préparé.' In an explanatory footnote, he added: 'Voir le panneau supérieur du vitrail de la cathédrale de Rouen.' In fact, he means the panel directly below the topmost one, but his reproduction of the top part of Langlois's drawing (as well as one further panel) would have made this clear to his readers. He was obliged to give the alternate possible endings because he had no medieval source himself.

Flaubert knew and used Lecointre-Dupont's obscure study, as the reader will have already perceived. But like his predecessors, Flaubert was a Romantic, too, in fact a 'romantique transcendant,' to borrow the term of praise he used of Baudelaire.[14] His use of his documentation was never servile, although he felt he needed it to set himself to dreaming ... in order the better to set his reader to dreaming:[15]

Alors le Lépreux l'étreignit; et ses yeux tout à coup prirent *une clarté d'étoiles*; ses cheveux s'allongèrent *comme les rais du soleil*; le souffle de ses narines avait *la douceur des roses*; *un nuage d'encens* s'éleva du foyer, les flots *chantaient*. Cependant une abondance de *délices*, une joie surhumaine descendait comme une inondation, dans l'âme de Julien pâmé; et celui dont les bras le serraient toujours, grandissait, grandissait, touchant de sa tête et de ses pieds les deux murs de la cabane. Le toit s'envola, le firmament se déployait. – Et Julien monta

---

13 Mlle Langlois's drawing is here far clearer than the present-day window, almost certainly because of poorly restored damage since her day.
14 *Correspondance*, IV, 408.
15 See Bart, 'Flaubert's Concept of the Novel,' *PMLA*, 80 (1965), 84-9.

vers *les espaces bleus*, face à face avec Notre Seigneur Jésus qui l'emportait dans le ciel.[16]

16 Pp. 124-5. For a study of the sense in which Flaubert did not so much find these
concepts in Lecointre-Dupont as he was rather stimulated by that text to use them,
because they corresponded to his own experiences and were part of his own habit-
ual vocabulary for describing these experiences, see Bart, 'Psyche into Myth ...'
   It is also important that the vocabulary of all three writers comes from the
standard terminology for recounting such experiences from the Song of Solomon
forward. Thus Giry, *Vie des saints* which fundamentally recapitulates St. Antoninus on Julian (*sub die 12 feb.*), interpolates the statement: 'Et alors le malade
parut brillant comme un Soleil.'

CHAPTER SIX

Flaubert's Contact with Lecointre-Dupont

It remains to determine how and when Flaubert came to know Lecointre-Dupont. Flaubert worked on his *Saint Julien* on two entirely separate occasions, the first in the summer of 1856 for a very brief period, the second in 1875-1876.[1] It is impossible to know certainly whether Flaubert read Lecointre-Dupont's article in 1856. The means by which he came to know it – which we shall discuss in a moment – were as available to him then as they were later. However, a first plan for the story, drawn up at this time, shows little which could not have come from Langlois or the *Legenda aurea*. (This plan will be discussed in detail in Chapter Seven, pp. 83-86.)

1 The importance of Lecointre-Dupont's account was first brought to light by Jean Giraud, 'La Genèse d'un chef-d'oeuvre: *La Légende de Saint Julien l'Hospitalier*,' *Revue d'histoire littéraire de la France*, 26 (1919), 87-93. Giraud's insight was further explored and substantiated by René Jasinski, 'Sur le "Saint Julien L'Hospitalier" de Flaubert,' *Revue d'histoire de la philosophie*, Nouvelle Série, fasc. 10, 15 April 1935, pp. 156-72. For the details of Flaubert's composition of the *Saint Julien*, see Bart, *Flaubert*, pp. 370 and 670ff. It has frequently been asserted – too hastily, we believe – that Flaubert worked briefly on the *Saint Julien* in 1874 while at Kaltbad-Rigi. The idea itself is improbable on the face of it; and the evidence adduced does not prove the contention. There is, to be sure, a notebook of Flaubert's in the Bibliothèque historique de la Ville de Paris (Flaubert: *Carnets de voyage*, No. 17), whose fly-leaf indicates he had this Notebook with him at Kaltbad-Rigi; and it has a number of entries concerning possible ideas for future works. Much of it is reproduced in Marie-Jeanne Durry, *Flaubert et ses projets inédits* (Paris: Nizet, s.d. [1950]). Notes on materials from hunting books also appear in the Notebook and Flaubert did use them in writing the *Saint Julien* – but these notes begin at the opposite end of the notebook and work backwards. Hence nothing can be determined from the Notebook itself about the date at which this second series of notes was made. Close examination of them shows that they come from nearly a dozen sources, many of them long: the sheer bulk of reading involved rules out the short stay in Switzerland, during which Flaubert was in ill health and hardly working at all. The matter will be discussed in detail in Bart's edition of *Saint Julien*, currently in preparation.

There is a very considerable packet of notes from his readings made at this time,[2] as well as a record at the Bibliothèque Municipale in Rouen of Flaubert's borrowings there then. Neither shows any evidence of Flaubert's having read Lecointre-Dupont.

If this were all the evidence, we could assert that Flaubert did not already know Lecointre-Dupont when he once again turned to Saint Julian in 1875. But there is one disturbing counter-indication. Julian, it will be recalled, must be absent from his castle at the moment of his parents' arrival. The *Legenda aurea* says only that he was away and 'by chance' (*casu*) returned; Langlois says merely that Julien was 'absent alors.' Alone among Flaubert's possible initial sources, Lecointre-Dupont (following the Prose Life) explains that he was away hunting. Flaubert planned his Tale that way already in 1856, as we shall see in Chapter Seven; and it may have been a recollection of Lecointre-Dupont which prompted him once again to make use of this explanation in 1875 while he was still in Brittany and thus before he could again have had access to Lecointre-Dupont.[3] Alternatively, the inner dynamics of Flaubert's story could have impelled him to reinvent this psychological parallel, which had already occurred to the originator of the Old French versions and to many others in the medieval period.[4] We see no means to determine which is the correct explanation. In any event, Flaubert again planned his story this way from the moment he began work on it in 1875. More important, however, is the fact that if he read Lecointre-Dupont in 1856, then when he again addressed himself to the Tale twenty years later, any memory he may have had of his predecessor was at best faint.[5]

2 B.N., N.A.F., 23663, where the earlier notes are readily distinguished by their handwriting, a means of dating which some of our predecessors have failed to utilize. These are the hunting notes and readings to which Dr Raitt refers (p. 362). The plan of 1856 is fol. 490 recto.

3 Once again, the Plans are B.N., N.A.F. 23663, fols. 490 recto, 492 recto, 493 recto, and 494 recto. Flaubert gives no indication that he had his previous Julian material with him in Concarneau. LaVallée, a further source whom we consider in Appendix E, also provides the hunting explanation; but Flaubert did not read LaVallée until his return to Paris.

4 In *The Rise of Romance* (New York and Oxford: Oxford University Press, 1971), Professor Eugène Vinaver, who tends to think rather strongly that Flaubert must have used the Prose Life itself, agrees that the parallel is in some sense immanent (pp. 114-16); thus the chances of Flaubert's having made it concrete independently are high. For a full discussion of this point, see Chapter Seven, pp. 86-93.

5 Raitt (and others) have proposed that Flaubert drew from Lecointre-Dupont his notion of displaying Julian's cruelty in hunting. This may indeed be so: disproof is impossible. Nevertheless, sadism was integral to Flaubert's temperament and had been so for many years prior even to 1856; it is therefore entirely possible that

On the other hand, all the medieval versions of the Julian legend have Julian's wife absent from the scene of the murder; in most texts Julian then goes to her, or calls her. Only the Prose Life and Lecointre-Dupont's retelling of it may be read to mean that Julian remained in the murder room and his wife came there unexpectedly to meet him: 'Au moment même, la chaste Basilisse, rayonnante de bonheur, accourait vers lui en lui tendant les bras ...' (Appendix B, p. 148). This is what she will do in Flaubert's rendering. Similarly, after the murder, Julian calls out in Flaubert's first scenario for the scene, and 'rien ne répond dans le château' (fol. 480 recto). This, too, corresponds to Lecointre-Dupont's account. Our hypothesis is that it must have been before this time in the redaction that Flaubert discovered (or rediscovered) Lecointre-Dupont.[6]

It will help in following our reasoning if the reader knows from the outset that – surprising though it may seem – Flaubert wrote each page or so of his Tale completely, rough drafts and all, through to its final form before passing to the next page. That is to say, there is no complete first draft of the entire manuscript, then a second, a third, and so on. When, after many drafts for a passage, Flaubert made his final copy of it, it was

Flaubert had long associated hunting with cruelty and hence with Julian; we do not feel that he needed Lecointre-Dupont (or, *a fortiori*, the Prose Life) to suggest its possible intrusion into a hunting tale. Hence, while not denying the possibility, we are loathe to see this as a conclusive argument in favour of 1856 for Flaubert's first reading of Lecointre-Dupont.

It has also been suggested that Flaubert learned from Lecointre-Dupont to use the occasional medieval words which appear in his retelling of the Legend; hence the reading must have taken place in 1856. Again, we feel this is possible but cannot find that this device could not have occurred to Flaubert unaided or from innumerable other readings. One recalls that Flaubert frequently used archaic terms in his letters.

6 In the Prose Life, she is nearby and comes to him upon hearing of his return (Appendix B, para. 51 and 53). But he does not cry out after the murder, as in Flaubert's drafts and in Lecointre-Dupont.

At a number of places – of which we find this one typical – Professor Jasinski (esp. pp. 167-72) points to striking resemblances between Flaubert's Tale and 'un curieux récit signé *lord Wigmore*' which appeared in *La France littéraire* in 1836. As this alleged source is not properly legendary, it lies just outside our area of concern; moreover, the claim does not appear, so far as we have observed, to have been widely accepted. We do, however, wish to demur from Professor Jasinski's conclusion that Flaubert must have seen and in some sense utilized '*lord Wigmore.*' The *récit* is an obvious derivative of the Julian legend, or an imitation of a part of it, or a fortuitous combination of the same ancient motifs as the Julian legend. We prefer to see the resemblances (which are real) as stemming from the traditions the two works have in common. Once such a derivation is posited, common episodes and details become inevitable in our view.

We make the same reservations concerning many of the *rencontres* to which Professor Jasinski points between Lecointre-Dupont and Flaubert.

in almost exactly that form that it went to the printer, for he confined later rewriting to only the most minor of alterations, largely deletions or occasional changes of a word or two. Hence he clearly had the story fairly well in mind before he wrote it out.[7] Therefore it is highly significant that extensive borrowings from Lecointre-Dupont occur only relatively late in the story. Part I up to the description of the hunting book (p. 85), he wrote in Brittany (see p. 79); it shows only occasional similarities to Lecointre-Dupont and these, we feel, are best explained as natural occurrences when two writers set out to use essentially the same folkloric material and natural detail related to it. Moreover, Flaubert and Lecointre-Dupont had both read the *Legenda aurea* and Langlois. As Flaubert had no thought of writing the *Saint Julien* when he went to Brittany (we shall shortly see this) and therefore took no books or notes with him, any similarities will have to be taken to be either coincidences or, at most, memories of the time twenty years before when he had last worked on the story.

Flaubert's letters from Brittany provide other and significant evidence which we must weigh before passing to his return to Paris and hence access to Lecointre-Dupont's text, presumably at the Bibliothèque Nationale. First, Flaubert wrote to his niece, apropos of his beginning to work on the *Légende de Saint Julien*: 'Si tu veux la connaître, prends *l'Essai sur la peinture sur verre*, de Langlois.'[8] Several inferences may be drawn. Since he had just been with his niece some ten days before and since she was obviously not familiar with the story (for he must tell her where to read it), the decision to return to *Saint Julien* can have come only after he had left her and reached Brittany. Second, he himself gives Langlois as his principal source, which concords with our thesis. Third, he obviously did not have

---

7   This complex matter was not understood by our predecessors. See, esp., C.A. Burns, 'The Manuscripts of Flaubert's *Trois Contes*,' *French Studies*, 8 (1954), 297-325. We regret that it is not possible here to enter into the full detail necessary to buttress the assertion that Flaubert composed the Tale in the fashion we describe. The proof depends upon a close examination of Flaubert's re-use of his manuscript sheets, his constant practice of turning them over to use the verso, *when he had completely finished with the recto*. Only when he had prepared his fair copy could he afford to re-use the sheet containing the last of his drafts for a given passage. Since such re-uses occur constantly, it is possible to chart his progress through the redaction and hence to make our assertion that he composed his fair copy as he went along. Bart will provide the full demonstration in his edition of the *Saint Julien*, referred to earlier. In the meantime, a considerable body of evidence appears in B.F. Bart, 'Flaubert and Hunting, *La Légende de Saint Julien l'Hospitalier*,' *Nineteenth Century French Studies*, 4 (1975-76), 31-52. All the notes in Carnet 17 were almost certainly made at the same time in Paris, upon Flaubert's arrival there from Concarneau.

8   *Correspondance*, VII, 262.

Langlois's volume with him, nor did he feel any need for it (since he did not ask her to send it to him). Five days later, after he had received her reply to his suggestion, he wrote again of the matter: 'Lis dans la *Légende dorée* l'histoire de saint Julien l'Hospitalier. Tu l'as mal comprise dans Langlois (où elle est pourtant bien racontée?).'[9] Jacobus da Varagine is, then, Flaubert's second acknowledged source.

Real similarities between Flaubert's text and that of Lecointre-Dupont begin only in Part II; and by then he had returned to Paris and could have had access to the article. There is evidence which we find of considerable weight that it was not until then that Flaubert came to know this work, or returned to it, as the case may be. First, the evidence that this did not happen until he was several pages into Part II. At the start of this second part, Julian flees his family's castle to avoid fulfilling the menacing prediction of the stag; in similar fashion, however, he later again flees his home (this time, the palace which was part of his wife's dowry) after committing his murder. Lecointre-Dupont provides an account of both of Julian's miserable wanderings. Flaubert does, indeed, seem to have made some use of both of these; but the real resemblances between Lecointre-Dupont's passage describing the first flight and Flaubert's text are to be found in Flaubert's account of the *second* flight! The most obvious example is Lecointre-Dupont's statement (concerning the first one): 'Longtemps il erra par sauvages terres nu-pieds et en pauvre habit. Comme un humble mendiant, il allait querant au hasard le toit et le pain de l'hospitalité. Souvent il eut mauvais lit et mauvais gîte, maintes fois même pas d'abri' (p. 143). Or, a few pages later, 'Julien ... implorait en vain un gîte pour sa nuit; chacun le repoussait comme un truant, et partout la porte et le pain lui étaient refusés' (page 145). These all appear as aspects of Julian's *second* flight in Flaubert's text, though in the form of resemblances: 'borrowing,' not plagiarism. There are, to be sure, a number of possible further borrowings by Flaubert in his account of the second flight which appear to have come from Lecointre-Dupont's own account of Julian's flight after the time of the murder; but our citations, which come from the first flight in Lecointre-Dupont, are as close as are the borrowings from the second one. Finally, we adduce these data as evidence only because the whole

---

9   *Correspondance*, VII, 265. The question mark at the end of the parenthesis, not present in the Conard edition, conforms to the autograph letter in the Lovenjoul Collection at Chantilly. We may gather that Flaubert is referring to a French translation, both because he does not call it the *Legenda aurea* and because, so far as we know, he had not taught his niece Latin (which would have been an even more unusual departure from norms of his day than the education he actually gave her). He owned the Brunet translation (Paris, 1843); we give the text in Appendix A.

end of Flaubert's Tale bears what we find to be undeniable marks of his having read Lecointre-Dupont with a view to using the material. If this tendency were lacking at the end of the Tale, we would not find the present data probative.

When, then, and how, did Flaubert come across Lecointre-Dupont? We believe it occurred very shortly after he wrote of Julian's first flight and immediately before he began the episode with the Emperor of Occitania, which leads to Julian's marriage. The last sentence before mention of the Emperor reads: 'C'est lui [Julien] et pas un autre, qui assomma la guivre de Milan et le dragon d'Oberbirbach' (p. 99). The odd pair of monsters does not come from Flaubert's memory. The initial draft for this passage carries: 'C'est lui et non x comme on l'a prétendu qui tua la x ...'[10] The next draft adds after 'x': '(tarasque d'Avignon).' But this draft also carries interlinear indications which lead us to Lecointre-Dupont, albeit indirectly. It is rewritten to read: 'C'est lui et non pas le sire de Uberti piémontais, lui et non pas le comte de Frankestein qui tua la guivre de Milan et le dragon d'Oberbirbach.'[11] The corrections use another pen and are not at the same angle to the bottom of the page as are the original notations: they are clearly a slightly later addition.

Where did Flaubert find these two heroes and their two monsters? In fact, he knew exactly where to look. Already from Brittany (and in the second of the letters from which we have already quoted), he had instructed his niece: 'Mets aussi de côté pour l'emporter à Paris les Légendes pieuses du moyen âge de Maury. C'est un petit in-8° broché en bleu qui se trouve en face des Buffon.'[12] This is an odd request at first sight, for Maury handles Julian in one line and a footnote. While it is possible that Flaubert had forgotten this, it seems to us more likely that he wanted the work for its rich stores of general information on medieval legends.[13] We may now return to Flaubert's draft, which had carried the suggestion 'tarasque d'Avignon.' The Index to Maury's book has an entry for the tarasque which referred Flaubert to page 147 and its footnote 1. The first paragraph of this footnote gave Flaubert the information he decided to

---

10 B.N., N.A.F. 23663, fol. 432 verso.
11 Fol. 462 verso, combined with the succeeding one, 456 recto.
12 Correspondance, VII, 265. The full data are: L.-F.-Alfred Maury, Essai sur les légendes pieuses du moyen-age. Paris: Ladrange, 1843.
13 It has even been suggested that he wanted access to it because he remembered that it had a footnote referring to Lecointre-Dupont. This may indeed be the case, but it is a rather cumbersome way to get a reference, when Flaubert knew he was going to be in Paris and would have access to Maury's volume in the Bibliothèque Nationale, to which he would have known he would have to go to make use of the reference.

use instead, on the *givre* [*sic*] *de Milan* killed by Uberti; and footnote 2 on the facing page mentioned Hans de Frankestein, buried in the church at Oberbirbach, whose tomb displayed a dragon, which popular fancy credited him with having killed.

It must have been either then, or at about this point in his redaction, that Flaubert looked up (or looked up again) what Maury had to say about Saint Julian, too. Here, in footnote 3 to page 72, Flaubert would have found the reference to Lecointre-Dupont.[14] From this point forward, Flaubert's possible borrowings from Lecointre-Dupont are frequent: we may assume the contact henceforth. Where Lecointre-Dupont's Romantic style or Romantic additions concorded with Flaubert's own imaginings of the medieval period, he adopted whatever was readily consonant.

In sum, then, the Middle Ages knew three separate major traditions concerning Saint Julian which have come down to us: a Latin one, a longer French prose one, and the version of the Rouen and Chartres windows. The Latin one remained current and became enshrined for the modern period in the *Legenda aurea* and in the Bollandists. An early – and, for our present period, an unrecovered – tradition perhaps related to the French prose one, lay behind the window at Rouen. Langlois, attempting to explain that window, did what he could to interpret it in the light of what he was able to make of its scenes and supplemented it with the *Legenda aurea*. To this he added passages Romantic in tone. Langlois and the *Legenda aurea* are Flaubert's initial sources. Lecointre-Dupont, stumbling, we do not know how, upon the Alençon manuscript, ostensibly retold its tale; but, having no suspicion that it was a completely typical version of the Old French Prose Life, he followed Langlois in making vague references to other 'légendaires' and in fact drew more and more upon Langlois as he neared the end of his account. Further, he went beyond Langlois in interpolating passages of a Romantic tone. Then, as Flaubert neared the midpoint of his redaction, he came upon (or returned to) Lecointre-Dupont and, finding the Romantic tone consonant with his views (especially where

14 Giraud first drew attention to this footnote. So far as we can determine, no absolutely convincing argument can be adduced from the presently known data to demonstrate categorically that Flaubert did not read Lecointre-Dupont in 1856: Indeed, we specifically acknowledge that he may have read the adaptation then. This would, moreover, explain the resemblances to Lecointre-Dupont which occur in the Tale prior to the moment we suggest for the reading or re-reading. These, however, we incline to see as coincidences: See our Notes to Appendix B. Nevertheless, the point remains that it is almost absurd to maintain that Flaubert took Lecointre-Dupont, which he does not appear to have owned, with him to Concarneau, but did not take Langlois or the *Legenda aurea*, both of which he did own. Hence, at the very most all reminiscences – the correct word – of Lecointre-Dupont in the opening pages must arise from a possible earlier reading.

Lecointre-Dupont derived from Langlois), he adapted Lecointre-Dupont's phrasings to his own purposes.

We may conclude that our predecessors were right in pointing to the window at Rouen, to the *Legenda aurea*, to Langlois, and to Lecointre-Dupont as the sources for Flaubert. All are involved; none is exclusive – but above all, as each in turn mirrors its predecessors in some measure, all are to some extent present constantly. And that is, perhaps, in the nature of the creative act. In any event, it is one of the outstanding characteristics of the shaping and reshaping of legend from the Middle Ages to Gustave Flaubert.

CHAPTER SEVEN

Flaubert and the Thirteenth-Century Prose Life of Saint Julian

The task of explaining how Flaubert came into contact with the legendary sources of the *Légende de Saint Julien l'Hospitalier*, and of explaining the use he made of them, is essentially completed with the preceding chapter. We could proceed at once to present the necessary documentation in our Appendices, were it not that a wholly different approach to the history of Flaubert's Tale has been current for some two decades: one which, being based on other premises, runs counter to our theses and leads to entirely other inferences and conclusions about Flaubert's use of legendary material.

We have discussed at length the impulses which lead to the creation of hagiographical legends, and have suggested that many resemblances between Flaubert's *Légende* and other forms of the Julian tale result from the logical imperatives of narrative sequence: the presence of common thematic elements or common motifs does not serve to prove that one text is the source, direct or indirect, of another. It is a simple matter to show by both internal and external evidence that such resemblances, in the case of certain modern texts, and probably in the case of the *Legenda aurea*, are not accidental, but reflect Flaubert's use of those texts as sources. So far, we have preferred to limit ourselves to the positive arguments which show rather clearly that Flaubert used as principal sources not only the *Legenda aurea*, but also Langlois's *Essai ... sur la peinture sur verre*, and Lecointre-Dupont's much-modified adaptation of the thirteenth-century Prose Life of Julian. But were these latter second-hand or abridged accounts Flaubert's only important contacts with medieval materials, or did he use and even imitate a manuscript of the medieval Prose Life itself?

The Prose Life hypothesis has often been repeated; it has important implications not only for Flaubert's method of composition but for the understanding of his attitude toward Julian's character, and of his motivation in presenting the saint as he did. We have deliberately sought to avoid taking issue with the theory in our previous chapters, in order to facilitate understanding of the rather complex genesis we have presented. It is now time to acknowledge the work of our predecessors, and to explain in detail why we cannot accept their assumptions and conclusions.

In an unpublished MA thesis presented at Manchester in 1944 (and hence at a time when access to continental libraries was blocked by the war), Miss Sheila Smith proposed that Flaubert had read, and on occasion must have misread, a particular medieval manuscript copy of the Old French Prose Life: B.N. Fr. 6447, which was not published until after his death. She alleged a large number of close textual correspondences between it and the text of Flaubert's *Légende*, and concluded that it was a major source, indeed an essential source, for his *Légende*. By all accounts, Miss Smith was unaware of the prior work of Giraud and Jasinski, which pointed to Lecointre-Dupont's Romanticized adaptation as the intermediary through which Flaubert's contact with the Prose Life came.

In its very simplest form, the Prose Life hypothesis runs as follows. In October of 1875, Flaubert was having difficulties (the nature of which he does not specify) with the creation of the Julian Tale. Yet in January he writes to George Sand that he is making progress, and promises completion of the 'bêtise *moyenageuse*' [*sic*] for the end of February. In point of fact, he refers to the work as finished on February 18th.[1] Interspersed with his remarks on his progress are vague references to various readings (he does not say what he is reading or why) and to visits made to the Bibliothèque Nationale. All this may indicate that while at the Nationale, Flaubert discovered and read the Prose Life in one of that library's manuscript collections of saints' Lives (see Appendix B); if so, he would surely have been influenced by the standard thirteenth-century version of the Prose Life.

At a glance, it is difficult to say whether the resemblances between the general outline of the medieval life and the *Légende de Saint Julien* result from such an influence, or are simply caused by the recognized fact that Flaubert knew and used Lecointre-Dupont's adaptation of the Prose Life. And matters of detail are always suspect, as we have pointed out in Chapter Two: they may be coincidences. As it will be seen, however, adherents of the Prose Life theory nevertheless assign the original medieval text considerable weight in the matter of composition, and especially in Flaubert's choice of the principal traits of Julian's character, as well as of certain structural elements, for his *Légende*. The alleged borrowings, from isolated translations of brief passages to the sequence of events itself, are so important and so exact as to constitute the next thing to plagiarism. The implication of the Prose Life theory, as it is stated in the works we are about to

---

1 *Correspondance*, VII, 279, 283, and 287.

discuss, is that Flaubert's *Saint Julien* should be thought of as a recasting of an authentic medieval text.

Miss Smith's thesis is still unpublished, and would have had no effect on our understanding of the *Légende de Saint Julien*, had its central positions not been given wide availability when Professor Eugène Vinaver reported her conclusions in an article published in 1953 ('Flaubert and the Legend of Saint Julian'; see our Bibliography, below, Section A, pp. 181-93, for details concerning the works discussed here). It is through this and subsequent restatements that we know Miss Smith's thesis, which has not been available to us in the original. Professor Vinaver's views were accepted without challenge when Professor Colin Duckworth prepared his student edition of the *Trois Contes* for Harrap (1959). Here, in a publication reissued and revised several times, Duckworth presented the Prose Life hypothesis as assured fact: his notes quote a great many of the alleged textual parallels, and he speculates at length upon the relationship of the Prose Life to the *Légende*, adducing many interesting details concerning the latter Tale's composition.

Reviewing this work a few years later (1964), the eminent Italian *Flaubertiste* Professor Sergio Cigada rejected the Prose Life hypothesis, using the only simple argument available. He noted that Flaubert could not possibly have borrowed from B.N. Fr. 6447, *because he lacked the requisite skills, both linguistic and palaeographic*, to read the manuscript. From our vantage point, the argument is conclusive and obvious: *cela saute aux yeux*. And there, conceivably, the matter might have rested. As a matter of simple logic, it seems impossible that Flaubert could have read nearly everything in a thirteenth-century manuscript accurately enough to imitate it and even transpose it into his text verbatim – this with no known training in medieval French – yet could make the limited number of mistakes, a half-dozen at most, and all quite elementary, which the proponents of the Prose Life theory ask us to believe he made in reading B.N. Fr. 6447, and which are central to their argument. Our readers who share this conviction may, without loss, turn at once to the final section of this Chapter, 'The Problem of Structure.'

'Cela saute aux yeux,' we have said. It proves, however, to be less simple than that. Suppose, on the contrary, that one were to assert in reply that Flaubert could indeed have found and read the manuscript – with help from a friend, for example. What possible answer can be made to that? A moment's reflection shows that logic is of little help here. We could deny the assertion only if it were possible to present a document, written either at the time of the redaction of the *Saint Julien* or during Flaubert's few remaining years, in which he said categorically and beyond the possibility of challenge that he had never been able to read medieval French manuscripts, indeed, that he had never tried. It will surprise no one that we (and other, like-minded *Flaubertistes*) are unable to produce such a document. Honesty compels us to confess that, if challenged by a contrary assertion, our case cannot be proven on this, the only simple ground. And the contrary assertion has, of course, been made, accompanied by quite an accumulation of evidence, all apparently convincing.

Dealing with this evidence requires very lengthy treatment, as is natural in any attempt to prove that something stated to exist does not exist. We return, then, to the history of the question, in order to list completely the points which we are to refute. Duckworth's popular edition was reprinted and revised; it provided the basis for Dr Baldick's Introduction to his translation of the *Three Tales* (1961). Only in 1965 was it challenged at length, in Dr A.W. Raitt's closely reasoned article in *French Studies*. Raitt discussed some of the circumstantial evidence thus far brought to bear on the question of how and when Flaubert could have read the manuscript, and examined the successive passages which Duckworth alleged (after Smith) as proof that Flaubert pillaged the Old French Life. Raitt demonstrated, to his satisfaction and ours, that the passages in question were coincidences, or could be more readily explained as coming from Lecointre-Dupont, the source which had been totally ignored in the Smith-Vinaver-Duckworth scheme. Again the matter seemed to have been settled.

Negative proofs are, we have said, always delicate matters. In a careful and detailed reply, Duckworth accepted Lecointre-Dupont as the source for most of the alleged borrowings from the medieval Life (1968). However, he retained three of his original positions and urged that both works be treated as concurrent sources for the *Légende*. We may state the implications of this argument in the terms we have used in Chapter Two: since three borrowings may be positively identified, we know that Flaubert read the work; thereafter all close resemblances may be adduced and discussed. The reader will have seen that, at this point, our task would be to evaluate the three 'source items' and that we should have to disprove their existence, if we wished to maintain (as we do) that Flaubert could not have used the manuscript.

But the controversy did not rest there, and in fact was to become enormously more complicated almost at once. Rejecting by implication Duckworth's concessions, and dismissing Raitt out of hand, Vinaver returned to the matter in two further publications ('La Légende de Saint Julien l'hospitalier et le problème du Roman,' and *The Rise of Romance*). Professor Vinaver's decision to maintain the Prose Life hypothesis requires the utmost care on our part, if we are to continue to disagree with the hypothesis. We cannot assume Duckworth's concessions to be final, as they are not acknowledged by Vinaver. Every one of them must be reargued on its merits, and this discussion will necessarily occupy a large part of this chapter.

But that is not all, for Vinaver also takes another related but different stand, urging that despite his insistence on the Prose Life as a source, it does not really matter whether Flaubert read the original or the version of Lecointre-Dupont: in either event, a spark of inspiration passed from the medieval author to Flaubert, a spark without which the *Légende* would not, could not have been what it is. With his customary finesse, Professor Vinaver then develops at length the vast implications of this direct contact, for medieval studies, for the novel, for Flaubert, and for creativity in general.

The reader will sense our malaise. This is a fascinating subject studied with great erudition, and its premises are asserted with all the authority of an acknowledged master. Unfortunately, it is still highly likely that Flaubert could not have read the document, even if he had known of its existence, which knowledge we do not think has been shown. Hence the original cannot have had the effect Vinaver claims, even if all the parallels are actually there, which we do not think is the case. More than that, the account of the Prose Life given by Lecointre-Dupont does not always say what it has been reported to say at crucial points, and we do not think it could have had the effect Vinaver describes either.

But – we have acknowledged the fact – a simple refutation based on Flaubert's lack of skills cannot be made. If we wish to maintain our position that the original Old French Prose Life is not involved in the redaction of Flaubert's *Saint Julien*, we must undertake to treat all of the points at issue. We shall study the numerous ramifications of the Prose Life hypothesis one at a time, with reference to the problem of Flaubert's access to the text, with reference in detail to the problem of the alleged probative resemblances between the medieval text and Flaubert's, with reference to the problem posed by the way Flaubert refers to his work in his Correspondence, and finally with reference to the structural, or broadly formal inspiration which Flaubert is sometimes said to have taken from a reading of the Prose Life, and which, it is claimed, he cannot have obtained anywhere else. It is apropos to invoke here some of the minor sources Flaubert used, but which do not belong to the sequence discussed in Chapters Three through Six. For the convenience of the reader, we summarize each section of our argument here.

A / *The Problem of Access*

There is a possibility that Flaubert knew of Ms. Fr. 6447 (or one of its several analogues – for, although the point has not been given much weight, there are a number of these that he might have consulted). We shall conclude that the arguments adduced in defense of the notion are very weak, but that others could be proposed. We cannot prove that Flaubert could not have found a manuscript of the Prose Life. It is only highly unlikely.

B / *The Problem of the Texts*

We shall examine the alleged detailed resemblances between the Prose Life and Flaubert. We shall not neglect the three retained by Duckworth; but we must also examine all the others, which Vinaver may be presumed to retain, since he dismissed Raitt's arguments. Each of the alleged borrowings will be discussed in its context and compared in detail with both Flaubert's text and the intermediary we presume, Lecointre-Dupont's adaptation. Only readings common to the three will not be treated in detail, since they obviously have no value as proofs. We shall urge reasons for thinking not a single one of the purported parallels is convincing.

We are also obliged to consider the question of whether Flaubert did or did not misread his suggested source in a few scattered spots, as these alleged misreadings are central to the thesis we are here opposing. Several of the essential 'borrowings' our predecessors insist upon are in fact radical misunderstandings of the medieval text. We shall show that these misreadings are impossible on palaeographic and philological grounds, and shall further suggest that the manuscript is so clear at these points that a reader *able* to make those mistakes would have been *unable* to imitate the text correctly elsewhere, since he would not have understood anything of what he was reading.

C / *The Problem of the Correspondence*

We shall examine the allegation according to which Flaubert's letters give evidence that, late in the redaction, he came upon Ms. Fr. 6447, and that it provided the indispensable 'fil du collier' without which he had been finding himself crippled in the writing of the Tale. Close examination and complete quotation will show that the *Correspondance* in fact indicates nothing of the sort. Neither have we been able to discover any evidence that the task of writing seemed to go faster after Flaubert came to Paris and its library in November of 1875.

D / *The Problem of Structure*

Finally, we shall turn to the larger and vaguer issues of the thematic and structural elements which Flaubert is alleged to have drawn from Ms. Fr. 6447 (or from Lecointre-Dupont, but in their original medieval form). For, if such elements could be shown to exist only in the Prose Life and in the *Légende* as printed, then we should have to acknowledge that somehow all our previous arguments had to be flawed. We shall show that the allegedly similar themes and structures are in fact present in Flaubert's very earliest plans for the story, or shared with third works known to be his sources, or so banal as to be inevitable, or in reality so profoundly dissimilar that they cannot be used either to sustain the burden of proving that Flaubert read the medieval Life, or to help us understand the *Légende* itself.

With this final demonstration, our argument will be complete: Flaubert did not read, and did not use, any manuscript of the medieval French Prose Life of Saint Julian. With this statement we shall, essentially, have returned to the position originally adopted by Cigada, and which has seemed logical to us all along: there is no reason to think Flaubert *could* have read the medieval original.

A / THE PROBLEM OF ACCESS

Let us begin with the practical question of how Flaubert would have had access to the collection of saints' lives in Ms. B.N. Fr. 6447 or perhaps a similar manuscript. We are obliged to discuss in some detail Duckworth's account of how it might have come about. His hypothesis (first stated in 'Flaubert and the Legend,' 107-08) is based on a misinterpretation of parts of a letter to him (which he quotes) from Marcel Thomas, now Conservateur en Chef of the Département des Manuscrits at the Bibliothèque Nationale. The letter mentions in passing that the Ancien supplément français of that collection, to which B.N. Fr. 6447 originally belonged, is treated in Léopold Delisle's *Cabinet des Manuscrits de la Bibliothèque Impériale* [*Nationale*], Vol. II (Paris: Imprimerie Nationale, 1874). Apparently unfamiliar with the work in question, Duckworth assumes that the *Cabinet des Manuscrits* is some sort of catalogue, and that Flaubert must have consulted it, learning thereby of the existence of B.N. Fr. 6447.[2] Duckworth grafts onto this hypothesis a suggestion that Flaubert may

---

2 Duckworth also seems to have been unaware that the Julian story occurs in some ten different B.N. manuscripts.

The question of whether Flaubert may have been inspired to seek out a genuine medieval book by a desire for physical *realia* in hand or at least in view (like the parrot of *Un Coeur simple* – or Carthage for *Salammbô* or the Rouen tympanum for *Hérodias*: see Duckworth, 'Flaubert and the Legend,' 109) is to a large extent moot. The people around him were certainly aware of the parrot, but never mention the B.N. manuscripts, and neither does Flaubert. In any case his use of the Rouen Julian window is perfectly well established, for those who think he needed a real object before him.

have been aided in his search and subsequent reading of the manuscript by his friend Frédéric Baudry, himself a librarian (though not necessarily a medievalist) and therefore a 'colleague' of Léopold Delisle. This hypothesis is repeated in Duckworth's revised edition of the *Trois Contes* (1969, pp. 54-5).

It should be pointed out that Delisle's *Cabinet* is not a catalogue of manuscripts but the standard history of the creation of the Bibliothèque Nationale's present-day manuscript collection, and of the accession and origin of its various *fonds* (its subtitle is *Etude sur la formation de ce dépôt* [i.e. of the *Cabinet des Manuscrits*]) as well as of the successive administrations of the Nationale. As for Frédéric Baudry, he may well have known Delisle, who was one of the foremost scholars of his time; but Baudry worked at Versailles, the Arsenal, and the Mazarine, and never at the Bibliothèque Nationale, so far as is known. In any case, his qualifications as a medievalist remain to be shown.[3] Finally, it is absolutely unnecessary to assume Flaubert thought of consulting any Bibliothèque Nationale catalogue at all, not even the handwritten ones available to him then (see our Bibliography, No. 4): if he had felt he needed to look at a medieval manuscript, his thoughts would most likely have turned to Alençon. Duckworth agrees that Flaubert used Lecointre-Dupont, and the latter is explicit about the nature and location of his source. Far from mentioning any Paris manuscripts, he in fact implies his is unique.

Nevertheless, we acknowledge that Flaubert could possibly have found the manuscripts of the Prose Life (though we find no reason to settle on a particular one, e.g. Fr. 6447) in the same catalogues available to Langlois or Lecointre-Dupont but used by neither; and also, by Flaubert's time, Paulin Paris had published his *Manuscrits françois de la Bibliothèque du Roi* (1836-1848), with numerous details on the first few hundred manuscripts of the Ancien Fonds, several of which contain the standard saints' lives in prose. However, at the risk of repeating ourselves, we doubt seriously (with Cigada) that Flaubert could have made sense of the thirteenth-century text, if indeed he ever tried to do so. The medieval 'lettre de forme' is not in fact easily read by an inexperienced person, however cultivated, despite Professor Vinaver's argument. Only a few minutes spent in any palaeography seminar should suffice to show the general applicability of this principle.[4] More important, for we do not know which friend might

---

3 For his biography and principal works, see Balteau, Prévost, *et al.*, *Dictionnaire de biographie française*, V (Paris: Letouzey et Ané, 1951), 897-8. He did not join the Académie des Inscriptions et Belles-Lettres, to which Delisle belonged, until 1879.

4 'La Légende,' 115-16. In any case, B.N. Fr. 6447, to which Vinaver refers, apparently without having it in hand at the time, is written in a round *libraria*, rather than the more familiar, more angular hand most often called *lettre de forme*.

have helped Flaubert, the greatest problem for anyone reading Old French manuscripts, unless he or she is an expert in the language, is not the script at all, but the sense of the text. It is not impossible that one of the experts of the time read and explained the Prose Life to Flaubert and that the latter never mentioned the experience to anyone who has left us a record of this; but it is a very risky assumption.

B / THE PROBLEM OF THE TEXTS

Despite the force of this line of argument, we should have to abandon our position if it were possible to affirm, beyond any doubt, that Flaubert's Tale contains multiple textual reminiscences of the Prose Life, of the type easily proven in the case of Langlois's or of Lecointre-Dupont's adaptations. Miss Smith claims that there are a number of parallels and coincidences of this type. We cannot pronounce on the validity of all of these claims; but in the instances which Vinaver and Duckworth have made available in their published work, the resemblances do not strike us as being at all compelling.[5] Most of the parallels cited by Duckworth in the notes to his edition prove, upon examination, to be passages which occur at the same point in all three texts: the Prose Life, Lecointre-Dupont's adaptation of the Prose Life, and Flaubert's text. Thus, of course, no matter how many of this sort there are, they do not show that Flaubert used the Prose Life, because Lecointre-Dupont is already acknowledged by all to have been one of his principal sources.[6]

There are, however, some more complicated cases. In a few places Duckworth notes verbal similarities between Flaubert's text and a statement in the Prose Life *but in a very different kind of context*: thus, for example, in Note 95 ('Il ne refuse nul encontre de *chevalier* ne de serjant. Tant par est de ses armes preus et aventureus que il est issus de mainte presse le jor et de mainte mellee u uns autres eust esté *ocis*.' B.N. Fr. 6447, fol. 214a; Appendix B, para. 64), the Prose Life is claimed as source for Flaubert's description of Julian's first exile ('En tournant sa masse d'armes, il se débarrassa de quatorze *chevaliers*. Il défit, en champ clos, tous ceux qui se proposèrent. Plus de vingt fois, on le crut *mort*'). The reader may judge for himself whether this parallel seems striking enough to justify calling the first 'indisputably the source' of the second. There are only two common terms, and the statements made about Julian are very different

5 See esp. Vinaver, 'Flaubert and the Legend,' 1953, 233-5, and Duckworth, *Trois Contes*, 194-210, or 'Flaubert and the Legend,' 109-12.

6 Such is the case for Duckworth's Notes 23 (the word *fêtes* occurs in Lecointre-Dupont and is not in the Prose Life), 30, 31, 32 (which is somewhat contradictory in any case), 70, 99, and 148.

(a demurrer which applies to other purported similarities in the series that follows). For our present purposes, it is equally important to note that Flaubert's lines are not in the same context as the Prose Life's and do not even relate to the same incident: the Life is describing Julian's exploits in the service of the knight whose widow he will marry, long after Julian has been to the Orient and returned. The two stories do not in fact parallel each other at all during their accounts of Julian's first exile – a circumstance easily and naturally explained by our hypothesis that Flaubert, following Maury's note, began to make direct use of Lecointre-Dupont only at this point, but hard to understand if we accept the hypothesis that his *Légende* is influenced from beginning to end by the Prose Life.

Further and similar transplants create the parallels stated to exist in Duckworth's Notes 110, 116, and 118. In Note 110, Julian's refusal to accept severance pay at the Jerusalem leprosarium which he has served for many years (Prose Life) is equated with his refusal to accept money for his service to the Emperor of Occitania (*Légende*; there is, once again, no such episode in the medieval lives). The first detail is a hagiographic commonplace, the second is imperative in the *Légende*, where Julian must refuse all other recompense, since he is finally to receive the hand of the Emperor's daughter. Flaubert is following neither Lecointre-Dupont nor the Prose Life here. The error is more serious in the case of Note 116, for the central notion of hunting is involved: the knight who in the Prose Life calls Julian 'mauvais' does *not* in fact mention hunting, despite Duckworth's affirmation that he does (text in Appendix B, para. 15). The same must be said of Note 118: Duckworth implies that in the Prose Life Julian spends the whole night before his fatal hunt and absence 'wondering whether to go or stay'; but the reference is not to the hunt in the Life but to another incident entirely, to Julian's original, and much more important decision concerning the propriety of breaking off his pilgrimage to Compostella.

In the Introduction to the *Trois Contes* another radical switch in context is made. Duckworth points out (p. 60) that in the Prose Life Julian's parents go to sleep in his bed 'bras a bras, bouce a bouce,'[7] and that when Julian takes the leper to his body to warm him, Flaubert writes: 'Julien s'étala dessus complètement, bouche contre bouche ...' We have already discussed this passage (above, p. 47). Duckworth suggests that the transposition of the 'bouche contre bouche' detail from the parents' distant couch results from the fact that both scenes take place in bed. This seems too strained to have probative force. The two incidents are widely separated, and the sequence of events in Flaubert's ending is in any case his

---

7 Appendix B, para. 51; both Duckworth's edition (Note 128) and his 'Flaubert and the Legend' (p. 111) read incorrectly *le bras a bras*.

own invention, appearing in no other version in quite the same form. As we have shown in Chapter Five, the idea of close physical contact, mouth and all, came from Lecointre-Dupont's description of how Julian carried the leper to the boat (to the extent that it came from any textual source at all): 'le front rongé d'ulcères du lépreux retomba sur le front de son hôte, et le sang livide des plaies du pauvre roula sur les joues et sur la bouche de Julien ...' (see Appendix B, page 151).[8]

To buttress the notion that Flaubert took the 'bouche contre bouche' detail from the unrelated bed-scene involving the parents, Duckworth also invokes the fact that in the Prose Life, as will be recalled, Julian's wife is present at the leper's arrival and offers him her warmth (see above, pp. 47-48). We see no parallel here and no reason for Flaubert to have associated the two scenes, for in the Prose Life, precisely, there *is* no bed scene involving the leper: the wife is just lying down when the leper undergoes his transformation. (We reproduce this scene in connection with the Alençon text in Appendix B.) Lecointre-Dupont, however, *does* have a bed-scene. It is one of his own invention, as we have remarked above (p. 49), for his manuscript source breaks off just before this point, and he had no way of knowing how it would have ended. In any case Flaubert is not following either the thirteenth- or the nineteenth-century text here, for Julian's wife is not present. He also omits the later scene of symbolic martyrdom at the hands of robbers, as we remarked elsewhere. We see no reason to think Flaubert would have associated the scene of Julian's contact with the leper and the scene of the parents being put to bed.

There are also one or two minor lapses in the notes, but they need not detain us long. In Note 32 *deduit de chiens et d'oisiaus* is translated as 'hunting with hounds and hawks,' which is a bit forced: *deduit* simply means 'pleasure' (cf. *deduit de bois* in the same sentence of the Prose Life) and not specifically 'hunting'; but the context is clear, and in any case Duckworth agrees that Flaubert must have understood his source to mean that Julian loved hunting, at which point all reference to the Prose Life is superfluous, since Lecointre-Dupont says the same thing, only explicitly. Lecointre-Dupont's sentence: 'il fut, comme on est à cet âge, amateur passionné de déduits de chasse, de chiens et d'oiseaux' also furnishes a source for the phrase 'en gazouillant comme un oiseau,' applied to Julian in one of Flaubert's manuscript drafts, if we consider, with Duckworth, that Flaubert would here have associated hunting and singing ('Flaubert

8 Lecointre-Dupont's text is in fact based on a similar passage in the Prose Life:
   '... li mesiaux mist son front contre le sien, si qu'il alena adés en la bouche
   Julien. ...' Alençon, B.M. 27, fol. 5 verso; see Appendix B, para. 74. Thus the passage probably belongs in the series of double parallels cited in Note 6 above.

and the Legend,' 110). In fact the whole description of Julian's childhood occurs in a section of the draft which Flaubert composed in the autumn, at Concarneau.[9]

In Note 83 it is claimed that the Prose Life parallels the *Légende* in showing Julian 'devoid of pity'; yet, as the note itself makes clear, Julian does not kill the stag in the Prose Life (nor does he in Lecointre-Dupont), as he does in Flaubert. The parallel claimed in Note 96 is also exaggerated: Flaubert in fact makes no mention of alms, although the Prose Life does (and Lecointre-Dupont does not).

The cases of Notes 124, 138, and 141 are more interesting. Note 124 is correct but incomplete. Dr Duckworth claims the thirteenth-century prose version of the legend is the only one to show Julian's wife giving food to the weary parents. But Lecointre-Dupont furnishes, at this point, a few lines from a popular lament about Julian (see Appendix B, page 148) in which the parents' meal is specifically mentioned.

It is also suggested (Note 138) that Flaubert had Julian's parents buried at a monastery three days distant from his castle because of material in the Prose Life. Examination of the Old French text at this point (in B.N. Fr. 6447 or any similar *légendier*) shows that Julian and his wife went off into the woods after the murder, remaining there for three days (see the Alençon text in Appendix B, para. 59). Here, by the way, they gathered the various foods discussed below in connection with 'coquillages.' The author then switches subject entirely, to discuss the actions of Julian's companions, who were led to discover the parents' bodies and to bury them in a *moustier*.[10] The two passages must be presumed somehow to have fused – become conflated (in this place and only in this place) – in the mind of the *puissant prosateur*. Two arguments, one familiar, one less so, seem to us to indicate that it did not happen. First of all, the language and the hand are as clear here as they are anywhere else, and we have no reason to think Flaubert would suddenly have become confused (let us say, lost his place), thus unintentionally combining two statements which, in the manuscript, are thirty-five lines (the better part of a column) apart, and which, above all, refer to two entirely different situations – this in a story which he is said to have understood so well that he could plagiarize it as needed. In the second place, the two texts, even when conflated, cannot in any possible sense mean that the *moustier* is three days' journey from anywhere: the time reference occurs in the *first* passage and describes the length of

---

9 For the dating of the sections of this draft, see above, page 55, and cf. our discussion of chronology below, pp. 78-79.

10 The latter word Flaubert is required to have misunderstood as meaning 'monastery' rather than 'church.' (See Appendix B, p. 131.)

or ⁊ sans argent. ⁊ nen porta cascuns ke vne
chape. Ensi sen fuient pmi. ⁊ bois. ⁊ souuent
se regardent ke nus ne les siue p̃ els retorner.
Ensi furent ii. iij. iors ou bois. ke onques
ne mangierent fors glant ⁊ souue. ⁊ au
tres fruis ke il galloient p les buissons. Di v̾
lairai ester de iulien ⁊ de sa feme. si v̾ dirai des
chis ki estoient el bois por cachier coment il re
uindrent. Ensi come il cerkoient la forest por
les bestes ke il queroient. se st̃ areste deles vn
buisson v il auoient veu. i. cheurel. ⁊ lauueore
rent. ⁊ le vaureur ocirre. Qnt il loe comencaa

il galloient

The *libraria* Gothic hand of Ms. B.N. Fr. 6447, fol. 217a, enlarged.
Prose Life, paras. 59-60. Note *glant* in line 5, and the abbreviated form
conquilloient in line 6 (isolated enlargement below). The Prose Life
hypothesis claims that Flaubert misread the former and the last syllable
of the latter yet interpreted the abbreviated syllables of the latter correctly.

time Julian and his wife spent in the forest. The *moustier* (not a mona-stery, but the chapel or a local church) is mentioned only as the place where Julian's former subjects buried his parents. It is, at best, misleading the reader to translate the subjects of 'Ensi furent il .iij. jors au bois' and 'Adont ont [il] fait les corps ensevelir' by the same pronoun *they*; the first *il* of course refers to Julian and his wife, the second to Julian's retainers.

Note 141 is rather more difficult. The matter of a manuscript reading *conquilloient* as source (misunderstood) for Flaubert's having Julian eat 'coquillages,' during his second exile, is complex. First, we have examined Ms. B.N. Fr. 6447, and it seems to us to weaken the hypothesis of its use considerably. In the manuscript the word is written, as one might expect, with the standard medieval abbreviations for the opening syllables, speci-fically for [kõ] and [ki] ('Tironian nine' and *q* with superscript *i*). While we doubt, as Vinaver does, Flaubert's knowledge of the medieval abbrevia-tion system, let that be assumed. The remainder of the word is written with perfect clarity and fully spelled out: '-lloient.' The whole word may be roughly reproduced typographically as $9q^{i}lloient$. It seems to us defi-cient in logic to urge that a reader (Flaubert or a helper) who could recog-nize the Tironian mark for *com-* and the abbreviation for *qui* (and thus interpret *conqui-*, or the even more rare resolution *coqui-*) would then be unable to read a normal hand writing the remainder in full. More impor-tant (for we have no reason to believe Flaubert consulted B.N. Fr. 6447 rather than any other manuscript), the suggested misreading turns a verb into a noun, and thereby makes nonsense of the sentence.[11]

Finally, Flaubert's drafts show first the word *polypes* and not 'coquil-lages' (fol. 439 recto); and hunting for and eating crustaceans on the beach was a personal experience of Flaubert's, here lent to Julian.[12]

Flaubert's alleged misreading of *glant* ms. as *plantes*, which Duckworth proposes in the same note, is similarly improbable; the latter word is femi-nine, and thus longer both palaeographically and phonetically (making a slip during the *dictée intérieure* unlikely); and Gothic *g* and *p* are no more alike than those in modern printed books.

Notes 90 and 133 may also be explained without recourse to the Prose Life hypothesis, and the explanation is of interest for the light it sheds on the relationship between a narrative composition and its presumed sources, as a general matter. In note 90, Duckworth points out that Flaubert's 'le

11 Let us note in passing that Alençon 27, for example, has the not uncommon graphy *concuilloient*, which does not resemble *coquillages* by *any* stretch of the imagination.
12 Oee (all in the Conard edition) *Notes de Voyages*, I, 385; also *Tentation de Saint Antoine*, p. 458, and *Trois contes*, p. 19. See also, in his letters, Flaubert's fre-quent references to *coquillages* on the beach at Concarneau.

vent tanna sa peau' resembles a line in the Prose Life: 'tant ala par glace et par pleuve ke sa char devint toute noire.' There is a change of agent (wind for rain and hail or snow), and there is no verbal similarity whatsoever, but that does not perhaps suffice to allow us to dismiss the parallel entirely.

Those facts do, however, suggest what is the most likely explanation of this minor resemblance. We have here, on a small scale, the same phenomenon discussed at length above in connection with the universality of motifs: in the description of Julian's first exile, we are dealing with *clichés*, in this case one which has occurred to both authors naturally, without any need to assume any borrowing. Examination of Flaubert's drafts here will help us understand how the reading came to assume its final form. It is the result of a certain amount of revision. The first time a reference to Julian's appearance occurs, it reads, not surprisingly: 'son teint se hâla' (B.N., N.A.F., 23663, fol. 430 verso). The need for an agent must have made itself felt, however, for on fol. 458 verso (the first revision), 'son teint se hâla' has been crossed out, and a new sentence inserted: 'le soleil et la pluie tannèrent sa peau.' It is obvious what Flaubert has in mind. Living out of doors, Julian undergoes the changes in appearance which the weather – *and the sun* – bring on. Finally on fol. 432 recto (a somewhat later revision) the wind is mentioned for the first time: 'Le vent, le soleil et la pluie tannèrent sa peau.' (The first two terms are later transposed.) It is not until the text is in nearly final form that the sentence we know, 'le vent tanna sa peau,' is created by the removal of the sun and the rain.

The multiple states of this line serve as a useful reminder of just how complex a process the composition of the *Légende* was. Flaubert was not copying anything; he was making his text up as he went from draft to draft. At times it is closer to the Prose Life than at others, although the original statement seems to have little to do with the medieval text, and the only term the two texts actually have in common is ephemeral (*la pluie*) and does not appear in Flaubert's *Légende* as printed. The original reading 'son teint se hâla' and the presence of the sun in several readings indicates that Flaubert thought of Julian as having been sunburned, rather than weatherburned as in the Prose Life, right up to his final draft; yet the final draft is clearly not radically new, not the result of sudden contact with some new source, but the product of a creative evolution. The drafts show Flaubert turning over, in his own mind, the variables of what is in fact the most banal of situations. Formally, his text may not be described as a recasting of the thirteenth-century statement with every word changed, but demonstrably representing an attempt at saying the same thing. It is intrinsically different, because it is of his own making: it is a new statement of a commonplace, or a micro-motif.

Note 133 allows us to expand upon this notion of coincidence in expression. It refers to the moment at which Julian returns to his room and finds in his bed a man and a woman, his parents, whom he takes to be his wife with a lover. The point here – in each and every version – is that he must not be able to see their faces, although it is day.[13] Why can Flaubert's Julian not see? Because the window does not admit enough light: 'les *vitraux* garnis de plomb obscurcissaient la pâleur de l'aube.' And the thirteenth-century prose gives the same cause, or nearly so: 'La cambre n'estoit mie mult clere, car la *fenestre* estoit entreclose.' Lecointre-Dupont, however, slips up and contradicts his manuscript: '... à la clarté douteuse de la *porte* entr'ouverte, il entrevoit dans son lit deux personnes endormies.'

Here is a very small agreement between Flaubert and the Prose Life against Lecointre-Dupont. The latter mentions the door at a place where the two others mention the window. (For the one, it is open; for the other, it is closed.) The latter speaks of seeing, where Flaubert and one clause of the Prose Life (later contradicted) speak of not seeing or not seeing well (see Note 13 above). Can it be doubted that this vague *rencontre*, like the preceding one, is due to pure coincidence? It must be dark for a reason. There are only two possibilities, rhetorically speaking: either one expects (but does not get) light from the window, or one expects (but does not get) light from the door. Just as the Prose Life chose the window arbitrarily, and Lecointre-Dupont chose the door arbitrarily, so Flaubert has chosen the window, in his turn, no doubt arbitrarily – but more logically and naturally than it might seem at a glance, since Lecointre-Dupont's door

---

13 We must insist that the question is not where the feeble light in the room is coming from, but why Julian does not recognize his own parents until too late: thus Flaubert's long and to some extent original description of how Julian touches first his father's beard, then his mother's long hair, then the beard again. In B.N. Fr. 6447, on the other hand, Julian can see well enough to distinguish two persons, one of each sex, but he cannot tell who they are: 'La cambre n'estoit mie mult clere, car la fenestre estoit entreclose, si c'on i veoit mult peu. Il vint vers son lit, si *esgarda* cels ki i gisent, et quide por voir ke il ait home avoec sa feme, et *la veue li trescanja por la dame qu'il avoit veue* el lit. [...] Au lit s'en vient comme hors del sens et les a ans .ij. decolés' (fol. 216 verso; Duckworth prints erroneously *Si con il veoit mult peu*, and thus translates the first sentence misleadingly. The Alençon text is similar, see Appendix B, para. 52). Compare Lecointre-Dupont: '... il vole droit à sa chambre, et, à la clarté douteuse de la porte entr'ouverte, il *entrevoit* dans son lit deux personnes endormies. Sa femme est adultère, songe-t-il, et il frappe ...' (Appendix B, page 148), and Flaubert: 'Les vitraux garnis de plomb obscurcissaient la pâleur de l'aube. Julien *se prit les pieds* dans des vêtements, par terre ... il avançait vers le lit, *perdu* dans les ténèbres ... il *sentit* contre sa bouche l'impression d'une barbe ... il crut voir ... le fantôme de sa femme, *une lumière à la main.*' Thus the degree of visibility (or illumination) and the reasons for the confusion are not the same in any two of the texts under consideration.

opens only onto a corridor, but the *aube* is *necessarily* beyond the window. (It is past noon in the Prose Life, by the way.) This is precisely what we have in mind when we claim that coincidence may be used to explain certain resemblances between two texts without reference to the commonly accepted meanings of the terms *source* and *influence*.[14]

'A minor point?' asks Duckworth of the window coincidence. He continues: 'Certainly – but what is important *cumulatively* is the fact that in these examples Flaubert's version includes details which bring it closer to [B.N. Fr. 6447] than to Lecointre-Dupont' ('Flaubert and the Legend,' 111). *Res ipsa loquitur*. We find no accumulation of details of the type Duckworth and Vinaver suggest. We have examined every example of textual coincidence that our predecessors have put forth. Most of these parallels are not probative, because the same text, or a genuinely similar one, occurs in Lecointre-Dupont. Others are created by critics' minor misunderstandings or misreadings of the thirteenth-century text, which have led to exaggerated claims. A few result from more complex presuppositions, which we have sought to disprove. We do not accept, notably, any suggestion that Flaubert copied isolated phrases or short clauses from the manuscript, then transferred them from one context to another far away, in which they find a new and radically different application, or that he attributed actions to protagonists the Prose Life does not attribute them to: to say he did is to warp the only functional definition of a source. And we find it improbable that Flaubert could have been the victim of the rare and peculiar misreadings our predecessors have attributed to him. Finally, coincidence seems to us a probable explanation for more than one parallel between Flaubert's tale and other, earlier forms of the legend (for further examples see Chapter Two, pp. 19-20).[15]

C / THE PROBLEM OF THE CORRESPONDENCE

Thus, a detailed examination of the text of the *Légende de Saint Julien* gives us no reason to think Flaubert ever saw or used the Prose Life. We

14 Much the same can be said of Dr Duckworth's presentation of a second similarity in the same episode. In both the Prose Life and the *Légende*, Julian's wife closes something when she leaves the parents alone in the room. We consider that natural, even inevitable, just as it is inevitable that Julian should open the door when he arrives. In any case the alleged parallel is imperfect: in the Prose Life the wife closes the door, but in the *Légende* she does not, she closes the window.

15 It is not necessary, nor would it be scholarly, for us to list *in extenso* the places where Flaubert *might* have used, but did not use traits of the Old French text which are not in Lecointre-Dupont; such possibilities will surely occur to every reader. One is the place where, during his wanderings, Julian is not only refused lodging but accused of being a danger to the virtue of any host's daughter: B.N. Fr. 6447, fol. 212c; Alençon 27, fol. 175a, text in Appendix B, para. 13.

shall now study the little that is known about the Tale's composition, in order to discover whether the external history of the *Légende* can furnish any support for the Prose Life hypothesis. For the textual similarities we have been discussing are not the only indications that the proponents of this theory have offered. In search of circumstantial evidence to buttress their claim that Flaubert used some manuscript version of the thirteenth-century life, our predecessors have presented a chronology for the *Légende*'s composition.

According to their account, a desperate Flaubert struggled throughout the autumn of 1875 to give some kind of shape to his Tale, but floundered painfully, unable to give his story coherence, or to find a central theme for it. (Indeed, his Correspondence does contain several complaints of slow progress, depression, and the like, for he is still in the grip of the nervous trouble brought on by Commanville's ruin.) Only upon discovering a Paris manuscript of the Prose Life[16] was Flaubert galvanized into action: 'he seemed unexpectedly to see the work clearly for the first time' (Duckworth, *Trois Contes*, 36). The difficulties disappeared. His rate of composition shot up, and he finished the Tale in a very short time.

This scheme is based on various references in the *Correspondance*.[17] All of the references in question are, we think, much better read in the context of the letters in which they appear, and in the context of the entire correspondence for this period. To take only one obvious example, there is a passage in a letter of Flaubert to George Sand (December 11, 1875, *Correspondance*, VII, 279) which reads:

> Vous savez que j'ai quitté mon grand roman pour écrire une petite bêtise *moyenâgeuse* qui n'aura pas plus de trente pages. Cela me met dans un milieu plus propre que le monde moderne et me fait du bien. Puis je cherche un roman contemporain, mais je balance entre plusieurs embryons d'idées. Je voudrais faire quelque chose de serré et de violent. Le fil du collier (c'est-à-dire le principal) me manque encore.

16 In November, 'soon after his arrival' in Paris, according to Vinaver, *Rise*, 117; his later date, December or January (*ibid.*, footnote 8), agrees more with his interpretation of the letter of December 11, which he quotes; but see our Note 17, below. Duckworth dates the discovery of the Prose Life February 6, the date of a letter to George Sand in which Flaubert mentions having had 'différentes lectures à expédier,' without saying what they were *or in what connection* he was doing them. This latter date, at least, seems impossible: it would require us to think that Flaubert wrote his Tale essentially in less than two weeks. Never in his life is he known to have written so fast.

17 See Duckworth, *Trois Contes*, 34-7, and 'Flaubert and the Legend,' Note 18, p. 113, or Vinaver, *Rise*, 117-18, and 'La Légende,' 107-08.

Surprising as it may seem, this passage has been used (with a minor difference in punctuation) to support the Prose Life theory: since Flaubert can say 'le fil du collier me manque' on December 11, it is clear he does not yet have his Tale well in hand! But the fact that he changes the subject of his statements after the second sentence of the quotation *must* be taken into account. The work for which he has not found the *fil du collier*, for which he is hesitating *entre plusieurs embryons d'idées*, is the second novel and *not* the *Saint Julien*. The *bêtise moyenâgeuse* (not 'moyennageuse') is already under way: [il] 'me fait du bien.' The last sentence of the passage is a semi-asyndetic juxtaposition of a type familiar to those even slightly acquainted with Flaubert's epistolary style.

Moreover, the often-repeated notion that Flaubert's rate of composition changed suddenly, under the influence of some new source he had found in Paris, fails to take into account the totality of the available evidence and the nature of Flaubert's work habits.

To begin with, one must remember that Flaubert always composed slowly, at least by comparison with most writers. From beginning to end, the average rate for *Madame Bovary* is about one-fifth of a page per day, which is about the rate for *Saint Julien*, insofar as such statements have any meaning. Also, examination of the draft, which is sequential in its composition, shows that the rate of work was irregular. Despite what one may gather from some remarks in the Correspondence, the writing was only a fraction more rapid at the very end than in the autumn in Brittany (during which latter period Flaubert was, after all, recovering from a near nervous breakdown), and very slow only in the first weeks after his November arrival in Paris. At least some of the delay in the *Légende*'s completion may be attributed to a halt in production before Flaubert's trip to Paris, a halt caused not by *impuissance* but by the strongly felt and stated need to consult particular books not available at Concarneau.

Flaubert's rate of composition for the *Saint Julien* can be fairly well charted for the time in Concarneau with the help of his *Correspondance*, in which he often speaks of the work. He began desultory work on the Tale on September 22 or 23 (letter to Caroline, *Correspondance*, VII, 262). On the 25th, he had completed one-half page of a plan (his second), which was ultimately to cover three pages written on one side each, and which was eventually heavily rewritten, although, so far as we can determine, it is not possible to know when the rewriting was done. By October 4, he had completed his second plan and he may have begun writing on October 5 (see *Correspondance*, VII, 266ff). By October 8, he had completed 'à peu près une page' (VII, 270). We remind the reader that this means completion through to near-final form, as was his practice for the *Julien* (see above, page 54). And before the 19th, he had completed about six pages.[18] By that time, he had reached the point in the manuscript where Julian's introduction to hunting is described, with details concerning his hunting pack and his falcons. It is perfectly natural, then, that he should write on October 17th to Caroline:

> le petit Julien l'Hospitalier [not 'le petit Julien'] n'avance guère et m'occupe un peu; c'est là le principal. Enfin je ne croupis plus dans l'oisiveté qui me dévorait [hardly the words of a man unable to write] ; mais j'aurais besoin de quelques livres sur le moyen âge! Et puis, ce n'est pas commode à écrire, cette histoire-là! Je persévère néanmoins, je suis vertueux. (VII, 273)

The situation may at least be guessed at, for the successive drafts at this point show a striking progression. At first Flaubert wrote approximately what any educated Frenchman of his day would have known about hunting without being a hunter himself; but afterwards he rewrote what he had done, on the basis of a vast and thorough documentation, whose use is one of the most interesting features of this part of his Tale.[19] We suspect strongly that around October 20 he stopped writing almost entirely, having done what he could to sketch out the passage, and not being inclined to continue without putting it into nearly final form, as he had the preceding pages. He very likely put the *Julien* aside to await his return to Paris and access to a library. 'Ce n'est pas commode à écrire, cette histoire-là' may mean almost anything, but in the light of the sentence which precedes it in the letter, there is good reason to think it is the detailed fabric of the story, its well-known documentary aspect, which Flaubert feels to be lacking, and not the basic thread. After all, the plan referred to on September 25 was already in existence, as was another, older plan (to be discussed later). On November 1st he left for Paris.

Thus despite his rather general remarks on the difficulty of writing in the state he was in, which our predecessors have taken as references to the Julian tale specifically, Flaubert actually prepared the detailed plan of the work and wrote some six pages of nearly finished manuscript in twenty-five or twenty-six days at Concarneau. The average rate is a little under one-quarter of a page a day. Once he was in Paris, he wrote fewer letters, and it is not as easy to follow him closely. By mid-November he was back at work; on December 9 he hoped to finish Part One in two weeks (*Supplé-*

18 The figure is variously given as 'six' or 'dix pages'; cf. *Correspondance, Supplément*, III, 223. The latter figure makes no sense for a number of reasons; thus we adopt the former figure, although it does not serve our thesis as well.

19 See Bart, 'Flaubert and Hunting: *La Légende de Saint-Julien l'Hospitalier*,' *Nineteenth-Century French Studies*, 4 (1975-76), 31-52.

ment, III, 228). If he maintained this rate of production (which one cannot tell), then he wrote the last six pages of Part One in forty to forty-five days (mid-November to the end of December), that is, at a rate of about one-seventh of a page a day. We are convinced that this slower rate evidences only the time spent in gathering the great amount of detailed information on the medieval and modern hunt, which he could not have gotten any sooner; nevertheless, it should also be remembered that he was, at the time, a well-known figure, and there were probably many demands on his time whenever he was in Paris.

As with all of Flaubert's works, when he approached within fifteen or so manuscript pages of the end, his tempo picked up. Parts Two and Three of the Tale occupy, in fact, fifteen pages of fair copy; these he finished on February 17 (*Correspondance*, VII, 287). Here, his story was already firmly in hand and required no documentation to speak of beyond what Langlois, the *Legenda aurea*, and Lecointre-Dupont had given him or could give him in an hour's reading. He probably wrote the fifteen pages between the end of December and mid-February, a rate of perhaps one-third of a page per day, or, on an average, one-twelfth faster than he had in Brittany, where he was in a severe neurotic depression, and a little more than twice as fast as he had in the few weeks after his arrival in Paris, when he had to read and annotate some twenty books for the hunting passages.

We do not think that such figures are meaningful beyond the obvious deductions we have made: that Flaubert writes faster when he does not pause for documentation, and still faster when he is approaching the end, spending more hours at his task, and concentrating more on it. The change in rate of writing towards the end (more precisely, a change in attitude, an increase in optimism, to judge by the tone of certain remarks in the Correspondence) is not unusual for Flaubert and above all not peculiar to the *Légende*. To link purported speed of composition with presumed ease of composition ('writing suddenly accelerated and became easier,' Duckworth, *Trois Contes*, 36) is disingenuous at the least.

This rapid set of calculations should serve to indicate the small value as evidence of an occasional statement such as 'J'ai travaillé tout l'après-midi, pour faire dix lignes!' (*Correspondance*, VII, 272; Flaubert adds: 'Mais *je n'en suis plus à me désespérer*,' emphasis ours). Such a remark may well refer to word-by-word composition, and not to any problem with 'seeing the work clearly as a whole.' The latter notion requires us to ignore completely the fact that Flaubert had written two outlines, corresponding largely to the story we have, before he ever reached Paris or could have had access to the Prose Life. (The outlines are discussed in the following section.) There is, in sum, no evidence in the circumstances of composition to support the idea that Flaubert suddenly discovered a new source upon his return to Paris in November, 1875, or in the winter of 1875-76.

D / THE PROBLEM OF STRUCTURE

1 / *Some General Considerations*

Thorough examination and, eventually, refutation of the idea that Flaubert received the form or structure of his *Saint Julien* from an original medieval manuscript source would require a rather precise definition of what is significant in the relationship between a text and its source, as well as fairly complete agreement on why literary influence is important, when it is. Both problems, except insofar as they affect the development of traditional legends, are beyond the scope of this study. Nevertheless, it is perhaps not useless to set down a few comparatively superficial reasons, structural and accessorily psychological, for our conviction that the *Légende de Saint Julien* does not have much in common with the medieval Life.

Principally, it has been claimed that Flaubert's work owes something essential to the Prose Life: the thematically vital idea of Julian's passion for hunting or blood lust, with its fatal consequences, and with all its analogical buttresses, notably the striking parallel between the two hunting sequences: the successful massacre which is terminated by the killing of the black stag, and the nightmare hunt which is the prelude to the parricide scene.[20] Our predecessors were certain that Flaubert must have consulted B.N. Fr. 6447 or a similar manuscript and that he must thus have seized upon those features, which they thought characterized the medieval Life, as they characterize the *Légende*. Commentators have written at considerable length about the contact between two authors separated by a gulf of centuries, about the similarities between the creative impulse which drove the thirteenth-century writer to build a coherent and motivated story upon the skeletal account of the *Legenda aurea*,[21] and Flaubert's

20 See especially Duckworth, *Trois Contes* (1969), 36-7; Vinaver, 'La Légende,' 108ff., and *Rise of Romance*, 120-22, where the idea of symmetry is emphasized, and those of bloodlust and of psychological motivation in general are strenuously attacked -- an attitude to which we shall have occasion to refer later.

21 This latter idea requires us to assume the *Legenda aurea* is a direct source of the Prose Life. In fact it is not even possible to determine which is older. The preserved text of the Prose Life may be a half-century older than Jacobus's compilation (see Chapter One, page 8), and in any case, the latter's sources are, for the most part, unknown – a fact obliquely recognized by such statements as Maurice Hélin's: '[Jacobus] arranged, according to the liturgical year, the stories *which he had read or heard told*' (*A History of Medieval Latin Literature*, tr. Jean Chapman Snow, New York: William Salloch, 1949, p. 118. Italics ours). More recent commentators recognize the importance of Bartholomew of Trent's *Liber epilogorum* as a source for Jacobus, but are still not certain in matters of detail. 'Etwa 235 Quellenwerke werden neben noch nicht gezählten Hinweisen auf mündliche Informationen in der *Legenda aurea* angeführt. Die letzteren beweisen, dass Vora-

desire to elaborate, with guidance from his medieval predecessor, the complex structure of his *Saint Julien*.

The image of contact between two creative spirits is a good one, and holds true even though the contact in question was made, as it surely was, with the quintessentially Romantic creations of Lecointre-Dupont and LaVallée (which we reproduce in our Appendices B and E) rather than with any genuinely medieval form of the legend. The situation, where structural resemblances between the medieval text and Flaubert's *Conte* are concerned, is much the same as that discussed above in connection with readings common to the *Légende*, the Prose Life, and Lecointre-Dupont: Ockham's Razor prevents our considering that Flaubert borrowed from a conjectured source that which is present in a known source. Thus, for example, the parallel symmetries of the hunting scenes in the Prose Life and in the *Légende* are, structurally speaking, to be found in Lecointre-Dupont and even to a certain extent in LaVallée. But final determination here is as difficult as it has been since the beginning of this study. What one author can invent, another can also; what a given structure suggests to one, it may suggest to another, independently, in another time and another culture. Influence, on the level of theme and structure just as in matters of detail, may be practically undetectable, and its study requires even more caution than usual.

Nevertheless, whatever its implications, our present task is not itself a matter of criticism, of understanding the general mechanisms of creation. We are dealing, fortunately, with a specific question of literary history, and with specific texts having particular social and esthetic histories. That principle is worth a moment's attention. It is obviously risky to claim that a text written around 1250 at the latest is basically similar to one written well over six hundred years later – we shall see precisely how risky before the end of this chapter. Let us first recall that the *Saint Julien* is, despite certain theories, the product of a given age and of its habits, just as it is the work of a man whose practices and predilections are known. Our preceding chapters show clearly the primordial importance for the genesis of the *Légende* of nineteenth-century sources, whose language, images, and attitudes Flaubert may be expected to have grasped thoroughly and quickly.

gine tatsächlich auch Inhalte aus der verbalen Tradition in sein Werk aufgenommen hat,' write Maria von Nagy and N. Christoph de Nagy, *Die Legenda aurea und ihr Verfasser Jacobus de Voragine* (Berne and Munich: Francke, 1971), p. 26; cf. *New Cath. Encyc.*, VII, 813.

As we suggest elsewhere, the development of the legend is sporadic, and may surely not be accounted for adequately by the references that Vinaver has made to Bartholomew, Jacobus and the Prose Life (in that precise order) without qualifying reference to possible intermediate stages or lost parallels.

We think it unnecessary to postulate anything as unusual as Flaubert's secret, direct use of a medieval book or his intuitive grasp of its portent.[22]

Hence, to take a specific example, the absence in Flaubert's work of a very important feature of the Prose Life: the striking analogy between the parricide and Julian's own beheading, the latter being the historically real medieval equivalent of Julian's apotheosis in Flaubert. The radical difference between the medieval text and the modern may be explained only with difficulty if we assume Flaubert understood the medieval life and looked to it for guidance; but Flaubert's text is accounted for immediately if we agree he used only Lecointre-Dupont's résumé of the defective Alençon manuscript. Conversely, and more usefully, we may state that it is not necessary for students of the *Légende*'s genesis to bother with speculations about Flaubert's having suppressed these details for 'dramatic intensity' when, in fact, they were not in his source.

2 / *The Evidence of the Plan of* 1856

It is, indeed, difficult to understand how speculation along the lines just discussed can have gone on as long as it has, in view of the unsurprising fact that Flaubert is known to have had the basic structure, psychological tone, and *mouvements* of his entire Tale, much as it was printed, firmly in mind long before he came to Paris in 1875. He even wrote out (as was indeed his custom for all of his works) the entire plan of his story, once in short form, and again, much later, in expanded form, but in an otherwise remarkably similar fashion. Raitt has already pointed out the existence and nature of these outlines ('The Composition,' 359). But – as our predecessors were not able to determine from the sources available to them – the brief outline now preserved as fol. 490 recto of B.N., N.A.F. 23663 is much earlier than hitherto claimed: it was not written in 1875, but in 1856. It can be dated by the handwriting, which corresponds to that of Flaubert's autographs datable to that year, and which differs from that of the older Flaubert. It is probably this work which is referred to in his letter of June 1, 1856 (to Louis Bouilhet): 'Je prépare ma légende et je corrige Saint Antoine. ... Si j'étais un gars, je m'en retournerais à Paris ... avec

22 We cannot adhere to Vinaver's dictum that 'ce qui compte ... ce n'est pas de savoir de quelle version de sa source Flaubert s'est servi, mais de reconnaître que grâce à cette source, c'est-à-dire grâce à un texte français du treizième siècle enfin retrouvé, il découvrit pour la première fois ce qui lui manquait pour donner à son conte la forme voulue' ('La Légende,' 117). Our study, if it has any meaning at all, shows very clearly that the medieval Prose Life and Lecointre-Dupont's quite un-medieval text are fundamentally different both in themselves and in the possibilities which they offered Flaubert.

Saint-Antoine fini et *Saint-Julien l'Hospitalier* écrit' (*Correspondance*, IV, 104). The plan prepared in 1875, to which Flaubert refers in a letter of September 25 of that year, is the more detailed, but similar one, now preserved as fols. 492 recto, 493 recto, and 494 recto of B.N., N.A.F. 23663.[23]

The simpler and older of the plans shows clearly that Flaubert had the symmetrical double hunt and the bloodlust theme firmly in mind two decades before he is claimed to have seen B.N. Fr. 6447 or a similar text. The outline is worth reproducing, in approximately diplomatic form, because of what it shows about how Flaubert conceived the movement of his *Légende*, and how he saw Julian's character, from the very beginning of his work on the Tale.[24]

St Julien L'hospitalier

I.   éducation – château.
       amour de la chasse.
II.   Prédiction du cerf.
       – un soir d'octobre. bruyère –
              brouillard.
                 Julien sent une gde volupté
    à le tuer.
    rentré chez lui, le soir, près de ses parents
  pleure. '– mère on m'a dit que je te tuerais.

       ses parents le consolent.
        La prédiction lui revient et par la
  peur de tuer il a envie de tuer
III.   il part. – guerroie. – pays lointains. vie d'aventures.
       refuse le combat quand la visière n'est pas
    levée. – honneurs. – le souvenir. souhaite presque
    Mariage.   que ses parents soient
                         morts

23 The words 'Je prépare ma légende' suffice, we think, to show that Flaubert was actually working on the Tale in 1856; Vinaver's statement that the work began in 1875 and not in 1856 is no doubt due to a slip of the pen (*Rise*, 117). In any case, the dating is not immediately essential, since no previous scholar has dated any of the outlines later than the autumn of 1875.
24 A diplomatic transcription of the 1856 Plan, including cancellations, and showing the exact placement of its elements with relationship to each other, will accompany Bart's edition of the *Légende de Saint Julien*.

IV. Dans son château (sombre . le bien différencier
     du paternel. – une mare au pied.
             une nuit. les bonnes gens. sa femme part le
                                chercher
le clair de lune l'avait excité à la chasse.
     rentre. – tue.
V. alla s'établir au bord d'un grand fleuve dans un

   pays froid.
       vie de misère.
               une nuit voix
  Le lépreux.
     passage.
     couchée

         Jésus Christ.
Et Voilà la légende de St Julien Lhospitalier telle
    qu'elle est racontée sur les vitraux de la cath
     de ma ville natale.

This plan clearly antedates any use Flaubert is supposed to have made of the Prose Life. Although it is not impossible that he may have read Lecointre-Dupont before he drafted it, nevertheless, the words 'sa femme part le chercher' in Part IV indicate rather strongly that he is not following that adaptation very closely. On first reading, the plan seems to speak for itself, but a few remarks are nevertheless in order.

Notably, the sequence *amour de la chasse – un soir d'octobre – bruyère – brouillard* was not written seriatim, but is an interlinear addition, and the vertical spacing clearly indicates it was made *after* the words *prédiction du cerf* were in place.[25] Was it at this moment that Flaubert first saw the possibility of the bloodlust theme? As he wrote the crucial line which follows: ('Julien sent une grande volupté à le tuer'), was he not obliged to return to the beginning, in order to insert the words 'amour de la chasse'? We obviously cannot be entirely sure; but the fact that 'amour de la chasse' is part of a correction, and thus certainly represents a second thought (probably intended to motivate the *volupté* of lines 6-7), is most suggestive, indeed redolent of psychological concerns. Much the same might be said of the clause 'souhaite presque que ses parents soient morts,' in Part III, which is

25 The left margin, it should be noted, is irregular throughout; the division into five (not three) parts is marginal, and probably was not envisaged from the start.

an addition following the end of line 15 ('... le souvenir'). Finally, the words 'par la peur de tuer il a envie de tuer,' embody the theme of the attraction of evil, the temptation of temptation, which appears in the *Légende* as printed ('... si je le voulais, pourtant?'). And it is an idea which in slightly different form is at least as old as the first *Tentation de Saint Antoine*.[26] Is it not natural that the theme should have been near the surface of Flaubert's mind as he worked with the *Tentation* again in 1856, and thus appear, in altered form, in the plan for *Saint Julien*? Finally, much has been made on occasion of the fact that when his parents arrive, Julian is away for a specific reason in the Prose Life: he is hunting. We need only glance at Section IV of the early plan to find a much more explicit, and much more significant statement of Julian's psychological ambience: 'le clair de lune l'avait excité à la chasse.'

That Flaubert had a source for some of the plan's emphases and for part of its sequence is obviously likely; that the source was Lecointre-Dupont's creation is entirely possible. But the essential fact remains this: to the extent that the *Saint Julien* reflects its medieval cousins, it is because Flaubert knew the texts for which we have documentary evidence of his knowledge. Nothing so far justifies the claim that he took anything from the Prose Life which was not available in sources everyone agrees he used. And furthermore, close examination of the texts will show that the parallel symmetries and the notion of bloodlust are, to an extent which our predecessors' theory fails to explain, themes peculiar to Flaubert's formulation of the legend, having the same marked importance nowhere else, not even in the Prose Life.

3 / Some Specific Elements and Their Sources

With the considerable accumulation of evidence which this chapter has presented so far, and with the text of the 1856 plan at hand, we may limit ourselves to a relatively rapid presentation of the ways in which the Prose Life and the *Légende de Saint Julien* differ in matters of structure, tone, and psychology. Our statements of what appears in the Prose Life often differ from what has been printed in the past; we refer our reader once and for all to our Appendix B, which contains the text.

For Vinaver, the *Légende* is a structural entity and not a psychological study; its essence is the resonant poetic symmetry between Julian's first hunt (the massacre) and the second (haunted) one. He finds that Flaubert

---

26 See Bart, *Flaubert*, pp. 180-1. Before writing *envie*, Flaubert wrote the letters *cra* (*craint?*), which he subsequently crossed out. The change may or may not be significant; *craint* would have created a redundancy.

received this structure from the medieval Life: 'le texte anonyme français lui révéla une certaine cohérence poétique possible. ... Ce qui a dû surtout frapper son imagination, c'était la présence dans ce texte de deux mouvements parallèles sur lesquels reposait sa délicate structure. ...'[27]

We are of the opinion that the briefest of comparisons between the Prose Life and Flaubert's text will show that the resemblance does not extend to this antithetical parallelism. The author of the Prose Life was in fact less concerned with hunting than the Prose Life theory would admit. His hunts are elementary narrative devices; they function as motifs of the type we discussed in Chapter One. The first hunt is given only bare-bones treatment in the Life (para. 4), and the second is not even described. Contrary to what the Prose Life theory implies, the Prose Life redactor, in recounting the second hunt (paras. 44 and 52), dwells almost exclusively upon the details of Julian's departure from his wife before the hunt, his conversation with her then, and the circumstances of his precipitous return (which the narrative urge elicits: we must know why Julian rushed home when and as he did). We find nothing in the Prose Life which might have prompted Flaubert to set up the contrasting pair of hunts the way he did.

It is true that in the original state of the expanded outline made in Concarneau in 1875, Flaubert refers to the second hunt as being a success, like the first. To the extent that the contrasting tones evoked by Vinaver are present in the *Légende* and essential to it (a matter for criticism rather than for history), then Flaubert did light upon them sometime around January 1, 1876, as he reworked this material. But the brilliant idea of the haunted second hunt cannot have come to him from the sources we have discussed so far, or from the Prose Life, since it does not occur in any of them.[28] Where did Flaubert get the idea of a spectral hunt? Probably from another of his known sources, the one pointed out in 1905, in a much-

---

27 'La Légende,' 117; cf. *Rise*, esp. 118-20. Vinaver's compelling description of the two movements in the *Légende* runs thus: 'Il y a entre eux une étrange symétrie: au réalisme brutal du massacre des animaux succède la prophétie surnaturelle; au rêve terrifiant du monde animal qui prépare une surnaturelle vengeance, succède l'horreur réelle des flaques de sang qui s'étalent sur le lit, par terre ...' ('La Légende,' 120). This has little to do with the spare style of the Prose Life. Nor is 'réalisme brutal' an entirely apt description of the first hunt, which Flaubert explicitly characterizes as being like a dream: 'avec la facilité que l'on éprouve dans les rêves.'

28 There is, of course, no second hunt at all in Langlois or in the *Legenda aurea*. Lecointre-Dupont and LaVallée do have two hunts, each preceding a crisis, and could thus have furnished that much gross poetic symmetry to Flaubert. But neither gives the second hunt any supernatural or dreamlike tone, nor do they go into any detail at all.

neglected article by René Descharmes.[29] In the letter to Bouilhet from which we have already quoted (June 1, 1856, see pp. 83-84 above), Flaubert mentions that he has just re-read *Pécopin*: 'je n'ai aucune peur de la resemblance' (*Correspondance*, IV, 105). The *Légende du Beau Pécopin et de la belle Bauldour* is a section of Victor Hugo's *Rhin*, then some sixteen years old.[30] Hugo's tale is rather less legendary than phantasmagoric ('C'est une légende que du moins vous ne trouverez en aucun légendaire,' 185), and it does not partake of the filiation we have discussed in Chapters Two through Six. It is a monument to imagination, a confusing accumulation of impossible adventures having little to do with Flaubert's tightly structured tale of Fate. It gives the story of handsome Pécopin and fair Bauldour: the former's passion for hunting leads him to leave his fiancée for a hunt which is only the first of a long series of fantastic adventures that keep him away from home for five years. Trying to return, he is trapped in the evil *bois des pas perdus*; but Pécopin suddenly sees before him an aged hunter who offers him safety and Bauldour on one condition: the young man must accompany him on a hunt, which will last through the night. Pécopin accepts. His host is the Devil. They whirl away on the Black Hunt, pursuing a supernatural stag through dream forests across half the world.[31] Mists swirl about Pécopin; he cannot free his feet from his stirrups. When it is all over, the ghastly hunt has cost Pécopin his happiness: he has the horrible experience of finding, upon his return to the natural world, that his fiancée has aged one hundred years and is a repulsive crone (223-6).

But equally important is the fact that (whatever the appearance) *Pécopin* does represent an attempt at a more or less coherent structure, made evident through clear references to earlier events. A talisman protects Pécopin from death and aging; it is one he received long before, from a sultana, with a prophetic message. The Devil is lame and hunchbacked; Pécopin was present when he received both deformities. And above all, as Descharmes pointed out, the *Pécopin* contains two antithetical hunts as does the *Saint Julien*: 'Chacune des deux légendes repose sur deux aventures de chasse, et de plus l'action de chacune d'elles se déroule principalement [this is a bit exaggerated] en deux chasses qui s'opposent l'une à l'autre' (67). For indeed, Pécopin's first adventure, the one which separated him from his intended, was a successful hunt, during which he killed an eagle, a kite, and a vulture. The birds appear to him again as visions during the

29 See '*Saint-Julien l'Hospitalier* et *Pécopin*,' *Revue biblio-iconographique*, Troisième Série, 12 (1905), pp. 1-7, 67-75.
30 *Le Rhin: Lettres à un ami* (Paris: Imprimerie Nationale, 1906), pp. 185-228; it is letter XXI in volume one of the 5th series.
31 See esp. pp. 205-6, and 209 ff. The stag is huge, has sixteen points, and bells in the thickets, as does Flaubert's, but these are no doubt mere coincidences.

haunted hunt of the Devil.[32] And at the end of the tale, the birds of the forest reproach the hunter his first hunt, in sonorous Hugolian alexandrines (228).

The resemblance of which Flaubert was not afraid, therefore, was surely that between his plans for the *Saint Julien* and Hugo's extended description of Pécopin's supernatural night. As things stood, Flaubert was no doubt right:[33] the plan of 1856 gives no indication that Julian's hunts are to have any kind of supernatural overtones, and the contrast between the two hunts is not made clear. But there is every reason to think that twenty years later, when he took the Julian story in hand again, Flaubert had not forgotten Hugo's tale. He may even have re-read it once again during this period, in the Nationale; we do not know. It has precisely the fantastic atmosphere and the extensive details of which the Prose Life has absolutely none, and it may very well have been the ultimate source for the tone of Flaubert's second hunting scene, and thus for the idea of contrast. Dr Duckworth gives an interesting textual parallel between one of Flaubert's drafts for the *Saint Julien* and Hugo's tale, in Note 132. At the very least, we have here another Romantic text, similar in ways to the *Légende*, which Flaubert can be shown to have known, which indeed he himself tells us he read. It appears that we need not seek so far afield as the thirteenth century to find the idea of the haunted hunt or that of the ghostly forest (even if they occurred in the Prose Life, as we have seen they do not).

It is, however, equally important to recall that the ghostly forest is, of course, to be found in other texts besides *Pécopin*. It is yet another Romantic motif, and probably one of the best known. To limit ourselves to a single example from earlier in the century: a young man is wandering in the forest in which he will meet the ghost of his wronged fiancée. It is silent, mysterious, and as he goes deeper into it, 'elle devenait à chaque instant plus touffue et plus sombre; la lune avait peine à glisser de temps en temps un pâle et furtif rayon à travers les branches.' Finally the young man hears snatches of phantom song. He suddenly finds himself in a strange clearing, 'tout entourée de hauts châtaigniers et mystérieusement éclairée par la lune.' The text happens to be Alphonse Karr's 'Les Willis,' which Flaubert may well have read, as Karr was a very popular author; but

---

32 See esp. pp. 190-200 and 210-11. The Devil chooses to lure Pécopin into the Black Hunt because he has learned from a dismissed domestic of his passion for the chase; see p. 222.

33 Had he known how his *meute de chasse* was to turn out, he might have thought otherwise. Cf. *Pécopin*, 207. There are similar parallels between Julian's experiences as a traveller — especially in his first flight, where we think Lecointre-Dupont's influence is not yet making itself felt -- and the fantastic adventures Hugo lends to Pécopin.

it did not necessarily influence the form of the *Saint Julien* either.[34] The point is that the effects sought and obtained by Flaubert are part of a tradition, just as the details of the storm, and the attributes of leprosy, discussed in Chapter Five, were part of one, a greater one than the direct line from Langlois and Lecointre-Dupont to Flaubert would imply; and just as the characteristics of the medieval Saint Julian were also parts of a very different tradition. Seen in this context of widespread similarities – which is the context we have attempted to define in Chapters One and Two – the insistence on B.N. Fr. 6447 or any original Prose Life text, indeed on any text at all to the exclusion of others, appears not as a simple material error, but as dangerously close to being a major historical misunderstanding.

Thus far, we have not challenged the assertion that the medieval Prose Life of Saint Julian and Flaubert's Tale are significantly alike in terms of pure structure, or sequence of events. But close analysis shows that there are flaws in the purported parallel symmetries of the two works. The animal's prediction – an element so striking that it can be said to give the story a great part of its character and interest in both folklore and literature – and its result, Julian's first flight, are both present in all our major written versions including the Prose Life and Flaubert. But it is worth pointing out that despite what has been said on occasion, the thirteenth-century author and Flaubert, at six centuries' remove, make rather different literary uses of these structural elements.

Upon hearing the prediction, Flaubert's Julian undertakes what might be called unrepentant flight. It is as though he cannot understand, or cannot admit, that his horrible deed is written into his character, and will not be conjured by a change in milieu. He separates himself from his family (a bit tardily, considering the two accidents which follow the stag's prediction), but he continues to live as a knight, and to live surrounded by violence. The renown which is the principal result of his first flight is gained not only by desperate courage but also by the skilled exercise of his soldierly profession. Success, here as in the first hunt, is attained through slaughter. Thus the juxtaposition of battle and hunt gives Julian's character uniformity right up to the time of his horrible mistake. Here, at least, the structural parallel between the first hunt and the second, with their sequels, seems no more important than the psychological concern with Julian's fatal passion. Bloodlust in whatever form (recreational or military) is essential. Flaubert's Julian is even ambivalent in a typically

34 See Karr's *Contes et Nouvelles* (Paris: Lecour, 1852), pp. 7-8. Karr once said unbecoming things about Louise Colet in print; see Bart, *Flaubert*, 142-3; Flaubert may thus have had occasion to know Karr personally. In any event, Karr was one of the most widely read authors of his day.

modern way, for along with the active extermination of enemies, there is even in his mind the ominous seed of his frightening crime: 'Si je le voulais, pourtant ...?'

This uniformity of character in the *Légende* has been overlooked in the effort to present parallels between the Prose Life and the *Légende*. For the results of the predictions, and the careers of the two Julians may, it seems to us, legitimately be considered dissimilar. The Prose Life, when examined closely, in fact gives us a curious, almost eccentric sequence, in medieval terms as well as in terms of Flaubert's handling of the action. The medieval French prose author's Julian has the mentality of his saintly class, i.e., no marked individual psychology at all: more specifically, he is *not* haunted by the *volupté* of killing. And above all, his flight from home is immediate and total: carried out as penance, it involves complete rejection of his original social self. When he becomes a beggar and a menial servant, he ceases to be a knight.

Yet we may not read into his abnegation the implication that he is aware of some fatal flaw in himself, the prelude to sin, or its analogue. For his sense of innocence is what dooms him. He comes to realize he is doing penance for a crime he has not committed, a crime which does not exist, and which he does not find himself tempted to commit, a crime which only Fate could ever bring about. 'Dex! Que vois je querant et truandant? Encor n'ai ge pas fet le pechié de quoi je ai eu maintes males jornees. Ce me vient de grant paor et de grant folie, que avant faz la penitence que le pechié; et bien sai qu'il n'avendra ja, ne ne m'en savra ja Diex gré, car je nel faz pas pour lui.'[35] Thus he takes up the knightly life again – and the crime becomes inevitable, because his penance, no matter how illogical, no longer stands between him and the parricide.[36]

35 Alençon 27, fol. 175c; see Appendix B, para. 16. Julian is lying awake thinking of the words of his host, who has taunted him for his sloth and summoned him to quit his pilgrimage and become a knight, as his birth requires. This is the passage Duckworth refers to in his Note 118, discussed above. Previously, Julian has tended lepers and cleaned stables in Jerusalem. It may be added here that the medieval Julian has visited the Pope, only to be told that the talking beast was a *fantosme* and not to be trusted; and that the worst the animal had said to him was: 'Enfes, ne m'oci mie ... tu occirras ton pere et ta mere a un cop; ja cele part n'iras, nus ne le te puet destorner fors Dieu' (Appendix B, para. 4). Compare Flaubert's 'coeur féroce. ...'

36 There is, it would seem, at least a little generalized determinism here, and very little or nothing in the way of individual psychology. Julian's mental processes – often made manifest through exteriorized monologues of the type just quoted are, and are supposed to be, those of any man faced with temptation. This phenomenon, unlike the precise sequence of events (which was practically a given by the time the Prose Life was written) is perfectly ordinary, and will even seem banal to anyone who has had occasion to read many such Lives.

Within the uncommon sequence of events in the Prose Life, then, the author's options, while real, are limited. He is obliged even here to link as best as he can the bits and pieces of legend which traditional motifs represent. He finally describes a series of changes in Julian's estate (one after the prediction; another after the knight's taunts; another after the parricide; and another upon the success of the couple's penitence) which has no parallel in Flaubert's work.

The theme of cruelty, which Duckworth considers to be the Prose Life's principal contribution to the *Légende*, is also in fact largely new with Flaubert, and not to be found in the medieval versions. We must insist here upon the importance of a motif whose presence has been recognized (Vinaver, *Rise*, 115) but which has not been taken into account in the building of the Prose Life hypothesis. For the medieval author, the principal cause of Julian's fatal error is not his passion for hunting, but the fact that he has broken off his pilgrimage to Saint James of Compostella. The logic is as perfect and inexorable as Flaubert's logic of bloodthirstiness, for if Julian had continued on the path he had sworn to follow, he would never have taken his wife, and his wife would not have revealed his whereabouts to his parents, nor put them in her bed; indeed Julian would not have been in the region at all. Nor does hunting enter into his decision to end his pilgrimage. Instead, he is the victim of a standard medieval narrative cliché which requires, roughly, that a disguised knight cannot repress his knightly instincts for long: when his host reproaches him for his apparent slothfulness, Julian's combative ardour is awakened, and he falls at once into the sin of pride. This is one of the fundamental movements of the Old French text, and it is necessarily absent from Flaubert's (cf. paras. 15-17 with 54).

And, let us recall, the four-cornered parallel claimed to exist between the Prose Life's two hunting episodes, and the hunts in Flaubert, is far from perfect. Most notably, Flaubert's Julian kills the black stag cruelly, but the medieval Julian throws away his arrows, breaks his bow, and flees at once, leaving the talking animal (whatever it is) alive and unwounded. The reader should perhaps judge for himself whether the medieval account of the hunt (Appendix B, para. 4) is in its entirety the story of an obsessed man; in the detail of the stag's death, at least, it cannot be said to be. We find the obsession, in other words the bloodlust theme *per se*, to be Flaubert's idea.

Further accumulation of detail would only, we think, accentuate the obvious. We find it highly unlikely, and an unproven and unnecessary supposition, that Flaubert ever saw or used any medieval manuscript text of the thirteenth-century Prose Life of Saint Julian. Even if he did by chance see or hear of the Old French Life, he clearly chose not to follow it, for in contrast to the abundant reminiscences of his known nineteenth-century sources, his *Légende* has less in common with the medieval Life than has been claimed hitherto. Such resemblances as there are – and they are real – result from Flaubert's use of the Rouen window (as seen through the eyes of Langlois), of the *Legenda aurea* (probably in Brunet's translation), of LaVallée, and of Lecointre-Dupont. Even Hugo's *Pécopin*, with its fundamentally modern accumulation of details, a tendency almost unknown to the thirteenth-century French Prose Life, seems to have influenced the tone and ultimately the shape of the Tale. Flaubert's own creative conscience, his readings in other medieval works, and the logical flow of the legend itself, whose fixed elements he necessarily adopted, also contributed to the *Légende* in ways which commentators have been unwilling to recognize.[37]

There is no indication that Flaubert used the Prose Life concurrently with Lecointre-Dupont, or that he received his basic theme and structure from the Prose Life rather than the sources just mentioned; they are most likely to have been his own invention. There is no genuine parallel between the careers and characters of the medieval Julian and of Flaubert's nineteenth-century saint. The notion of minor borrowings of phrases and isolated words, some misread, is not supported by a close reading of the two texts with particular attention to the *contexts* of the passages in question. The circumstances of the *Légende*'s composition do not indicate any radical change in plan from 1856 on, or any sudden *prise de conscience* after November 1, 1875. And once again, the *Légende de Saint Julien l'Hospitalier* is, and must be understood to be, the work of a man who used, comprehended, and eventually drew upon sources from the nineteenth century, which passed on to him a tale whose form and tone are modern. They acted as filter between him and the historic Middle Ages.

---

37 Flaubert the man and writer did not receive the notions of sadism and penance from a (perhaps deservedly) obscure medieval redactor.

CHAPTER EIGHT

Epilogue

At the end of a necessarily long journey through the history of Flaubert's *Légende de Saint Julien l'Hospitalier*, it is worth asking what we have seen that will help in understanding the Tale. There is at least one primary answer, from which the others flow. Flaubert left us a problem of genre in the *Saint Julien*. Its title implies that his work is a 'legend,' and yet he included the story in the collection everyone knows as *Trois Contes*. A *conte*, or a novella, is not the same thing as a legend, as our early chapters show. It seems likely at first glance, and it has nearly always been assumed, that Flaubert's title is mere window-dressing of a kind associated with Hugo or Kipling – that is, that in spite of its title, the *Légende de Saint Julien* is a short story and must be treated as such, with all the implications that designation has for an author's approach to his characters, his story, and his sources. We have proven, we think, that Flaubert's Tale in fact shares important characteristics with typical legends: Its form is fixed by a tradition absent in the case of the novella, and many of its details must have been put into place in response to the shape of the tradition as Flaubert perceived it. That is why a detailed and comprehensive study of the legendary sources has been necessary for the *Saint Julien*. It shows clearly some of the differences between the way an author works when he is re-stating a traditional story, and the way he works when the mechanism of plot, and the details it elicits, are largely new at the time of writing.

Nonetheless, those who have written of the Tale and its literary value have tended to treat it in practice as the creation of one man, alone responsible for its flow and rhythm, and for its style and phraseology. Certain critics, such as Vinaver and Duckworth, have been aware of the possibility of important structural or verbal influence from a source other than Flaubert's own stock of creative material. But even they have insisted principally on the relatively limiting influence of a single relatively exotic source (the thirteenth-century Life of Saint Julian in Prose) which they claim Flaubert discovered, understood, and mined for specific sentences, or for structural elements which he imitated directly. In other words, even for Vinaver and Duckworth, whatever the single writer Flaubert did not give to his Julian story, he derived from another single writer, by a process of transposition, during which no tradition of textual or thematic development came into play.

Creation *ex nihilo*; or re-creation from a distant skeletal source such as the *Legenda aurea*; or specific creative decisions under the tutelage of a kindred (though distant) literary spirit: these are conceptions of the writer's art which easily fit the definition of the short story, the *conte*, or the novella. But, by the same token, they do not concord with the notion of legend. The legend is not a structure put into place where there was nothing before; it arises from the slow shaping, by processes of adaptation and accretion, of a story which owes elements of its form, and even of its expression, to several conscious creators, and not only to one. It is axiomatic that a legend has more than one form, with variants which do not obscure the essential resemblances among all the versions, but which give each version a particular flavour and particular emphases. And it is clear that any one manifestation of the legend, even the most literary in appearance, is best described not in terms of a single source or a restricted number of them, to which all or nearly all of its elements are traced, but by comparison with every available version of the same legend.

Understanding any of the forms of a legend, therefore, requires different critical processes from those required for the understanding of a short story. A legend's re-creator shows his personality and his powers, not in the conceiving of the tale he recounts, not necessarily in its ordering, but rather in his choice of detail and tone, of the images and accidents which surround the ancient structure and its themes. Whether he appears near the distant beginning of a line of written and accessible transmission, or long centuries later, the re-creator chooses to work with a version of a story which, whatever its age, has elements he cannot change.

The study of the legendary tale may therefore, paradoxically, be more revealing than that of the short story, since the choice of the legend itself, and the emphases chosen for its re-creation, often stem from the writer's deepest preoccupations; and they are readily compared with other versions of the same structure and motifs, thus showing by contrasts (some of which are quite sharp) the tendencies peculiar to one writer's mind.

The *Légende de Saint Julien l'Hospitalier* furnishes a clear and unusually potent example of the value that such distinctions and attitudes may have. For, in an important sense, it really is a legend, as *Un Coeur simple* and even *Hérodias* are not. Whether by chance or design, the title of the tale reveals its nature and the nature of its creation. In it Flaubert's gift of observation, his thirst for the unusual, his sense of detail, all found special applications, as his obsessions, his joys, and his anguish led him to write his Tale. It was not put together solely from the author's imagination and experiences, yet it is like no other Julian tale (least of all the medieval ones) precisely because of that imagination and those experiences. It does not even derive from the inspiration provided by a single source perceived as unified, for its sources (verbal and structural) are multiple versions of the same legend. In fact, the texts Flaubert knew are themselves related in complex ways to each other, so that the sources taken singly are themselves, like the *Légende*, only specific manifestations of a tradition largely accessible to us for study and appraisal.

We have explained for the first time that the sources of the *Légende* are predominantly nineteenth-century manifestations of the legend of Saint Julian, parricide, ferryman, and host. The texts we have studied in this regard date from the period between 1820 and 1850, and bear many recognizable marks of the atmosphere of the Romantic period. Thus, when Flaubert goes into frightening detail in the description of the leper Julian must embrace, when he writes of the terrible storm on Julian's last night on earth, when he describes Julian's ascent into heaven, he is following a Romantic tradition, traceable in the texts which external evidence shows he knew. And he follows that tradition not only on the level of tone and events, but at times almost word for word.

The legendary mode is ancient, but it succeeds over and over in conveying its ancient messages anew because those messages take on new forms with each set of retellings. The retellings of Lecointre-Dupont and of Langlois touched Flaubert for the same reason the imaginings of Hugo did: because they were put in his terms. Surely that is what is implied in Flaubert's rhetorical question, which stands at the beginning of this book: 'Comment a-t-il tiré ceci de cela?' *Cela*, the Rouen window, is raw material – of which, in fact, Flaubert made relatively little use. *Ceci*, the *Légende de Saint Julien*, is a specific product made from that and other raw material by particular techniques. Neither of the two may be made the exclusive study of literary scholarship, but we hope to have helped to show that even taken together, they are not the whole story. There is also the intricate *comment*.

Flaubert's specific choice of the traditional Julian story is, then, of paramount importance. The exact structure of the *Légende de Saint Julien* is a modern creation. Its symmetries and its shifting tones were given to it by Flaubert, as the texts show. Its phraseology and its details come from Flaubert's consultation of scholarly and imaginative works of his own time. But error and redemption are universal themes. The legend of Saint Julian is a story of salvation and rebirth in the face of overwhelming fate; and it happens that Flaubert gave it its final form only after the months of soul-searching which followed the collapse of his world, in the wake of his nephew Commanville's terrible financial debacle in 1873-4. We think we have touched here, through the methods of history, upon one of the reasons why the *Saint Julien* is a work of such evocative strength and such emotional power, or that at least we have defined one of the modes of its aesthetic success. It moves us profoundly because it reflects human experience in a special way, through a typology of error and redemption which is great precisely because it is not pure invention and is not peculiar to Gustave Flaubert. It is crucial to recognize here that what is 'medieval' in the *Saint Julien* is not the tone, not the masses of anachronistic details, not the tensions of the work's structure, but the theme of salvation against terrible odds. It is in that sense that Flaubert wrote a story which was not merely the limited reflection of his own state of mind or of the flawed medievalism of his age. His achievement is in large part the result of the way he went about writing – of his use of sources whose distant roots are in universal narrative habits (we have called those habits folklore). It is essential to the understanding of the achievement to realize that the removal of Julian's story from the realm of the everyday does not mean that the Tale is therefore an escapist romance or a failed attempt at historical recreation. The *Légende de Saint Julien l'Hospitalier* is, rather, a serious aesthetic undertaking in its own right. Where it is not modern, it is timeless.

APPENDIXES

The Life of Saint Julian in the *Legenda aurea* and Brunet's Translation

It is not possible to state with certainty what texts of the *Vita* of Saint Julian Hospitator in the *Legenda aurea* may have been used by Langlois in the early 1820's, by Lecointre-Dupont in the next decade, and by Flaubert on the several occasions then and later when he probably consulted the work. For that reason, we have elected to give here the best text currently available, that presented by Theodor Graesse. We cite from the second edition (Leipzig, 1850), regularizing the spelling to conform to modern practice but making no substantive changes. The passage occurs in Cap. XXX, 4.

Fuit etiam alius Julianus qui utrumque parentem nesciens occidit cumque is Julianus praedictus juvenis ac nobilis quadam die venationi insisteret et quendam cervum repertum insequeretur, subito cervus versus eum divino nutu se vertit eique dixit: tu me insequeris, qui patris et matris tuae occisor eris? Quod ille audiens vehementer extimuit et, ne sibi forte contingeret, quod a cervo audierat, relictis omnibus clam discessit, ad regionem valde remotam pervenit ibique cuidam principi adhaesit et tam strenue ubique et in bello et in pace se habuit, quod princeps eum militem fecit et quandam castellanam viduam in conjugem ei tradidit et castellum pro dote accepit. Interea parentes Juliani pro amissione filii Juliani nimium dolentes vagabundi ubique pergebant et filium suum sollicite quaerebant: tandem ad castrum, ubi Julianus praeerat, devenerunt. Tunc autem Julianus a castro casu recesserat. Quos cum uxor Juliani vidisset et, quinam essent, inquisivisset et illi omnia, quae filio suo acciderant, enarrassent, intellexit, quod viri sui parentes erant, ut puto, quia hoc a viro suo forte frequenter audierat. Ipsos igitur benigne suscepit et pro amore viri sui lectum iis dimisit et ipsa sibi alibi lectulum collocavit. Facto autem mane castellana ad ecclesiam perrexit et ecce Julianus mane veniens in thalamum quasi uxorem suam excitaturus intravit et inveniens duos pariter dormientes, uxorem cum adultero suo, silenter extracto gladio ambos pariter interemit. Exiens autem domum vidit uxorem eius ab ecclesia revertentem et admirans interrogavit, quinam essent illi, qui in suo lecto dormirent, at illa ait: parentes vestri sunt, qui vos diutissime quaesierunt, et eos in vestro thalamo collocavi. Quod ille audiens paene exanimis effectus amarissime flere coepit ac dicere: heu miser quid faciam?Quia dulcissimos meos parentes occidi; ecce impletum est verbum cervi, quod dum vitare volui, miserrimus adimplevi. Iam vale soror dulcissima, quia de caetero non quiescam, donec sciam, quod Deus poenitentiam meam acceperit. Cui illa: absit, dulcissime frater, ut te deseram et sine me abeas, sed quae fui tecum particeps gaudii, ero particeps et doloris. Tunc insimul recedentes iuxta quoddam magnum flumen, ubi multi periclitabantur, quoddam hospitale maximum statuerunt, ut ibi poenitentiam facerent et omnes, qui vellent transire fluvium, incessanter transveherent et hospitio universos pauperes reciperent. Post multum vero temporis media nocte, dum Julianus fessus quiesceret et gelu grave esset, audivit vocem miserabiliter lamentantem ac Julianum, ut se traduceret, lugubri voce invocantem: quod ille audiens concitus surrexit et iam gelu deficientem inveniens in domum suam portavit et ignem accendens ipsum calefacere studuit. Sed cum calefieri non posset et, ne ibi deficeret, timeret, ipsum in lectulum suum portavit et diligenter cooperuit. Post paululum ille, qui sic infirmus et quasi leprosus apparuerat, splendidus scandet ad aethera et hospiti suo dixit: Juliane, dominus misit me ad te, mandans tibi, quod tuam poenitentiam acceptavit et ambo post modicum in domino quiescetis. Sicque ille disparuit et Julianus cum uxore sua post modicum plenus bonis operibus et eleemosinis in domino requievit.

Flaubert owned the two-volume translation of the *Legenda aurea* by G. Brunet (Paris: Gosselin, 1843): see Chapter Two, Note 2. We may assume that at some time he read the life of Julian in it: on the whole it is an adequate translation. But two minor omissions in Brunet's translation suggest that Flaubert may also have read the Latin text at some time, for these omitted indications were adopted by Flaubert in his story. As they are small matters, however, and entirely natural, Flaubert could have introduced them in his *Légende* without any prompting from a source. The passage occurs in I, pp. 125-6.

Il y eut un autre Julien qui tua son père et sa mère par ignorance. Celui-ci était noble,[1] et dans sa jeunesse il alla un jour à la chasse, et il trouva un cerf qu'il poursuivit. Le cerf se retourna soudainement et lui dit:[2] 'Tu me

1 Brunet perhaps does not quite render the full force of *praedictus*. Flaubert will emphasize how remarkably promising the youth is, both at his birth by the two predictions of his future glories, and by the hopes his parents felt for him.
2 Brunet omits *divino nutu*. In the course of his Tale, Flaubert will show clearly that the stag is divinely inspired.

poursuis toi, qui tueras ton père et ta mère.' Et quand il entendit cela, il ne douta aucunement[3] qu'il n'advînt en effet ce qui lui avait été annoncé par le cerf, et alors il laissa tout et partit secrètement; et il vint en une contrée très-éloignée, et se mit là à servir un prince, et se comporta honorablement partout, à la guerre et à la cour.[4] Et alors le prince le fit chevalier, et lui donna pour femme une châtelaine qui était veuve, et il lui accorda[5] un château pour douaire. Pendant ce temps, les parents de Julien étaient désolés de la perte de leur fils, et ils allaient, tout éperdus, s'informant à chaque endroit si on n'avait pas des nouvelles de leur fils. Et enfin ils vinrent au château dont Julien était seigneur, et Julien par hasard était absent du château; et quand la femme de Julien les vit et qu'elle se fut enquise qui ils étaient et qu'ils eurent raconté tout ce qui était arrivé à Julien leur fils, elle comprit que c'était le père et la mère de son mari, car elle avait bien souvent entendu son mari lui dire ce qui lui était arrivé,[6] et elle les reçut très-bien et elle leur donna son lit,[7] et elle fit disposer un autre lit pour elle. Et le lendemain au matin, la châtelaine alla à l'église. Saint Julien vint le matin dans sa chambre pour éveiller[8] sa femme, et il trouva dans le lit deux personnes qui dormaient ensemble, il ne douta pas que ce ne fût sa femme et quelque débauché,[9] et, dans sa fureur, il tira son épée[10] et il les tua tous deux ensemble. Et quand il sortit de sa maison, il vit sa femme qui venait de l'église; et, tout plein de surprise, il lui demanda quels étaient ceux qui étaient dans son lit. Et elle dit: 'Ce sont votre père et votre mère, qui vous ont cherché si longtemps, et je les ai mis en votre chambre.' Et quand il entendit cela, il resta comme demi-mort, et il commença à pleurer très-amèrement et à dire: 'Hélas! malheureux, que ferai-je? car j'ai tué mon cher père et ma bonne mère! et ainsi la parole du cerf se trouve accomplie, et ce que je cherchais à éviter, par le plus grand des malheurs, je l'ai consommé! Adieu, ma soeur bien-aimée, car je n'aurai dorénavant aucun repos avant que je sache que Notre-Seigneur Jésus-Christ a agréé ma pénitence.' Et elle répondit: 'Cher frère, je ne peux consentir à ce tu me délaisses[11] et

3 A slight modification, which underplays the sense of *vehementer extimuit*. The sentence as a whole does not so clearly imply, as the Latin does, that Julian fled to avoid the curse; rather, he seems to think it inevitable.

4 'A la cour' is not quite the sense of *in pace*.

5 Latin: [*Julianus*] *accepit*.

6 Brunet omits the qualifying note of Jacobus da Varagine: *ut puto*. Thus what was probably an *ex post facto* attempt at explanation becomes an unqualified assertion.

7 Brunet omits *pro amore viri sui*.

8 Brunet fails to render the sense of *quasi*.

9 Brunet thus renders *cum adultero suo*.

10 Brunet omits *silenter* and significantly, adds the notion of *fureur*. Langlois cites this phrase in Latin, p. 171, Note 2.

11 This is not quite the Latin: *ut te deseram*.

que tu t'en ailles sans moi; car je prendrai ma part de ta douleur.'[12] Et alors ils s'en allèrent ensemble vers un très-grand fleuve, où beaucoup de gens périssaient, et ils fondèrent un hôpital en ce désert pour faire pénitence, et pour porter de l'autre côté de l'eau tous ceux qui voudraient passer, et tous les pauvres devaient être reçus en cet hôpital. Et longtemps après, comme Julien était à se reposer, très-fatigué, vers le milieu de la nuit, et qu'il gelait fortement, il entendit une voix qui pleurait piteusement et qui appelait Julien, afin de passer le fleuve. Entendant cela, le saint se leva tout ému, et il trouva un homme qui mourait de froid; et il le porta en sa maison, et il alluma du feu et il s'efforça de le réchauffer; et comme il ne pouvait y réussir, il craignit que ce malheureux ne vînt à expirer de froid, et il le porta en son lit et le recouvrit avec grand soin. Et peu après, celui qui lui était apparu ainsi malade et lépreux,[13] se montra très-resplendissant, et, s'élevant vers les cieux, il dit à son hôte: 'Julien, Notre-Seigneur m'a envoyé vers toi, et il te fait savoir qu'il a agréé ta pénitence, et vous deux vous reposerez en Notre-Seigneur dans un peu de temps.' Et il disparut aussitôt. Et peu après, Julien et sa femme, pleins de bonnes oeuvres et d'aumônes, reposèrent en Notre-Seigneur.

12 This is a less than faithful rendering of: *sed quae fui tecum particeps gaudii, ero particeps et doloris.*
13 Again Brunet omits *quasi.*

The Alençon Text of the Prose Life and Lecointre-Dupont's Adaptation

INTRODUCTION

We transcribe here the text of the thirteenth-century Life as it appears in Ms. Alençon B.M. 27, fol. 172 verso-182, fol. 5, with brief notes. As we refer to the Prose Life often in the course of our inquiry, and since our reading of it sometimes differs radically from what can be found in print, we have thought it important to place the text itself before our readers, in order that they may better judge our conclusions. Rudolf Tobler's transcription of B.N. Fr. 6447 is diplomatic, and thus often difficult to interpret.[1] The presence of punctuation (hypothetical, as in all editions of medieval works), of rough paragraph divisions, and of majuscules, and the distinction of *u, v, i,* and *j* should make our text more readable. We have chosen to reproduce the Alençon text rather than another, of course, because it is Lecointre-Dupont's acknowledged source, and thus at one remove Flaubert's. Comparison between it and Lecointre-Dupont's adaptation, which we also reproduce in this Appendix, will show clearly how the latter is a nearly pure manifestation of the Romantic tendencies we describe in our study.

The Alençon copy, interesting though it may be for the history of Flaubert's Tale, is of little or no importance in itself. We have not given it extensive critical treatment; only those variants which shed some light on its sense are systematically included. Neither have we attempted to give a definitive edition of the Prose Life itself. Under these circumstances, we hope that our having established our text on the basis of photographs rather than the original will be pardoned. At least two scholars have undertaken to include, in their recent theses, critical editions of the Prose Life: M.J.-P. Perrot in Paris, and Dr Carolyn T. Swan, at Northwestern Univer-

---

1 See 'Die Prosafassung der Legende vom heiligen Julian,' II, in *Archiv für das Studium der Neueren Sprachen und Literaturen,* 107 [1901], 79-102.

sity.[2] M. Perrot used as his base manuscript B.N. Fr. 17229, which on first examination at least, appears to be a better copy than Al. 27. We wish to thank M. Perrot here for his generosity in allowing us to consult his preliminary transcription of Fr. 17229. Dr Swan used Al. 27 as her base manuscript, but incorporated into her edition readings from other manuscripts, thus giving a text which is certainly different in some ways from that known to Lecointre-Dupont. For our present purposes, we have preferred to maintain all but a very few of the problematical readings of Al. 27, since we cannot be sure that Lecointre-Dupont was able to recognize them as problems, and we know in any case that he had seen no other Prose Life manuscript at the time he wrote his adaptation.

The manuscript Lecointre-Dupont used is described by Henri Omont in the *Catalogue des manuscrits des bibliothèques publiques de France*, II (Paris: Plon, 1888), 501-502.[3] The manuscript itself presents few points of interest; it is universally attributed to the fourteenth century, and contains, besides a series of saints' lives, the *Somme le roi* of Friar Laurent. The language of the copy does not require extensive commentary; it presents only rare dialectal features. There is no noteworthy decoration. The most important physical feature, for our purposes, is the absence of at least one leaf, presumably the last of the manuscript, which would have contained the ending of the Julian legend as we know it from the other *légendiers*. A division of volumes may once have followed the Julian story, which would explain why it is last in the book despite its place in the calendar. The next-to-last leaf of the preserved manuscript had clearly been detached at some point, for when Lecointre-Dupont used the manuscript, that leaf, the last surviving one of the Prose Life, was already bound as folio 5 (it should be 183).

The Prose Life itself poses interesting and largely neglected problems of literary history. We regret that the limitations of this study have not allowed us to pursue in any detail the still unanswered questions of its date, place of composition, sources, and relationship to the thirteenth-century Life of Julian in verse.

---

2 'The Old French Prose Legend of Saint Julian the Hospitaller,' 1973; cf. *Dissertation Abstracts International*, 34, 9 (March, 1974), 5998-A. There is no important reference to Flaubert. The text of the Prose Life is accurately given according to Alençon 27, and ingeniously emended. See also our Bibliography, No. 42.

3 One may also consult the notices by Paul Meyer in the *Bulletin de la Société des Anciens Textes*, 18 (1892) and in the *Histoire littéraire de la France*, 33 (1906), 431-2. The latter volume includes further references concerning the *légendiers*. We wish to thank the Institut de Recherches et d'Histoire des Textes of Paris, and especially Mme Bouly de Lesdain and Mlle Girard of the Section Romane, for their usual courteous and expert help in bibliographical matters.

We may not, however, neglect entirely two points which have some bearing on the study of Flaubert's *Légende*. First, it is important to realize that the Prose Life occurs in many *légendiers* and not just four or six as is sometimes stated. The Institut de Recherche et d'Histoire des Textes lists twenty-four copies of the Life in France and Belgium, but a few of the manuscripts contain only an abridged Life. At least ten complete copies are in the Bibliothèque Nationale: they are Fr. 183, 185, 987, 1546, 6447, 13496, 17229, 23112 and 23552, and N.A. Fr. 10128, in each of which we have examined the text personally. N.A. Fr. 10033, sometimes cited, is post-medieval and contains only an excerpt of a few lines.

Second, the rightful place of the Life in the history of the medieval legend has not been established, despite some speculation. The sparse evidence indicates, notably, that the Prose Life cannot derive from the Verse Life. Their parallels have been exaggerated.[4] Even superficial examination shows that their divergencies (already mentioned by both Toblers) are too numerous to allow us to think of either of the versions as only a copy or imitation of the other. They treat the prophecy scene differently: in the Verse Life, but not in the Prose, Julian (whose childhood incidentally is not described) kills the animal despite its warning of dire consequences, and thus brings upon himself a curse which would never have fallen on him, had he let it live. They give the Pope a different role; they differ about whether Julian was a servant or a knight in the Holy Land (see our Chapter Seven, page 69), and they do not agree on why he wanted to go to Compostella or even whether he went there at all. In the Prose Life, he promises to go, but does not go until too late; in the Verse, he goes twice. In the Verse Life, Christ appears openly; but we have argued that the original text of the Prose Life had an angel instead (Chapter Three, pp. 25-28). The Verse Life also introduces the character of the honest Gervais, a Breton merchant who befriends the fleeing Julian and is later accused of having done away with him.[5] The whole problem is further complicated by the fact (hitherto little noticed) that the Verse Life shows signs of being a hybrid version. It appears to be an entirely independent

---

4   The discussion is in R. Tobler, 'Prosafassung,' I, *Archiv*, 106 (1901), principally
     pp. 304-23; Meyer, *op. cit.*, p. 388; and Eugène Vinaver, *Rise of Romance*,
     p. 114, Note 1. The latter two authors reject Tobler's evidence without discussing
     the bulk of it, thus implying Tobler's work is less thorough than it proves to be
     when one reads it.
5   The Latin Life of Julian now in Bruges, with added appearances of the Breton
     Gervais, probably represents an expanded version of the Verse Life. Gaiffier's
     opinion concerning its priority is only a hypothesis (see 'La Légende de Saint
     Julien l'Hospitalier,' *Analecta Bollandiana*, 63 [1945], 161). The references in
     the Verse Life to a source are (like those in the Prose Life) a cliché common to
     many medieval authors in many situations; they prove nothing.

redaction, different in content and tone from the Prose Life, for some 2800 lines (to the point where Julian's parents learn his new identity – from a man, not from a woman as in the Prose Life). Then the Verse Life changes the circumstances of its recital to a form nearly identical with that of the Prose Life.[6] One of the results is a major inconsistency. When the Verse Life redactor has Julian summarize his life-story for his wife immediately after the murder (lines 3691-3754; there is no such episode in the Prose), the summary coincides not with the first part of the Verse Life, but with the Prose Life, in all the details just discussed and in others. The Verse thus explicitly contradicts itself, in peculiar and suggestive fashion. It is not entirely impossible that the Prose Life was in existence in some form, and came into the hands of the verse redactor, at the time the latter was writing (probably before 1267).[7]

This thorny but minor problem is important to us only because it affects the problem of filiation treated at length by Vinaver and referred to in our Chapter One (page 8). If the Verse Life redactor knew the Prose Life before 1267, or if the resemblances between the two are due to their reliance on a common source resembling the Prose Life, then it is clearly risky to assume that the Prose Life is later than the *Legenda Aurea*, as Vinaver has claimed. But we must not stray from our main purpose, which is to make clear what can be known of Flaubert's sources. The Prose Life is rather obviously not one of them, as may be seen from our Chapter Seven, and thus its history cannot detain us here.[8]

What follows is a summary transcription of the Prose Life as it appears in Alençon 27, with minor emendations and a minimum of notes for the non-specialist, intended to facilitate his reading of the text. The notes are arranged according to the divisions we have given the text. The transcription follows the usual conventions as set out by the Roques Commission in 1926, except in the matter of numerals, which (as is often the case) we have not been able to transcribe. We have also made liberal use of the diaeresis.

6   See Tobler, 'Prosafassung,' I, 315-22, and cf. our Note 5, chapter Two. It is after the change that the wording of the two texts begins to show marked similarities.
7   Dr Swan prefers to speak, in her abstract, of a common verse source for the two known Lives. The existence of multiple states of the story is indeed likely, as we have remarked in Chapter One. Any common source would presumably contain that material which appears in both Lives, and thus would surely make important parts of the literary legend of Julian somewhat older than the middle of the century; we have also expressed our suspicions in that regard, in Chapter One.
8   It seems to us to have no more literary merit, and no less, than any of a dozen or more Lives of similar form and generally similar content. This is, after all, the nature of the highly stereotyped genre to which the Prose Life belongs.

Following the Prose Life, we reproduce the text of Flaubert's principal source, 'La Légende de Saint-Julien le Pauvre d'après un manuscrit de la Bibliothèque d'Alençon,' as retold by G.-F.-G. Lecointre-Dupont. Lecointre-Dupont's article is not easily accessible today. It was first printed in the *Mémoires de la Société des Antiquaires de l'Ouest*, année 1838 (Poitiers, 1839), pp. 190-210, and was reprinted separately the same year (Poitiers: Saurin, 1839) with no change in the text but with new pagination. Both these publications contain, as we have remarked, a few crude copies made from certain of the panels shown in Langlois's drawing of the Julian window at Rouen, with no indication of their source.

Gabriel-François-Gérasime Lecointre-Dupont was born in Alençon (December 4, 1809) and was one of the founders of the Société des Antiquaires de l'Ouest. He died September 25, 1888, and his obituary appears in the *Bulletins de la Société des Antiquaires de l'Ouest* (the same publication as the *Mémoires*), deuxième série, IV (1886-1888), 525-39. The latter eulogy makes no mention of any training Lecointre-Dupont may have had in the area of medieval studies. His knowledge of medieval literary history was necessarily limited and his attitude toward the medieval past coloured by the doctrines of Romanticism, when, at age thirty, he undertook to retell the Julian story. His work is clearly not a transcription or summary of the medieval text he had before him, but (as our notes make clear) a dramatized account, with some important variations and numerous changes in detail. We note also the more important resemblances between Flaubert's text and the Lecointre-Dupont version, even when we do not consider that borrowing necessarily took place.

We have gone to considerable lengths to give both texts fairly complete annotation in this Appendix, despite the fact that the resulting critical apparatus takes on rather imposing dimensions. The notes are, indeed, indispensable, as they are important supplements to the statements we make in our Chapters Five, Six and Seven, and also incidentally support our remark (Chapter Six, Note 6) that we do not agree with Jasinski concerning Flaubert's use of 'Lord Wigmore' or even the extent to which Flaubert may have used Lecointre-Dupont.

In the Lecointre-Dupont text, numbers between parentheses on the line of printing refer to Lecointre-Dupont's own footnote, and superscript figures refer to our notes.

THE THIRTEENTH-CENTURY
PROSE LIFE OF SAINT JULIAN

1 / *Explanatory Prologue*

Uns preudon raconte la vie Monseignor Saint Julien que il a tranlatee de latin en romanz, et dit que cil qui l'escouteront volentiers i avront mult granz deliz. Juliens furent .ii.: li uns martirs, li autres confessors; li uns evesques, et li autres osteliers. Cil Juliens li martirs fu filz le conte d'Angiers, et fu osteliers, et n'ama onques nules richeces fors donner pour Dieu. Et herberga mult volentiers les povres pour Dieu, et onques n'en fu ennoiez. Et encontre avient que quant aucuns est destroiz d'ostel, si doit il dire la Pater Nostre en honor de lui et de sa fame, et pour l'ame de son pere et de sa mere, et Diex le conseille d'ostel; et l'a merité dou saint home.

2 / *The Mother's Premonitory Dream. Julian's Birth*

Li quans d'Anjou n'ot plus enfanz que Julien. Et quant la mere le conçut, si sonja la nuit que de son cors issoit une beste qui devoroit li et son seignor, et cele beste estoit en semblance d'omme ou de fame. Cil songes anoia mult a la fame. L'endemain ele ala a son chapelain et li conta son songe, et li chapelains li dist qu'ele ne s'esmoiast, car Dame Diex la semonoit de fere aumosne; et li amonesta qu'ele en feïst assez: car quanqu'ele avoit li avoit Dame Diex donné. Et cele crut son provoire, et fist ses conmandemanz, et fist toz les provoires revestir au Mans ou ele estoit, et cela son songe, et ne volt mie que l'en seüst pour quoi ele le fesoit. [173a] La dame porta son filz jusqu'a son terme. Et quant li enfes fu nez, tuit si parent en orent grant joie. Et conmanda li quans pour la joie de son enfant que tuit li prison des mers et de sa terre fussent delivré. Et cil qui le baptiserent et donnerent la foy li mistrent non Julien.

3 / *Julian's Youth. His Love for Hunting*

Li enfes crut, et fu mult biax, et mult blons, et bien tailliez, et bien plesanz et mult gracieus a touz ceus qui le veoient. Et la contesse sa mere l'ama tant qu'ele mist tout son cuer en lui amer; et quant ele venoit en .i. privé leu, et il li souvenoit de son songe, si ploroit. Et quant li enfes ot passé .vii. anz, si fu mult granz de son aage, et mult ama deduit de chiens et d'oisiax sor totes choses; et deduit de bois ama il tant, qu'a grant paine s'en pooit il .i. jor tenir, ne ja ne li anoiast.

4 / *The Hunt and Prediction. Julian Flees at Once*

Et ot .i. jor ses chiens lassez, et li loerent si compaignon qu'il s'en alast, car il lor annoit tote jor a aler parmi le bois. Et quant li enfes l'oï, si lor dist:

'Alez vous en, car je ne m'en iré pas encore, ainz irai querant aventure parmi cest bois.' Aprés prist son arc et s'en ala, et tiex i ot des compaignons qui le siuirent; mes il se destorna d'els au plus tost qu'il pot. Et quant il s'aperçut que si compaignon l'orent perdu, si tendi son arc; et vit une beste gesir en .i. buisson, et ala entour le buisson espiant conment il peüst la beste besser. Et einsint conme il volt traire a li, ele conmença a crier, et dit: 'Enfes, ne m'oci mie: je te dirai [173b] ta destinee qui t'avendra: Tu occirras ton pere et ta mere a .i. sol cop.' Quant li enfes oï parler einsint la beste, si detint sa saiete, et fu moult esbahiz, tant qu'il se porpensa et entesa sa saiete, et volt traire a la beste; et ele conmença a crier, et dit autel conme ele avoit devant dit. Si en fu li enfes moult esbahiz et espouantez, et entesa derechief sa saiete, et volt ferir la beste, quant ele conmença a crier, et dit: 'Enfes, ne m'oci mie, que je te di voir: tu occirras ton pere et ta mere a un cop; ja cele part n'iras, nus ne le te puet destorner fors Dieu.' Quant li enfes l'oï, si tressua d'angoisse, et prist son arc et ses saietes, si les brisa, et dist: 'Pute beste, tu as menti de quanque tu as dit, car je n'iré jamés en leu ou mon pere ne ma mere soient.' Et puis derompi ses cheveus et detort ses poinz, et dist: 'Diex, ou est la moie mort? Que ne me prent ele ançois que ce m'aviegne?' Il deschauça ses esperons et ses heuses, et les geta ilec, et s'en foï parmi le bois com hom desvez, car il vouloit mielz tot jorz estre en essil que aaler en leu ou il seüst ne son pere ne sa mere.

5 / His Mother's Anguish

Einsint s'en foï nuit et jor ausint com c'il deüst le monde conquerre par foïr. Et son pere le fist querre par tout le païs, mes il ne le troverent mie. Et sa mere faisoit chascun jor messe chanter, et fu en oroisons et en proieres que Diex li sauvast son fil et li renvoiast sain et sauf. Et se complaignoit [173c] chascun jor a Dame Dieu par li meïsmes, et disoit: 'Hé, Diex, con vous m'avez traïe! Car je ai perdue ma joie et tout mon confort que j'avoie en cest siecle, et nule chose que je oie ne que je n'oie ne me puet conforter. Lasse, chetive, que ferai je? Hé, Diex, pour quoi soffrez vous que je perde ma joie? Diex, ce festes vous, car vous estes poesteïs de totes choses fors de moi rendre mon fil. Biaux sire Diex, se je l'ai forfet vers vous, il ne le deüst pas comparer. Je vous pri que vous le me rendez, et prenez la venjance de mon cors, non pas du sien.' Ceste proiere faisoit la dame chascun jor, et fesoit aumosnes chascun jor plus que l'en ne vous porroit dire. Ele vestoit et pessoit les mesiaux et les contrez et les autres povres, et levoit, et couchoit, et trouvoit quanque mestier lor estoit.

6 / A Changed Julian Visits the Pope in Rome. The Pope Orders Him to Ignore the Prediction, and to Return Home to His Parents

Or leré ci ester de la dame, si vous dirai de l'enfant conment il ala a Romme nuz piez et en langes par sauvages terres, ausint com povres penëanz, et si ala en povre abit, et ne fu onques jor ne nuit que il n'eüst granz paines et granz travaus; mauvés hostiex et mauvais liz ot il maintes foiz, et souvent jut hors par defaute d'ostel, et ala tant par noif et par glace et par pluie que sa char devint tote noire et perse de l'angoisse des froiz. Et fu si povres et si atornez qu'an ne connoüst quil le veïst en tel abit. Tant ala li enfes qu'il vint a Rome. Et quant il pot avoir lieu et tans, si s'agenoilla as piez l'apostoille, et li conta [173d] toute s'aventure: qui filz il estoit, et dont il venoit; et quanque la beste li avoit dit li conta au mielz que il pot et que il sot, conment il occirroit son pere et sa mere a .i. sol cop, et endementieres qu'il disoit ceste parole chaï as piez l'apostolle tout pasmez et tout envers. Li apostolles se seigna et le redreça et li dist que ce fu fantosmes qui l'avoit deceü, et que il ne devoit mie croire, car ce seroit contre reson et contre nature et contre Escripture que beste qui n'a en soi sens ne entendement parlast. 'Je te conmant de par Dieu que tu voises arrieres, et sers ton pere et ta mere, et honore; et soies moult repentanz de ce que tu departis onques d'els pour ceste chose; et se tu lor as riens mesfet, prie lor par Dieu que il le te pardoingnent. Il seront mult lié de ta venue et mult joieus; et ne doutes riens que tu as oïe ne veüe, car ele ne te puet fere se bien non.'

7 / Julian Insists He Will Go to Jerusalem
Despite the Pope's Order. The Pope Blesses Him
and Gives Him the Pilgrim's Cross

Li enfes respondi a l'apostoille et dist: 'Sire, pour Dieu, n'en parlez jamés, car je vous di que jamés n'irai en terre ou j'aie parent ne parente, ne nul avoir terrien, ainz irai en la terre ou Diex fu morz et vis, et au Saint Sepulcre ou il fu couchiez. Sire, pour Dieu vous pri que vous me doigniez la croiz, car je veil aler Dieu servir de tot mon cuer et de toute ma pensee, et veil mielz que li Turc me preignent que je ne face ce que j'ai entrepris.' Atant se mist li enfes aus piez a l'apostoel a genoillons, et li pria doucement en plorant que il li donast la croiz pour celui qui en croiz fu mis. Li [174a] apostoilles fu mult en grant pensee du faire ou du lessier, tant que li enfes li dist 'Sire, pour Dieu merci, ne m'alez mie delaient, car ançois irai je sanz croiz que je n'i aille.' Quant li apostoilles le vit si engrant d'avoir la croiz, si li dist: 'Biax filz, Dame Dieu te doint bien faire, et te desfende de mal. Je te donré la croiz puisque tu la me demandes pour Dieu; et si t'aiderai de .xx. besanz, et Diex te doint part en toutes les aumosnes et en toutes les proieres que je ferai tant com je vivrai.' Atant osta li apostolles une atache de son mantel, si la seigna et gita sus eue benoite, et en fist croiz et la donna a l'enfant, et le doctrina mult bien et enseigna a bien faire et a eschiver pechié a son pooir. Li enfes retint bien les bones paroles que li bons hom li avoit dites, et se pena mult de bien fere.

8 / *Julian Visits Jerusalem as a Penitent*

Il prist congié a l'apostoille, et s'en ala droit a Brandiz ou il trouva assez pelerins, et loa nef avec eus, et s'en passa outre, et vindrent en Acre dedens .iii. semaines. Juliens fu mult liez; et tantost que il fu arrivez chanja il ses besanz a la monoie de la terre, et en donna pour Dieu a touz ceus qui li demendoient, et li plut moult a donner. En tel maniere donna il quanqu'il ot, car il avoit mielz estre povres que riches. Tant ala que il vint en Jherusalem touz deschauz et en mauvese robe; et fist ses oroisons et ses afflicions au Sepulcre tot em plorant, et pria Jhesucrist qu'il le gardast qu'il ne feïst le pechié que la beste li avoit [174b] dit; et fist ilueques mult grant duel, psource qu'il l'en souvenoit, et dist: 'Biax sire Diex, se tele mesaventure me doit avenir dont vous pri ge que vous me doingniez la mort ançois.' Quant il ot assez ploré et fet son duel, si issi hors de son mostier et ala conme povres penëanz en touz les leus ou il oï dire que l'en devoit pelerinage fere, et mena tres povre vie.

9 / *He Serves Seven Years in a Leprosarium Without Pay*

Et quant il ot son pelerinage fet, si s'arestut en Jherusalem aus mesiax, et fu touz nuz fors d'une pel de beste qu'il avoit vestue entour lui; ileques fist debonairement quanque l'en li conmanda. Il cura souvent les estables, et autres services faisoit il, et ne volt onques or ne argent prendre de son servise, car il le fesoit purement pour Dieu. Si conme il avient maintes foiz que quant .i. gentilz hom a lessié toutes terrienes richetés pour Dieu servir en religion, il se met plus engrant d'orer et de bien fere que ne fet .i. vilains qui onques n'ot se painne non et travail. Juliens soffri toutes les mesaises qu'il ot por Dieu doucement et debonairement si conme gentilz hon doit fere; onques une seule foiz ne li sonjast de chose qui li chanjast son cuer, pour quoi il lessast a servir. Einsint servi il .vii. anz en la meson aus malades, que onques ne li demanda nus qui il fu ne dont il estoit, car il estoit si povres et si nuz que nus ne cuidast qu'il [174c] fust filz de conte. Et mena si tres povre vie que mult fu changiez dedenz son terme; mes il fu si forz, et si preuz que il vai[n]quoit tous les autres ovriers et tous les sergens de l'ostel a ovrer.

10 / *Julian Undertakes a Pilgrimage to Saint James of Compostella in Hope of Hearing News of His Parents*

Et quant il ot ileques servi tot son terme si li prist talant d'aler a Saint Jaque pour ce que il verroit par aventure pelerins de son païs par le chemin, et lor demanderoit se li quens et la contesse d'Anjou vivoient encore; et se il oït dire pour voir que li uns d'eus fust trespassez de cel siecle, il s'en iroit en son païs, quar donques savoit il bien que la beste li avoit menti. Il vint

.i. jour a son mestre qui gardoit les ouvriers de la meson et li dist: 'Sire, donnez moi congié; je m'en veil aler en mon païs. Je entrai par vous ceanz et par vous m'en veil issir. Vous m'avez mult bien fait; Dex le vous rende.' Li mestres li respondi et li dist: 'Julien, vous nous avez mult bien serviz et longuement, si en devez avoir grant loier. Or demandez ce que vous voudroiz et vous l'avroiz.' 'Sire, fait Julien, je ne veil avoir nul loier fors ce que Dame Dex me donra. Je pren a vous congié, si m'en vois.' Li mestres envoia aprés lui .v. besanz, mes Julien les renvoia et dist que il n'en avoit cure, car il vint sanz or, et sanz ce s'en voloit aler.

11 / *After a Visit to Saint-Gilles, Julian sets out for Saint James With a Group of Pilgrims, Begging for Lodging Each Night*

Einsint s'en rala jusqu'a Acre et trova ileques les Templiers et autres genz qui voloient passer et avoient ja chargié lor nef. Cil passerent Julien ovec eus pour Deu et pour ce que il le virent povre. [174d] Il furent .xv. semaines sus mer, si en i ot mult de morz ainz qu'il arrivassent. Mes Juliens fu tot jorz sainz et hetiés. Et vint ovec ses conpaignons tresqu'a Saint Gile ou il sejorna .ij. mois; et aloit touz les jourz par la ville, et alloit demandant son pain pour Dex, et repairoit chiés .i. povre prestre de la ville qui le heberja pour Deu, et le coucha sus une nate. Einsint conme il ala .i. diemenche par la ville, si trouva en une maison pelerins a pié et a cheval, qui s'en voloient aler a Saint Jaque, et se estoient entrefiancié que li riche aideroient as povres a leur pooir en totes choses, et s'i porteroient loial conpaignie. Quant Juliens oï la bone conpaignie que li uns devoit porter a l'autre, se li prist talent d'aler ovec euls. Il se mit ovec eus, mes il ne porta or ne argent, car il avoit fiance en Dex le criatour qu'il l'en dorroit assez. En chascune ville ou il venoit, si demandoit de pain pour Deu et ostel a la nuit, et Dame Dex li donna tot jorz assez quanque mestier li estoit. Il faisoit chascun jor sa jornee ausint bien conme cil qui avoient lor forz chevaux, car il avoit mise toute s'entente en son pelerinage fere.

12 / *At the News of a Local War, the Group Turns Back; But Julian Goes On Alone, to the City of One of the Warring Lords*

Et ainsint alerent il .ix. jorz bien em pes; et au disieme virent il pelerins que il connoissoient bien. Il lor demanderent ou il aloient, et il lor distrent que il troveroient mult grant guerre dedenz .v. lilues, que .li. contes ont la tout le païs essillié, ne nus homs ne peut passer [175a], tant ait bon conduit ne fort. 'Nous i avons sejorné .ii. jors; or nous en retornons arriers.' Quant cil l'oïrent, si en furent mult esbahi et desconforté, si s'asistrent pour prendre conseil d'aler avant ou arriere; et quant il furent conseillié, si s'en retornerent tuit fors Julien. Cil s'en ala avant touz ceus, quar il se porpensa que il n'avoit que perdre, si en iront mult plus seurement. Tant ala

que il vint au chastel ou li uns des seignors repairoit qui maintenoit cele
guerre; et fu la ville si plaine de gent que nul n'i pooit ostel trover.

13 / He Cannot Find Lodgings. The Inhabitants Insult Him

Juliens demanda et a destre et a senestre ostel pour Deu, mes il ne trova
quil le herbarjast, ainz l'escharnissoient et l'apeloient ribaut et truant, et li
distrent que il avroit tost forstrete la fille son oste. Il ne leur respondi riens,
ainz pria Dex que il lor pardonnast la folie et la vilenie que il li disoient, et
a lui donnast ostel et viande. Ainsint ala il de rue en rue demandant ostel,
mes chascun l'escondisoit, et faisoit la sorde oreille, tant que il conmensa a
dire: 'Ha, Dex, sire, roi poissant, car me hesbergiez, quar je en ai grant mestier. Je ne vin onques mes en leu ou je ne trovasse ostel fors ore.'

14 / Finally A Knight Offers Him Hospitality

Endementires que il se plaingnoit ainsit, l'oï .i. chevaliers; et l'apela et li
demanda dont il venoit et quel vie il menoit et coment il avoit non. Juliens
li respondi mult sagement: 'Biau sire, je sui vostre povre homs [175b] qui
vois querant mon pain; mes je ne truis qui me veillie herbergier pour ceste
guerre, ainz sai bien que je gerré annuit hors, se Dame Dex d'ostel ne me
conseillie.' Li chevaliers li respondi: 'Dex t'a ostelé, car je te hebergerai hui
mes pour l'amor de lui.' Juliens lors si li enclina mult doucement et li dist:
'Sire, Dex vous en rende le guerredon.'

15 / The Knight Mocks His Poverty,
and Offers Him Instead Employment As a Man-At-Arms

Atant ala seoir au feu ovesques les genz mult liez. Cele nuit ot il bien quanque il covint, et li donna li sires de touz ses mes. Et quant il ot mengié il
apela devant lui pour ce que il le vit grant et bien menbru, et li demanda
quele vie il menoit. Juliens respondi mult sagement et dist: 'Sire, je sui uns
povres hom qui nulle riens ne quier fors ma viande.' 'Mauvés estes, fait li
sires, qui autre chose ne querez, car uns chiens ou une truie trueve assez
a mengier; et [si] n'est mie grant delit de vivre a[i]nsint conme une truie;
ne nus hom ne vaut riens qui est tot jor an povreté.' 'Sires, dist Juliens, nus
ne doit vivre pour son ventre emplir, mes que el servise Dame Dex entre,
il le covient parfaire. J'estoie esmeü pour aler a Saint Jaque, mes il me
semble que l'en ne puet passer pour ceste guerre.' 'Certes non, fet li chevaliers, car touz les pons et les plances du païs sunt despeciés, que nus n'i
peut passer, ne privé ne estrange. Mes demeure ovec moi, je te retendrai
pour sergent [175c] et avras .xii. deniers le jour; et se Dex te velt donner
proece et oster hors de la paresce ou tu es, tost te porroit venir grans biens.'
Julien li respondi: 'Sire, laissiez moi conseillier et le matin vous en savrai a

dire que je en ferai.' Li chevaliers li otroia mult debonerement et li promist mult de bien a faire.

16 / *Throughout a Restless Night, Julian Tries to Decide Whether to Renounce His Poverty and His Pilgrimage*

Ainsit ala Juliens concher, et fu toute nuit em pensee ou de l'aler ou du remaindre. Lors se conmença a desesperer de bien faire, et dist: 'Dex, que vois je querant et truandant? Encor n'ai ge pas fet le pechié de quoi je ai eu maintes males jornees. Ce me vient de grant paor et de grant folie que avant faz la penitance que le pechié; et bien sai qu'il n'avendra ja, ne ne m'en savra ja Diex gre, car je nel faz pas pour lui. Fox fui quant j'entrepris onques tel chose dont je ne puis avoir ne pris ne lox, et nus ne me doit prisier se ge sui tout jorz truanz ne mandianz, et je en doi avoir grant honte, por ce que je sui fiulz de conte et de contesse, et li plus gentis hon de touz mes encessors. Jamés plus truanz ne serai, car ce est vil vie et mauvese, de quoi nus prodons n'a envie. Je maintendré chevalerie ausi conme firent mi parant qui vesquirent a grant honor. Je ne voi pas conment nus hom qui ci sejourneroit peüst ocirre le conte d'Anjou; et s'il venoit par aventure pour guerroier, conment [175d] i(1) vendroit sa fame? Et se ele i venoit, conment les occirroie je andeus a .i. cop par ma chevalerie? Car ma mere ne set porter armes. Si m'aist Diex, je ne tendrai plus cest essil, car trop i ai ma jovente perdue.' Einsint se dementa Juliens cele nuit, et regreta ses parenz.

17 / *The Next Day, Julian Enters the Knight's Service*

L'endemain quant ses sires leva, Juliens vint devant lui, et si se pena mult de lui servir, et fu liez et joieus de ce qu'il volt servise prendre. Quant li chevaliers le vit si bien servir, si li demanda s'il estoit conseilliez de demorer avecques lui. 'Sire, fet Juliens, oïl, car je ne veil mes mener si povre vie conme j'ai fet, ainz veil une autre essaier qui me sera plus honorable, et si vous servirai miex et plus volentiers que garçons qui soit en vostre cort.' 'Julien, fet li chevaliers, et je vous retieng; et si vous conment que vous soiez totjorz pres de moi quant vous me verrez en estor ne en mellee.' 'Sire, s'irai ge se je puis.'

18 / *The City's Livestock Is In Danger. The Count Goes Out to Defend His Property*

Endementres qu'il parloient einsint leva li criz en la vile que lor anemi estoient a la porte du chastel, et avoient ja pris de lor genz assez, et emmenoient par force la proie. La vile fu maintenant escomeüe, et cria l'en as armes. Li sires demanda ses armes hastivement, si s'arma; et Juliens l'arma, et mist grant cure en lui atorner. Li autre s'armerent einsint, et pristrent lor glaives et lor javeloz et lor autres armes, si sont ensemble issu hors de la porte; et li quens qui estoit sires du chastel, et qui menoit la guerre, issi touz premerains, et mena [176a] .ii. chevaliers avec lui atot .xl. autres chevaliers fors [et] bien combatanz, et aconsurent lor anemis entre .i. gué et une montaigne. Tantost lesserent aler les chevax et les firent par force avaler de la montaigne. A l'avaler qui firent, en chaïrent plus de .c. pardesus les testes des chevax. Ilec conmencerent il un estor grant et fort, et lor corurent sus de toutes parz, et escrierent lor enseignes. Li quens qui plus ot preude gent et hardie, resqueut sa proie et mena ses anemis par force jusqu'au gué, et les embati dedenz. Ilecques fu li estors mult granz et mult fiers, et mult i ot ocis de gent et d'une part et d'autre; mes li quans ot meudre gent et plus hardie, si fist ses anemis passer le gué a force, et cil se desfendirent mult fierement encontre.

19 / Julian Rushes Out Unarmed, But Soon Finds a Horse and Gear

Juliens vint isnelement touz nuz fors de sa cote, .i. baston en sa main, car il n'avoit autre armeüre; et vit les bons chevax qui gisoient si en parfont einsint qu'il ne s'en pooient mouvoir, et les sergenz et les chevaliers si morz et affolez assez plus que l'en ne vous porroit dire. Maintenant gita son baston fors, et prist armes les meillors qu'il trova en la place et les plus beles, et trait hors du sanc .i. destrier fort et isnel, si sailli sus, la lance ou poing, et passa le gué jusqu'a l'estor.

20 / Unrecognized, He Fights By the Knight's Side

Il vit son seignor enmi la presse, si la rompi et vint a li, si li aida mult bien, car onques tele part n'ala, ne a chevalier ne se prist que Juliens ne [176b] li fust au costé; et se il prenoit chevalier, Juliens sesissoit maintenant par le frain. Ainsint li aida il mult longuement, mes ses sires ne se prist mie garde qu'il estoit, car il ne cuidoit mie que li truanz qu'il avoit herbergiez osast enprendre tel hardement qu'il venist a l'estor. Li chevaliers estoit mult preuz et mult hardiz, car il se metoit tout jorz en la grant presse. Et Juliens le(s) siuoit tot jorz a l'esperon, et li ot le jor mult grant mestier; et le resqueut maintes foiz, tant que cil ocistrent soz lui son destrier.

21 / The Knight's Horse Having Been Killed, Julian Gives Him His. The Knight Learns Who Has Rescued Him Thus

Juliens li bailla celui qu'il avoit gaaignié, et le remonta a force. Adont dist li chevaliers: 'Qui estes vous qui m'avez donné cheval et qui tote jor m'avez si bien servi?' 'Sire, fet Juliens, je sui cil que vous retenistes hui matin.' Li chevaliers le regarda et dist: 'Juliens, moult estes preuz et hardiz. Tote devez avoir l'onor et le pris de ceste bataille. Et sachiez de voir que le guerredon de vostre servise vous rendré je bien.' Juliens l'en mercia doucement, et li conta ou il avoit pris le cheval et les armes. 'Juliens, fet li chevaliers, or lessons ce ester, si venez aprés moi de grant eslés, car de totes parz poez vous veoir nos anemis.' Atant lessent chevax aler et vont aider lor compaigno[n]s qui estoient en la mellee. Juliens les passa touz em proesce fere, car il n'adreça a nul home qu'il ne li feïst les arçons widier.

22 / *The Knight and His Friends Marvel at Julian's Prowess*

Ses sires s'aresta touz quoiz enmi la presse pour esgarder ce que Juliens faisoit, et apela ses compaignons et lor mostra conment son truant qu'il avoit herbergié enchauçoit lor anemis. [176c] 'Seignors, fet il, se Diex m'ait, vous ne veïstes onques si povre ribaut conme il estoit hui matin quant je le reting. Or le secoron, car il en a grant mestier.' A cest mot broche le cheval, si s'est mis en la presse, et li autre tuit aprés, quanque cheval pueent rendre; et s'esforcierent si de ferir que tot le champ widerent de lor anemis. Cil s'en vont fuiant quanqu'il pueent jusqu'a lor lices. Li quans ne sa gent ne les vodrent enchaucier plus, ainz s'en retornerent atant, et vindrent a lor chastel atout le gaaing qu'il orent fet le jor.

23 / *After Their Victory, Julian and the Knight Return to Supper. Julian Is Rewarded. The Knight Speaks of Him at the Count's Court*

Mes Juliens en ot tout le pris et le los, si com ses sires dist qui a son ostel l'emena avoec li, et li donna neuve robe et li fist baillier tot son hernois a garder, et pour sa proesce l'en anora mult. Ne demoura mie granment que l'en demanda l'eue par le chastel. Li sires Julien(s) qui a l'ostel demoroit fust mult bien serviz. Li chevaliers s'en ala a cort, et trouva le conte et tote sa gent mult liez et joieus de la bone aventure qui lor estoit avenue, et en tindrent grant parole; et que que chascuns en die, li chevaliers Julien reconuit certainement que .i. truanz que il herberga pour Dieu qui ostel ne pooit trouver avoit toz les autres vaincuz de bien fere. Puis lor conmença a conter conment il conquist son cheval et ses armes, et conment il passa le gué et le resquelt quant son cheval li fu ocis, et le fist monter sus .i. autre qu'il avoit gaaigné par sa proesce. Quant [176d] li quans oï ce, si dist au chevalier: 'Frans hon, pour Dieu, gardez le bien, et li donnez assez du vostre tant qu'il ait bien son estouvoir.' 'Sire, dist li chevaliers, se je avoie fin or molu, si l'en donroie ge partie, et si ne quier que jamés de moi se departe.'

24 / *Despite the Esteem Shown Him, Julian Can Think of Nothing But The Joy of Combat*

Li chevaliers revint en son ostel chantant et demenant grant joie. L'endemain fist avoir a Julien quanque mestier li fu. Bien le fist vestir et chaucier, et li trova bone armeüre. Juliens en ot mult grant joie en son cuer de son hernois que l'en li apareille, mes nule riens ne li plest tant com estre en estor. Li jor li anoia mult quant il ne porta armes, et disoit en son cuer:

'Diex, pour quoi sejornons nous hui? Pourquoi ne nous armons nous et alons prendre lor proie? Ja en eüssent il hier menee la nostre se nous ne l'eüssions resqueusse. Diex, fet il, pourquoi sont cil chevalier en ceste ville? Car m'eüst li quans conmandé que je fusse .i. jor lor conestables, et que je peüsse d'eus fere ma volenté! Jamés le jor n'avroient repos. Ce n'est mie grant lox quant en desfent, car a force lor convient fere.'

25 / Another Attack Comes

Or a Juliens quanqu'il veult fors de ce qu'il ne trueve li ou esprover. Au tiers jor aprés, orent assemblé lor anemis .iii.c. chevaliers et toutes les menues genz de partoutes les contrees, et pristrent la proie a ceus du chastel a force, et chacerent lor gent en la vile. Li criz leva, et la noise que lor anemi enmainnent la proie, et si estoient ja venu(e) jusqu'au rues du chastel. Lors oïssiez cors et buisines soner. Tuit [177a] s'armerent hastivement et enchaucerent lor anemis a grant force, et les aconsistrent en la montaigne delez .i. pre, et firent ilec un grant estor et mult perillieus. Maint home i perdi l'ame cel jor.

26 / Julian's Love of Battle Leads Him to Take Many Risks

Juliens garda toutjors son seignor, et se tint mult pres de lui, mes onques nus fox ne nus yvres ne fu si entalantez de combatre conme estoit Juliens. Maint home aida le jor a ocirre, et ses sires regarda le jor souvent conment il se contenoit. Il ne venoit en nulle presse ou il n'eüst tost fet entree. Il ne refusoit nule encontre de chevalier ne de sergent. Tant estoit bien aidanz de ses armes, et aventureus, que il essi le jor de mainte grant presse et de mainte mellee ou uns autres eüst esté ocis; et chascuns qui l'esgarda dist que onques mes ne vit home qui si bien s'aidast.

27 / His Companions Think Him Foolhardy.
His Thirst for Honor Makes Him Refuse All Advice. The Victory is His

Il entreprist plus de cent choses le jor qui le greverent, dont il vint bien a chief, si que chascuns tenoit son hardement a folie. Assez plus fist que nus autres, et si ne pot onques estre lassez le jor, ainz fu totjorz en bone vertu. La ou la bataille estoit plus fiere se mist il toutjorz en la presse, si que ses sires ne l'en pooit oster, ainz li dit souvent: 'Julien, trai toi arriere, car totes noz genz sont si lassees qui ne se pueent mes aider, ne il ne te veulent mie lessier seul ci.' Juliens qui entendoit a lox conquerre ne se volt retorner pour home qui en peüst parler. Grant partie du jor estoit alé ançois qu'il les peüssent vaintre. Mes quelque talant qu'il eüssent, les mistrent [177b] il touz a la fuie par le hardement Julien. Assez en i ot morz et pris plus que je ne vous porroie nombrer. Jusqu'a lor lices vont fuiant, et ilecques se rassemblent tuit, et li autre ne les vodrent plus chacier, ainz sont venu arriere.

28 / *The Count Takes Julian Into His Service*

Cel jor ot bien veü li quans quanque Juliens ot fet. Il point vers lui a grant eslés et deslaça son hiaume et le bailla a .i. escuier. Lors acola Julien et le besa plus de cent foiz de route, et si li dist: 'Biax amis, je vous promet grant loier pour vostre grant servise, et si vous pri que vous soiez de ma mesnie, et je vous ferai chevalier mult par tens.' Juliens l'en mercie mult, et li dist: 'Sire, je ai seignor qui avant ier me retint pour Dieu, et je sai bien qu'il l'en peseroit se je le lessoie pour autrui servir.' 'Certes, fet li quans, non fera, ançois proiera encore que l'en vous face chevalier.' Atant e vous le seignor Julien qui volentiers et debonerement otroie que Julien soit au conte, et dit que grant asmone fera s'il le fet chevalier, car mult est preuz et hardiz.

29 / *Recognizing His Noble Quality, the Count Knights Him*

Li quans l'en mena avec lui jusqu'a la tor, si l'a fet desa[r]mer, puis l'esgarda mult longuement, et li sembla mult biax et mult bien fez de toz membres, et li dist ses cuers qu'il estoit gentilz hom. Li quans si conmença a aler et a trere vers lui, et li dist: 'Si m'aist Diex, je ne cuidoie mie que vous fussiez tiex conme vous iestes, ne si biaus ne si bien tailliez, car je ne vi onques home a estre miex taillié a chevalier que vous estes. [177c] Bon cheval en destre vous doine, et bones armes, que vous n'i faudroiz mie.' Juliens l'en mercia mult courtoisement, et se fist mult liez de ce que li quans li avoit promis. Einsint le fist li quans tote la semaine garder jusqu'au diemenche qu'il le fist chevalier a grant apareillement et a grant feste.

30 / *Julian Lives as a Knight. The Count Is Killed In Ambush*

Einsint fu Juliens feiz chevaliers, et oblia Saint Jaque et son pelerinage; ne li souvint de nule rien du monde fors d'armes, ou il avoit mis toute s'entente. Des preësces et des estors qu'il fist en sa chevalierie nouvelement et des secors qu'il fist tant com la guerre dura, ne vous avroie je hui dit la moitié. De ses anemis fu il totjorz doutez, et sor toz les autres. La guerre dura mult longuement, et lor ocist dedenz l'an plus de cent chevaliers. Mes entor la feste Saint Jehan issi li quans fors desarmez pour lui esbanoier, si fu parmi le cors feruz de ses anemis, et ne vesqui puis que .iii. jorz. Et quant il fu morz, sa gent firent aussi grant duel pour lui com l'en puet por nul home fere, et ce ne fu mie merveille, car il furent puis desconfit souvent de lor anemis, qui ne lor voloient doner trives ne fere pes a els, ainz guerroient mielz qu'il ne souloient, et plus hardiement.

31 / *The Young Countess Cannot Keep Her Discouraged Army Together. Her Counsellors Urge Her to Remarry. They Have Someone in Mind For Her: Julian*

Or vous dirai de la contesse conment ele maintint sa guerre. Ele n'avoit mie .xx. anz, mes Diex ne fist onques fame de sa valor; et ce fu puis chose bien esprovee. Car ausint conme la rose seurmonte toutes autres flors en biauté, ausint estoit ele plus [177d] bele et plus sage des autres dames du païs; et onques en son tens ne fu fame si plaine de bontez ne de si ferme foy. Mes la guerre ou ele estoit avoit tout le païs gasté et destruit. Chascun jor veoit ele prendre sa proie, et ne li pooit ne secorre ne aidier de nule part, ne secors n'atendoit, ainz ploroit souvent pour la honte et pour la perte que si anemi li faisoient. Ele ne pooit riens veoir dont ele ne fust dolente, car ele veoit sa terre apovroier et aler a noiant, et sa gent la vouloient guerpir; ne ele ne trouvoit en qui ele se fiast, ne trouvoit aide ne secors en nul leu du monde ou ele le seüst demander, tant que tuit si haut home de son païs furent venu .i. jor a li, si li distrent: 'Dame, pour Dieu merci, l'en vous assaut chascun jor, et onques puis que vostre sires fu morz ne vous finerent cil qui nous hëent de desconfire; et nous ont lessié li François et li autre preudom de hors, si n'a entour vostre chastel forteresce qui ne soit en grant aventure de perdre. Tote vostre terre perdrez se vous ne crëez vos conseulz. Dame, pour Dieu, prenez seignor qui vous gardera vostre terre et vostre honor desfendra de nos anemis. Car se vous aviez chevetainne que vous eüssiez pris par noz lox et par noz conseulz, lors serions nous en grant pes et en bone, dont nous somes ore en grant gerre. Et sachiez certainement que le plus bel et le plus large et le mielz vaillant et le meillor chevalier que onques [178a] nus de nous veïst vous voulons doner a seignor.' La dame demora mult a respondre; nepourquant si demanda ele qui cis chevaliers est que il li ont tant loé, car ele prendroit volentiers le plus preuz du monde, et si en avroit grant mestier. 'Dame, fet chascuns, Juliens est preuz et vaillanz et sages plus que chevaliers que nous veïssons onques en noz tens. De sa largesse ne parot nus, car mult a donné robes de vair, de gris, et armes et chevax qu'il a conquis par proesce. Mult donne a ceus qui en ont mestier, et qui li demandent, et si ne recroit onques. Tot avrions perdu se il n'estoit, car tote nostre resqueusse est en lui, si savons bien que il desfendroit bien la terre puis que ele seroit venue en sa main.'

32 / The Countess Is of High Birth, and Hesitates to Marry a Man of Unknown Family. But the Council Insists, and She Acquiesces

La dame respondi maintenant: 'Seignors, fet ele, je vous pri por Dieu que vous me conseilliez en bone foy, car je sui a vous a conseillier, et si ne vous merveilliez mie de ce que je vous dirai. Je ne di mie que Juliens ne soit mult preuz de grant maniere; mes je ne me voldroie marier a nul fuer a home estrange dont je ne seüsse l'estracion, car je ne voudroie mie fere chose dont je eüsse reproichier. Uns princes de haut parage et de grant afere m'a novelement requise. Et si ne contredi ge mie Julien, car en lui a grant chevalerie et grant largesce et grant bonte, mes il n'est mie de connoissance, et si me desplest mult de ce qu'il vint onques en cest païs querant son pain; ne en cest païs ne vint puis home quil le conneüst. Je sui parante la roïne [178b] de France, et tuit mi parent sont haut home: conte, baron, chastelain. Bien tendrai m'anor endroit moi.' 'Dame, fet chascuns, il ne puet autrement estre, car nous savons bien certainement que Diex l'envoïa pour nous en cest païs; ne vous n'i devez mie avoir honte, car ce la roïne de France estoit en autel point, si le devroit ele prendre volentiers. Dame, ne vous savons autrement conseillier, ainz vous disons bien que se honte ne blasme en venoit a vous que ce seroit sus nous.' La dame respondi mult doucement: 'Se vous le me donnez, je ne le refus mie, ainz sui preste de fere voz volentez, car je ne vous ose escondire. Or doint Diex qu'il m'atourt a preu et a honor.'

33 / Julian is Brought to the Court, and the Marriage Takes Place at Once

Lors font grant joie a la cort de ce que la dame a respondu si debonerement, et rendent graces et merciz a Dame Dieu et envoierent maintenant pour Julien a son ostel, et le convoierent a cort, si que il se merveilla pour quoi il le fesoient. Quant il vint ou palés amont, tuit se leverent contre lui et li porterent grant honor plus que il ne souloient. Un hauz hom le prist par la main, et le fist seoir ou plus haut leu delez lui, si li dist: 'Julien, vous avroiz dedens brief terme le bien que Diex vous a promis. Vous savez bien que cist païs est touz gastez par la guerre, si avrions mestier d'un preudome quil le gardast bien, si avons esgardé que vous avroiz madame la contesse a fame qui en est mult joiant de ce que si preudome avra a mari.' Juliens les mercie doucement [178c] de lor avancement et de lor promesse. Atant ont la dame amenee, qui s'estoit vestue et apareilliee de la meillor robe que ele ot, et quant Juliens la vit venir, si corut contre li, et la prist par la main. Maintenant font .i. prestre revestir a mult grant joie, qui les espousa. De son doner ne de son despendre ne vous dirai ge ore plus, car il s'en sot bien aidier.

34 / That Night, the Countess Asks Julian About His Family. He Replies That He is Noble, But Refuses to Reveal His Origins

Grant cort et grant feste tint le jor, et quant ce vint au vespre, et lor liz fu apareilliez et saigniez, si se couchierent. La dame le reçut entre ses braz; ele l'acole doucement et bese, et li dist: 'Sire, pour Dieu, ne vous poist il mie de ce que je vous demanderai, puis que il est einsint que vous m'avez espousee. Volentiers voudroie savoir ou vous fustes nez, et quele gent vostre parant sont, car vous estes si preuz que vous ne devez mie avoir honte du dire.' 'Dame, je vous di pour voir que mes peres fu totjorz sires de païs et de la terre ou il fu nez, et si fu fil de conte et de contesse. Mes ventance ne vaut ci rien, car je n'i avroie home qui le me tesmoignast.' 'Sire, pour Dieu, et en quel terre porroie je envoier querre vos paranz que il me venissent aidier a guerroier?' Quant Juliens l'oï, si se repenti de ce que li avoit dit, car se sa fame envoiast querre ses paranz, bien porroit avenir ce que la beste li avoit dit. 'Dame, fet il, ne vous poist il mie, je ne nonmeré jamés ma contree, ne jamés ne seroi si liez, se je l'oi nomer, que je ne soie corrociez.'

35 / But, at Her Insistence, He Tells His Wife the Names of His Father and Mother

'Sire, fet ele, [178d] or le me pardonnez ceste foiz por Dieu. Jamés nel vous demanderai, mes seulement le non de vostre pere et de vostre mere me dites. Ja ne savrai pour ce dont vous estes.' 'Dame, fet il, mon pere si a non Jeufroi, et ma mere Anme. Or vous prie pour Dieu que vous ne me demandez plus, car vous n'i porriez rien gaaigner.' La dame se tint atant tote coie, et retint mult bien les nons en son cuer; neporquant si l'en fu il mult petit, car ele cuida qu'il le deïst par ventance. Grant joie li fist la nuit si conme ele dut fere a son seignor.

36 / Julian Defeats His Enemies Quickly

L'endemain firent grant despens et granz noces, et cil du païs se penerent mult d'anorer lor novel seignor. Trestuit cel jor li firent homage et bone seürté; et Juliens conmença maintenant sa guerre. Chevaliers et sergenz manda, et il en i vint a grant planté. De totes pars corut sus a ses anemis chascun jor, et les greva durement. Et quant il virent qu'il ne porroient avoir duree, si li prierent doucement que il lor donast trives, ou il feïst pes a euls; mes il n'en volt onques oïr parole, ainz les envaï chascun jor plus a plus. Cil ce sont .i. jor assemblé, si vindrent a lui pour crier merci, et li baillierent les cles de toz lor recez et de totes lor forteresces, et li amenerent lor filz en ostages; mes Juliens lor a tout pardonné, et lor chastiaus et lor forteresces et lor terres lor a rendu, et si les a touz lessiez en pes.

37 / In Peace, Julian Takes Up Hunting With His Old Delight

Or sera Juliens en repos, puisque sa guerre est finee; il n'a plus cure de corre en proie, [179a] ainz est revenuz a sa nature; il fet chiens querre par tot le païs, car nus deduiz ne li plest autant com d'estre en bois et en pes. Einsint demora Juliens ilecques .v. anz, et .vii. anz devant estoit issuz de son païs.

38 / His Parents, Uneasy, Finally Agree to Go Out As Pilgrims to Seek News of Their Son

Et endementres qu'il demora ilecques tu li quans Jeufroi d'Anjou son pere en son païs mult a malese de ce que il ne savoit nule novele de son filz, tant que grant talant li prist d'aler a Saint Gile nuz piez et en langes; et dit qu'il ne menra avec lui que .i. seul sergent et .i. somier qui portera ses deniers et sa robe. La contesse voit bien que ses sires s'apareille d'aler, si l'apela en une chambre priveement a conseil, et li demanda ou il veut aler. 'Dame, fet il, je veil aler a Saint Gile nuz piez et en langes purement, que Diex me doint oïr bones noveles de mon fil se il est vis; et s'il est morz, que Diex en ait merci.' Lors conmença la contesse a soupirer, et dist: 'Sire, je irai avec vous; n'i vaut riens desanester, car je ne m'en tendraie por rien. Pieç'a que je l'avoie enpensé, si com vous dites, le pelerinage a fere.' 'Dame, fet il, vous ne savez de quoi vous voulez entremetre. Vous ne porriez sosfrir la paine d'aler deschauce. Mon oirre me porroiz atarger; si ne me feroiz se mal non.' 'Sire, fet ele, pour Dieu merci, il n'est riens quil le me peüst destorner. Ne doutez mie que ja par moi ne sejorneroiz jor; ainz ai assez plus grant paor de vous que de moi. Et si sai bien que Diex nous mosterra apert miracle de nostre filz, et por ce nous devrions nous [179b] haster. Une pucele sanz plus menrai o moi por moi servir.' 'Dame, fet il, quant vous le voulez enprendre, vous n'en seroiz ja escondite.'

39 / *They Travel to Saint-Gilles*

Li quans apareilla isnelement son hernois, et la contesse le sien. Entor Pentecoste se sont esmeü en tapinage. La dame s'esforça mult d'aler, et ne li greva riens, ce li semble, porce qu'ele le faisoit pour son filz. Et a touz les povres qu'il encontrerent donnerent de lor argent, et cuiderent bien lor fil trouver par les ausmosnes qu'il font. La contesse e mult liee de ce qu'ele erre mielz qu'ele ne seult. Plus de .c. povres pelerins siuoient lor route, dont li plus estoient d'els atendant. Quant il vindrent a Saint Gile si alerent droit au mostier et firent ilec lor offrendes que Diex lor doint par son conmandement avoiement de lor enfant.

40 / *From Saint-Gilles, They Set Off*
for Saint James of Compostella With A Group

Quant il orent leurs offrandes fetes, si sont alé prendre lor ostex, et sejornerent .v. jorz en la vile, et troverent pelerins qui devoient aler a Saint Jaque, dont la contesse fu liee, et pria mult le conte qu'il alassent avec euls. 'Dame, volentiers iroie, se ge ne vous cuidoie grever.' 'Sire, pour Dieu, de tout ce ne dout je rien, ainz vous pri que nous en aillons demain avec euls.' 'Dame, et nous en iron demain, desque vous le voulez.'

41 / *They Arrive at Julian's Stronghold, and Take Lodgings*
With a Widow Who Tells the Story of the Beggar Turned Lord

Au matin si tost conme il virent le jor, se sunt mis au chemin, et vont tant que il sont venu au chastel dont lor filz estoit sires et quans; et pristrent ostel chiés une veve dame qui n'avoit nul enfant. Quant il orent la nuit mengié, si s'alerent esbanoier [179c] en .i. prael ou leur ostesse les mena.

'Dame, fet la contesse, conment a non li sires de cest chastel? C'est li plus
biax et li mielz seanz que je aie veü en ceste voie.' La borjoise li conmança
a dire: 'Dame, se Diex m'ait, vous n'oïstes onques parler de tiex merveilles;
mes fortune conseille ceus qu'ele veult. Les uns monte, les autres abesse.
Bien a passé .v. anz que une grant guerre fu en cest païs si que toute la
terre en fu gastee; et vint .i. povres penëanz en ceste vile son pain querant,
et devint sergent par son hardement: puis fu tres bons chevaliers. Et avint
.i. jor que nostre sires fu ocis; et pria l'en le chevalier que il preïst la dame,
et ele le prist par le lox de sa gent por ce que c'estoit li plus hardiz qu'an
seüst en cest païs. Puis prist il ses anemis par force, si se vencha si bien
d'eus que nus ne li ose mes riens fe[re].'

42 / The Widow Names and Describes Julian

'[Dou]ce dame, dist la con[tesse], dit[es] moi conment il a non et conment il se vit et quel forme il a.' 'Dame, fet ele, il a non Juliens, et si ne vit
onques plus [bel] home. N'a pas .xxx. anz; il a blons chevex, gent cors et
grant enforcheüre, grant vix et grant front, si a les elz [vairs].' Quant la
contesse l'entent, si a grant joie, si que la joie qu'ele ot li toli grant piece
la parole; et li quans refut mult liez. Maintenant demanda a la borjoise quel
deduit il amoit plus, et ele dit qu'il n'amoit nul deduit tant conme de
chiens, dont il avoit grant planté. Lors dit la contesse en plorant: 'Sire,
dedenz brief terme avrons le guerredon [179d] dou servise que nous avons
fet a Monseignor Saint Gile'; et puis a parfondement soupiré, et recleime
Saint Marie de fin cuer en plorant. 'Sire, pour Dieu, fet ele a son seignor,
alez vous couchier.'

43 / Alone in Their Room, the Couple
Plan to See Their Son on the Next Day

La contesse a la chambre bien fermee, por ce qu'ele ne veult mie que nus
i sorviegne qui lor conseil oïe. 'Sire, fet ele, avez oï com deümes estre con-
chié du deable; mes Diex nous vost sa ravoier por nous metre hors de tris-
tece et de paine, ou nous avons esté maint jor. Or avons trouvé nostre fil.
Si nous convendra demain sejorner. Mes cist nons Juliens est conmuns a
totes genz, et maint home ainment forest et deduit de chiens et d'oisiaus
plus que d'autres; mes se Diex plest, ja por ce ne serons deceü, car se ge
l'avoie une foiz veü, je savroie bien s'il seroit mes filz.' 'Dame, fet li quans,
bien matin le verrons, et si vous dirai conment: nous entrerons demain priveement el chastel, si nous tendrons demain devant la chapele, et se l'en
nous demande riens, nous dirons que nous sommes pelerin, si orrions
volentiers messe, et verrions volentiers le conte dont nous avons oï dire si
grant bien.' Einsint vont tote nuit devisant conment il feront l'endemain, si
que onques la nuit ne dormirent.

44 / Meanwhile, Julian Announces to His Wife That He Is
Going Hunting. She Is To Prepare Their Baths For His Return

Or vous lairai du conte et de la contesse, si vous dirai de Julien qui au
matin veult aler chacier. Il apela sa fame, si li dist: 'Dame, fetes moi demain .i. baing apareillier contre ma venue.' 'Sire, fet la dame, a vostre
talant sera [180a] fet; et si vous creant que je en ferai .i. fere por moi, si
que ge serai baingnie encontre vostre venue; mes je vous pri que vous revaigniez par tens.' La dame conmenda a ses puceles que li baing fussent
apareillié a tierce ou ançois, et eles si firent.

45 / The Parents Go to the Chapel and Learn That Julian Is Absent

Li quans et la contesse d'Anjou se sont par matin levé, et vindrent par le
chastel, et troverent la premiere porte overte, et alerent tresqu'a la chapele,
et firent lor oroisons dehors a l'uis simplement. Quant il orent ilecques
longuement esté, si vint ilecques li chapelains, et les salua doucement. Cil
se leverent encontre lui et li demanderent se li sires vendroit a la chapele
pour oïr messe. 'Par foy, fet li chapelains, je cuit qu'il soit pieça au bois;
mes il revendra dedenz midi.' 'Et sa fame il vendra ele?' 'Oïl; orendroit, fet
il, li chanterai messe, car ele ne se tendroit .i. jor de la semaine de messe
oïr pour nule chose.' Atant est li chapelains entrez en la chapele, et eulz
aprés lui, si sont asis en .i. angle desoz .i. degré.

46 / They Speak With His Wife, Alone

Atant vint la contesse du chastel a la chapele, et .ii. [chevaliers] o li, et
oï messe del Saint Esperit. La contesse d'Anjou vint a son seignor, si li
dist: 'Sire, vez ci la contesse; parlons a li ainz qu'ele s'en voist. Ele nous
savra a dire ce dont nous sonmes en doute; et contons li tote nostre aventure, conment nous avons nostre filz perdu et conment nous fesons cest
voiage pour lui, car il ne puet estre qu'il ne li ait conté conment il issi de
son païs.' Il vindrent a la dame et li distrent qu'il vouloient parler priveement. La dame dit maintenant [180b] a ses genz qu'il se tresissent en
sus.

47 / The Mother Tells Their Story

La contesse d'Anjou conmença sa reson: 'Dame, fet ele, nous fesons penitance pour .i. pechié qui nous avint par mescheance. Mes sires que vous
veëz ci est quans d'Anjou, et je en sui contesse; si alons a Saint Jasque nuz
piez et en langes pour .i. nostre fil que nous avons perdu mult a lonc tens;
et si n'oi onques plus enfant. Je le norri .xvi. anz avecques moy. Il amoit
bois sor tote riens, si ne sai par quele aventure il fu alez eu bois bien a .xii.
anz. Par tout le païs le feïsmes querre, mes n'en oïmes puis noveles; si

avons puis oï dire que .i. tiex hom est ci arivez, et avons grant fiance que
se soit il, pource qu'il a autel non. Car mes filz si a non Julien.' A cest mot
li failli la parole, et devint plus jaune que cire.

48 / The Wife's Curiosity Is Satisfied: She Knows Who Julian's Parents Are

Quant la dame les oï ainsint parler, si en fu mult lie, et demanda lors nons.
Or savra ele quanque ses sires li a celé. La contesse li dit: 'Mes sires a non
Jeufroi, et j'ai non Anme. Tote la terre d'Anjou et du Maine est nostre.'
La dame reconut bien lor nons, si lor chaï maintenant as piez, et lor cria
merci, et rendi a nostre seignor graces de ce qu'il les i avoit envoiez. 'Certes,
fet ele, je ne cuidoie mie en ma vie que vous ja venissiez çà; mes or sai ge
bien certainement que vous avez vostre fil trové.' La contesse d'Anjou fu
mult esbahie, et conmença a plorer de joie, et li quans ausint. La dame du
chastel mercie mult Dame Dieu quant ele a pere et mere recovré.

49 / She Invites Them to the Castle

Quant ele les vit en langes et deschauz, si [180c] pensa qu'il avoient grant
mestier d'aaisier, conme cil qui mult estoient travaillié, por ce meïsmement
qu'il n'avoient mie acostumé a aler einsint. Ele lor a dit: 'Vostre filz est
alez eu bois chacier, si revendra assez tost, car je ai fait fere .i. baing pour
lui et .i. autre pour moi; si vous i convient baignier ambedeus, car trop
estes travaillié; et si me merveil mult conment vous poez le travail soffrir.
Je sai bien que je morroie. Je vous baigneré en mes chambres priveement,
si que nus ne savra qui vous seroiz.' 'Dame, fet la contesse d'Anjou, vostre
merci, nous n'en avons mestier.' 'Si feroiz, fet ele, douce mere, je le vous
pri, et si ne vous prie onques mes de rien. Vous baigneroiz en mon baing,
et mes peres el baing son filz, si seroiz baigniez ainz vostre filz reviegne del
bois.' Li quans qui de joie sospire dit: 'Si m'ait Diex, bele fille, je ne baing-
nasse mie volentiers mon veil; mes je ne vous os escondire, car je vous ainz
autant ou plus com se je vous eüsse engendree, et puis que vous le voulez,
vostre volenté en sera fete.'

50 / She Gives Them the Baths She Has Prepared

Atant les mena la contesse en sa chambre, et une de ses puceles sanz plus a
qui ele dist: 'Damoisele, gardez que nus n'entre çaienz, et si m'aidiez a baig-
ner et a servir ces pelerins que j'ai ci retenuz, et gardez que nus ne sache
qu'il soient çaienz, si conme vous voulez avoir m'amor.' 'Dame, fet ele, nus
ne savra par moy'; puis trempe les bainz et apareille; et la dame en fu mult
liee de ce qu'il furent si prest. Lors entra chascuns [180d] en sa cuve, et la
dame les fist bien encortiner de blans draps, et lor aporta a mengier. Maintes foiz les baisa avant qu'il fussent baignié, si que la pucele s'en merveilla.

51 / *She Puts the Parents Into the Bed She and Julian Share,*
Dismisses the Servants, and Goes to a Far Room

Et quant ce vint vers midi, si dit la dame au conte: 'Biau pere, entre vous et ma mere iroiz couchier en mon lit, ou ge et mon seignor gisons, et je serai apareillie quant mes sires vendra, si le menrai au lit ou je vous avrai couchiez.' Il font le conmandement a la dame, si se vont couchier. Ele les couche et cuevre mult bien, puis ist de la chambre et clot l'uis. Cil sont maintenant endormi braz a braz, bouche a bouche. Quant la dame vint en la sale, si la conmanda a vuidier de touz ceus qui i estoient, pour ce que il ne feïssent noise a ceus qui estoient couchiez. La dame c'est alee esbatre en une chambre loing d'iluec.

52 / *Near Noon, Julian Remembers He Should Be At Home.*
He Leaves His Companions and Rushes to the Castle.
Finding the Couple In Bed, He Kills Them Both In Anger

Et quant ce vint vers midi si souvint a Julien de ce qu'il avoit dit a sa fame, et li fu avis que bien estoit eure de repairier. Maintenant lessa ses conpaignons et ses chiens, si s'en vint poignant vers son ostel la plus droite voie, que il sot venuz jusqu'a sa cort, mes nus ne vient encontre lui pour son estrier tenir, car tuit s'en furent alé a lor ostex, si conme la dame lor ot conmandé. Juliens descent du cheval et va en la chambre ou son pere et sa mere gisoient. La chambre n'estoit mie mult clere, car la fenestre estoit entreclose, si qu'an i veoit mult pou. Il vient vers son lit, si esgarde ceux qui i estoient, et cuide pour voir qu'il ait couchié [181a] home avec sa fame. Li anemis le deçut d'ire et d'a[n]goisse, si sacha s'espee conme home desvez, et dit: 'Mult est mauvés qui fame croit.' Lors li vient en corage qu'il les ocie endeus. Au lit vient com home hors du sens, si les a endeus ocis et decolez.

53 / *His Wife Arrives on the Scene and Announces*
the Presence of the Parents to Julian

Mult fu liez de ce qu'il les avoit endeus ocis, car il cuida bien estre venchiez. Endementres que il terdoit s'espee vint la novele a sa fame que il estoit venuz et que il estoit en la chambre alez. La dame li cria maintenant a haute voiz: 'Sire, soiez mult liez et mult joieus, car je ai herbergiez tiex ostes dont vous vous merveilleroiz mult. Li quans Jeufroi d'Anjou et Anme la contesse sont ceanz. Ha, sire, pourquoi me seliez vous qu'il fust vostre peres? Certes, nul ne devroit tel prince celer. A Saint Jaque vont nuz piez et en langes a pou de gent. Je les ai retenuz et baigniez et couchez en mon lit. Ouvrez cele fenestre, si les verrez.'

54 / *Julian Vents His Great Despair*

Quant Juliens l'oï si chaï pasmez; et quant il revint, si conmença a dire:
'Ahi, dolanz, chaitif, pourquoi vif je tant, et porquoi fui onques nez?
Certes, Diex ne fu onques a mon nestre, mes li deables, qui plus a pois-
sance. Si est bien droiz que ses oevres parent. Saint Jaque, j'estoie vostre
pelerins, mes li deables m'a trait a lui. Si renie Dieu, et vos, et foi, et charité, et pelerinage, por son servise fere. Sauvage beste felonesse, vous le
m'avez bien dit, mes je le tornai tot a fable. Ha, dame, com je sui morz
[181b] et deceüz! N'i vaut noiant confort, ainz m'en devroient porter li
deable tot vif, quant j'ai mon pere et ma mere ocis. Or venez devant, dame,
et si verroiz quel martire j'ai fet.' A cest mot deront ces cheveus et se hurte
a .i. marbre si qu'il chaï tot envers pasmez, et jut ilecques ausint conme
morz.

55 / *His Wife Finds the Bodies and Bewails The Disaster In Her Turn*

La dame qui au lit ala descouvrir le cors, si li en prist si grant pitié qu'a pou
que li cuers ne li creva ou ventre d'angoisse. Et se torna d'autre part et vit
son seignor pasmé, et cuida bien qu'il fust morz. 'Deable, fet ele, soiez en
moy, puisque nous devons estre vostre. Ahi, fet ele, lasse, maleüree, pour
quoi sui je onques conceüe? Toz cist maux est venuz par moi. Je ai ocis
euls et mon seignor. Certes je morrai aprés.' Atant c'est a un marbre hurtee
si que pasmee chaï a terre.

56 / *The Wife, Coming to Her Senses, Takes the Blame Onto Herself*

Or sont cil pasmé et li autre sont mort. Juliens se dreça premierement, mes
onques ne li souvint de chose qu'il eüst fete; et quant il ot grant piece esté,
si li resouvint de son pechié. Maintenant chaï pasmez a terre. Puis est la
dame revenue a mult grant paine de pasmoison, et se couche sor son seignor, et fet mult grant duel. 'Ahi, frans hon, fet ele, mar me veïstes onques.
Bien sai que por moi les avez ocis; pour moi avez Dieu perdu. Or le perdrai
aprés pour vous.'

57 / *But Julian, Coming to His, Announces His Intention*
to Resume His Life of Poverty. His Wife Insists on Accompanying Him

Atant Juliens se dreça en estant: 'Dame, fet il, a Dieu vous conmant je.
Einsint conme je ving, ça m'en rirai, et en tel habit; ne nule riens plus
[181c] ne veil porter.' 'Sire, fet ele, se Diex plet, je ne serai ja si de mauvese maniere vers vous que je einsint vous les. Je livrerai mon cors a paine
et a honte por cest homicide que j'ai fet. Car quant je ving au mostier, et
je les connui, je les reting, et les baignai au mielz que je poi, et les couchai

la ou il sont mort; et por ce en doi ge avoir tote la colpe, car se ge les eüsse arriere envoiez en lor ostel, il ne fussent pas ocis, dont il m'est avis par reson que je sui cause de lor mort. Certes grant desloiautez feroiz se vous ne me lessiez aler avec vous, car se je m'en vois par moi, tiex me verra seule qui me fera force et anui. Sire, por Dieu solement mi lessiez les nuiz trere a vostre ostel, et je ne vous demant plus.'

58 / He Replies That She is Too Weak to Stand Such a Life, But She Will Not Be Put Off

'Dame, pour Dieu, fet Juliens, lessiez ester, car vous ne porriez endurer mes travax ne mes paines, car pieç'a que je les ai aprises. Si demorez par mon lox, et fetes messes chanter, et fetes aumosnes et oroisons por noz pechiez espeneïr.' 'Certes, sire, fet ele, je n'i demorré mie, ainz rendrai mon cors a Dieu pour le pechié, ne ja ne l'en fera eschange, ainz irai mes toz les jors de ma vie par estranges terres nuz piez et en langes, ne jamés, se Diex plest, n'avré aise en ma vie, ainz serai en povreté et en essil.' 'Dame, fet Juliens, puisque vous desirrez les paines et les travax a sosfrir, vous vendroiz avecques moi jusqu'a tant que nous avrons nostre penitance parfete. Mes sachiez que jamés paine ne nous [181d] faudra, mes tant avrons de confort que nous ferons ensemble le bien et le mal que Diex nous donra.' 'Sire, dist ele, or dites vous raison: car se vous fussiez rois de France, si en deüsse je estre roïne par droit; et quant Diex nous a einsint destiné, si soions parçonier de quanqu'il nous donna; et li prions doucement que il nous let vivre ensemble, et nous delivre de cest pechié.'

59 / In Rags, They Flee Into the Woods, Where They Must Forage For Food

Atant s'en sont torné nuz piez et en langes, sanz or et sanz argent, ne n'en porta chascuns que une chaspe. Einsint s'en fuient parmi .i. bois, et sovent se regardent que nus ne les puisse siure pour euls retorner. Einsint furent il .iii. jors ou bois, que onques ne mengierent fors glant et faine et autre fruit qu'il concuilloient par ses buissons.

60 / Julian's Companions Are Warned By A Talking Deer

Or vous leré ester de Julien et de sa fame, si vous diré des chevaliers qui estoient ou bois pour chacier, conment il revindrent. Einsint com il serchoient par la forest pour les bestes que il queroient, si se sont aresté delez .i. buisson ou il orent veü .i. chevrel, et l'avironerent, et le vouloient ocirre, quant il conmença a crier: 'Estez! Ne m'ociez mie, mes entendez que je vous dirai. Alez au chastel isnelement, si troveroiz en la chambre vostre seignor mult grant martire.'

61 / *They Discover the Parents' Bodies, But Cannot Find Julian*

Quant il orent la beste einsint oï parler, si en furent mult esbahi et esperdu; mes onques puis ne demorerent, ainz alerent au chastel, et trouverent eu lit lor seignor cel martire. 'Ha, Diex, font il, qui a ce fet? ' Par [182a] la sale vont et vienent et quierent lor seignor tant qu'il en furent tuit anoié. Granz [cris] demenoient conmunement, et regretoient souvent Julien lor seignor. Au lit revienent, si enportent les cors en la sale.

62 / *The Chaplain's Story. The Bodies Are Buried*

Par la vile est la novele alee que l'en a en la cort trouvez .ii. pelerins ocis. Li chapelains i est maintenant venuz et dit: 'Je les trovai hui matin a l'uis de la chapele orant, et me demanderent se li quans [et la contesse orroient messe ici, et je lor dis que li quens] estoit alez chacier grant piece avoit. Quant le messe fu chantee, si ala cele dame a la contesse, et dist que ele voloit parler a li; et quant il orent longuement parlé, la contesse les mena en sa chambre, et lor fist mult grant joie. Et cuit que ce fust ses peres et la dame sa mere.' Adont ont fet les cors ensevelir, et les mistrent en une biere et les porterent au mostier et les enfoïrent a grant honor.

63 / *The Wife's Suffering in the Woods.*
The Couple Make A Vow of Chastity

Atant vous lesserai de ceus, et vous dirai de Julien et de sa fame qui s'en fuient parmi les bois conme desvez. La dame qui mult estoit sage ne tenoit mie grant paroles ne de boivre ne de mengier; quant mains en a, Diex en rent graces et merciz. Mult souvent fet senglanz ses piez a pierres, et puis dit entre ses denz coiement: 'Sire Diex, aorez soiez vous, car or sai ge bien que vous me covoitiez.' Et quant Juliens la regarde, si l'en prist grant pitiez, si que li travaux qu'ele sueffre li est plus griés que le siens. Andui ont voé a Dieu que ja mes n'avront charnel conpaignie ensemble. Et Juliens dit qu'il fera le pelerinage qu'il avoit promis a Saint Jasque, et d'ilecques a Rome.

64 / *They Visit the Pope, Who Gives Further Advice*

Et vindrent [182b] devant l'apostoille, si li chaïrent as piez; et Juliens li dist que il estoit li pelerins cui il avoit doné les besanz, et que ce estoit avenu que la beste li avoit dit. Et conment et en quel maniere il li avint li a tot conté par ordre. Il en souvint bien a l'apostoille qu'il li avoit dit, si li dist: 'Amis, je n'oï onques mes parler de tel aventure, fors vous. Soiez bien confés, et bien repentanz, et priez Dieu qu'il le vous pardoint, et vous doint espace de vie que vous l'aiez espeneï; et gardez que vous ne vous repentez de bien fere, mes travailliez vous durement et penez, et Diex par son plesir vous doint tenir bone conpaignie.' Atant les seigne, et si les lesse, et cil s'en vont tendrement plorant.

65 / *Their Wanderings Last Seven Years*

Onques de .vii. anz ne finerent d'aler par le monde, et n'avoient riens fors ce qu'en lor donoit. Travax et paines orent tant com il en porent endurer. Et quant il sont venu a Saint Gile, il vont tot jors lor pain querant, mes onques nule mie n'en estooient a l'endemain, car il ne queroient fors au jor la viande.

66 / *Reaching the River Gardon, They Discover a Ferry Whose Owners Refuse Passage To Any Who Cannot Pay*

Tant sont alé qu'il sont venu a Gardon, une eue de Provence, mult roide et mult parfonde; mes il n'i passeront mie se il n'ont argent, car il n'i a ne pont ne gué ou il puissent passer. Mes dui vilain felon et engrés passoient les genz, et chascuns que il passoient paoit .ii. angevins a l'entree de la nef sor le rivage. Nus n'estoit si povres ne si mesaisiez qu'an la nef meist le pié [182c] se argent ou gage ne lor lessoir; et s'il i entroit par aventure, il le getoient en l'eue.

67 / *The Ferrymen Insult Julian and His Wife*

Or se puet Juliens esmaier se Diex ne le conforte. Il vint droit cele part et vit ceus que l'en prenoit et tolot le lor ainz qu'il vosissent movoir lor nef. Mes il n'i osa aproichier, ainz lor conmença a dire: 'Seignors, por Dieu, passez nous; vous n'avez mie assez charge, et nous n'avons argent ne gage dont nous vous puissons consirrer.' 'Haï, mauvés truant, lessiez vostre truande et nous vous passeron; mes vous n'estes mie si enyvrez! Raler vous en poez, se vous ne paiez .iiii. angevins.' Il lor respondi: 'Si m'ait Diex, nous n'avons or ne argent; mes passez nous pour Dieu.' 'Fuiez, font li vilain, que çaienz ne metroiz vous le pié.' Lor nef enpaintrent de la rive, si s'en sont outre passez. Et Juliens remest dolanz et corrociez, si se conmance a porpenser conment il porroit outre passer. 'Dame, fet il, ci ne passerons nous mie.' 'Non, sire, fet ele, ainz nous covendra aler arriere, ou atendre tant que Diex nous amaint tiex genz qui nous facent outre passer avec eus. Sainz Giles nous amena ça, si fera Diex tant por s'amor qu'il nous fera passer.' Atant sont li pautonnier retorné, si les escrient: 'Ahi, truans, font il, desoz ces buissons vous deüssiez seoir, car li vens vous grieve trop ici; si deüssiez vos neuz escorre, car il n'i passera hui tant de gent que vous i passiez pour noiant.' Juliens ne leur respont mot, ta [nt ne l] e sevent lesdengier. Il voit mult gent aler a la nef, mes il doute tant les vilains qu'il n'i ose aler.

68 / *The Wife Suggests They Work Until They Can Buy*
A Boat and Give Travellers Free Passage. When They Have
Acquired Some Money, She Further Suggests They Build a Hostel

'Sire, [182d] pour Dieu, fet la dame, soion touzjourz sor cest rivage, si porchaçon tant que nous puissons avoir une nef. Jamés nus hom ne sera sosfreteus que nous ne passons pour Dieu.' Cest conseil lor plot mult. Maintenant ont lor chapes vendues; et granz travax et granz paines sosfrirent par le païs ainz qu'il eüssent gueres gaaignié. Nepourquant, tant ont pourchacié que par lor porchaz ont nef conquise. Puis ont fet une loge sus la rive de l'eue, et garderent le passage prés d'un an, tant qu'il orent .1. soulz assemblez que l'en lor ot donnez par charité; si s'est la dame porpensee que de deniers assembler seut venir grant perdicion. 'Sire, fet ele, je ne quier pas deniers assembler, ne je ne vueil jesir en ostel ou il ait denier qui soit miens. Feson fere une grant meson ou nous puisson herbergier ceus pour amor Dieu qui mestier en avront.' 'Dame, fet il, je m'i acort bien.' L'ostel font apareillier; et quant il fu prés, si herbergierent et passerent touz ceus qui mestier en avoient.

69 / *She Cares For the Poor. One Day Seven Years Later,*
a Great Storm Comes Up. No One Appears at the Hostel

La dame de servir ne cesse; touz les deschauce et lieve et couche et passe et rapasse; et quanque lor donna, il donoient pour Dieu, si que nule rien ne lor remanoit, ne de nule rien n'avoient defaute. Einsint ont il esté ilecques .vii. anz, si que granz renonz estoit d'eus parmi le païs; et tuit li truant du païs avoient bien l'ostel apris, et i venoient sovent, tant que .i. jor leva .i. orage si grant et mult orrible, qui dura le jor et la nuit si que nus ne se pot movoir de son ostel, et la dame estoit tote jor en son ostel et a son huis ou ele [5a] atendoit ostes; et mult estoit dolente de ce qu'ele n'en cuida nul avoir. 'Dex, fet ele, par vostre plesir, donez moi tex ostes com vous plera, et je les servirai bien a mon pooir.' Li jorz ala, la nuit vint, et ostes ne vint de nule part.

70 / *The Griefstricken Wife Fears God's Displeasure.*
Julian Attempts to Console Her

Quant la dame vit ce, si en fu mult dolent, car ele ot paor que Diex ne se fust corrociez a euls. Mult fist lede chiere, et plora, et cria merci a nostre seigneur. Juliens qui la vit corrociee li demanda qu'ele avoit. 'Sire, fet ele, je ai grant paor que Diex ne se soit corrociez a nous quant il ne nous envoie hostes, car onques puis que nous venismes ça ne nous avint que nous fussons sanz ostes fors anuit.' 'Dame, fet il, il a hui si fort pleü que nus hons ne pot issir fors d'ostel; et se Dame Diex ne nous donne toz noz voloirs, por ce ne devons nous pas cuidier qu'il soit corrociez a nous.'

71 / Unable to Sleep, the Wife Hears A Voice Crying Over the River

De ce ont lessié ester, si se sont alé couchier; mes por tot l'or du monde ne dormist la dame, ainz se plaint de la pluie et du tens oscur qui li ont tolu ses ostes. Endementres qu'ele dist ces paroles, si oï une voiz outre l'eue criant: 'Frans Juliens, pour Dieu, passe moi.' La dame qui aillors n'avoit son cuer c'est assise en son lit, et la voiz s'escria: 'Frans Julien, por Dieu, passe moy, car mult sui plains de mesaise.'

72 / When Julian Says He Dares Not Go Out, She Says She Will Go Help The Unknown Traveller Herself

Juliens se vouloit endormir, quant sa fame le conmença a sachier, et li dist: 'Levez sus tost, car il me semble que je aie une voiz oïe outre l'eue. Alez [5b] le querre, que c'est aucun povres qui vous atant.' 'Dame, fet il, ne vous poist mie, je n'i oseroie aler, car l'eue est mult roide et parfonde, et li venz est si forz que la nef seroit mult tost emplie d'eue. Par jor i aroi ge assez a fere.' 'Sire, fet ele, or voi ge bien que vous ne prenez mie en gre ce que Diex vous consent a avoir. Ne vaut riens qui se repent, car il pert quanqu'il a devant fet. Jesez vous tot quoi tot belement, et je l'irai querre.' Lors se conmança a vestir.

73 / Thereupon, Julian Sets Out Himself, and Crosses the River With Difficulty

Quant Juliens la vit si li conmança a dire· 'Dame, s'il vous plest, je l'irai querre, car je veil mielz sosfrir le travail que vous. Mes alumez de cest pesaz sor cest rivage.' La dame a le feu alumé, si le porte au rivage; et Juliens la suit maintenant, et entra en la nef, puis s'enpaint enmi l'eue, si nage outre a grant painne, et ot grant paor ainz qu'il fust outre passez; mes il ot totjorz en remembrance la passion Jhesucrist qui le conforta.

74 / He Learns the Traveller Is A Leper

Quant Juliens fu a la rive, si sailli hors de la nef et dist: 'Ou estes vous qui m'apelastes? Vous n'estes si povres ne si las que ja por ce vous aie plus vil. Metez vous du tot en ma menaie; je ne vous ferai se bien non.' 'Sire, fet li povres, je ne vous demant fors que vous me prestez l'ostel huimés, car je sui uns povres mesiax mult meseaisiez et mult foibles.' Juliens vient a lui, si li dist: 'Levez tost sus, si vous en venez avecques moy a la nef.' 'Par foy, fet li mesiax, je sui si foibles que je n'i puis par moy aler, se vous ne me portez entre vos braz.' 'Volentiers [5c] te porteré, fet Juliens, mes di moi conment et en quel maniere.' 'Je sui, fet il, tant desfet que je ne sai

conment ne en quel maniere, et neporquant prenez moy par les cuises, si
me levez contre vostre piz. Ne vous chaut s'il vous grieve, mes sosfrez tot
por l'amor de Dame Dieu, qui vous rende par sa grace le bien que vous me
feroiz por lui.' Juliens, qui estoit fors et preuz, le prist par les cuises et le
leva contremont son piz, et li mesiax mist son front contre le sien, si qu'il
alena adés en la bouche Julien; et il ne s'en corroça onques. Einsint le porta
Juliens jusqu'a sa nef en l'eue, et naja a force tant qu'il est outre passez.

75 / The Wife and Julian Carry the Leper Into the Hostel

La dame qui son feu faisoit sor le rivage li conmença a demander: 'Sire,
pour Dieu, que aportez vous?' 'Dame, fet il, .i. povre mesiau mult desfet et
mult mesaisié, qui mult avroit grant mestier d'aide.' A cest mot est venue
la dame a la nef, si entra enz le feu en la main, et vit celui qui mult estoit
mesaisiez; et l'en prist grant pitiez, et dit que ele est tote preste de fere son
servise a son pooir. Li mesiax li dit: 'Dame, je ne me puis de ci movoir, ne
jamés n'en seré meüz se vous ne m'en portez entre vos braz.' La dame le
sesi d'une part, et Juliens d'autre, et einsint l'enporterent a lor ostel au
plus doucement que il porent.

76 / The Leper Is Freezing, But Fire and Food
Cannot Warm Him. He Says He Will Die of Cold That Night

La dame l'asist sor .i. cossin, et puis si li dist que nule chose qu'ele face ne
li griét. 'Dame, fet il, je sui plus froiz que glace. Fetes le feu pour moi eschaufer, et si me donnez a mengier hastivement, car je sui encor geüns.'
[5d] La dame tantost l'afuble, et si li fet le feu, et li apareille a mengier
de ce que ele pot avoir, et l'esforça durement de mengier, et cil li fist sem-
blant qu'il eüst grant faim, si menja durement. Et quant il ot mengié et
beü, si refroida il, si qu'il dist por voir qu'il moroit de froit la nuit. La dame
li fist le feu de seche buche, et de tant com li feus estoit plus granz refroida
li mesiax plus.

77 / The Leper Explains That the Only Thing
That Can Warm Him Is Contact With A Woman's Body

'Dame, fet il, je sui de tel mal plains que nule chose ne me puet eschaufer
fors une seule, se l'en le me voloit fere.' 'Certes, fet la dame, soz ciel n'a
riens que je peüsse fere pour vous aidier que je ne feïsse hastivement.'
'Dame, fet il, il me covenist char de fame por moi eschaufer, ou autrement
je n'eschauferoie jamés pour aise que je eüsse. Juliens, pour Dieu vous pri
que vous me prestez vostre fame anuit mes; si gerra pres de moi pour moi
eschaufer. Ja l'avez vous totes les nuiz eüe; bien la me poez anuit mes prester. Je ne demorré anuit ceanz se ge ne l'ai, car pour lui se ge ça venuz. Juliens l'ot, si le resgarde, et li dit: 'Frere, je ne l'ai mie en garde por prester. Je

ai eu mùlt d'ostes, et si ne m'en requist onques mes nus de ce que vous me requerez; ne je ne quist que ele le feïst pas por moi.' 'Sire, por Dieu, dit la dame, ne l'esconduisié vous mie. Je ai mise tote ma vie en Dieu servir; je n'escondi mie a fere cest servise pour lui. Ma char a la seue atouchera se il einsint doit eschaufer. Mes alez couchier tost, et je coucherai o lui par charité.' 'Dame, fet il, je n'osaie por vous, mes quant ...'

It is here that the Alençon Manuscript breaks off.
The remaining text of the Prose Life is given here
according to the reading of Ms. B.N. Fr.6447, fol. 218 verso.

[78] The Wife Is Just About to Lie Down
When She Discovers The Leper Has Disappeared

'Dame, fet il, je ne l'osoie creanter por vos; mais quant vos le creantés, je le voel bien.' Juliens se couche d'une part. 'Dame, fet li mesiaus, couchiés moi tost en mon lit.' Et ele si fist, et puis covri le feu et vint au lit por jesir. Mais ele ne trueve mie le mesiel. Et taste partout et demande ke il pooit estre devenus. 'Je m'en esmaie molt de ce ke je nel puis trouver.' Juliens saut sus maintenant, si alume le feu, et vait de toutes pars alumant et querant, mais il nel trueve mie dedens l'ostel.

[79] The Leper Speaks to Her From Outside, Explaining That
Their Sin Is Pardoned. He Adds That Thenceforth Any Traveller
Without Lodging Need Only Say the Lord's Prayer In Remembrance
of Julian and His Wife and Parents, and He Will Find Shelter

La dame en fu toute esbahie, si corut a l'uis et le trova fermé. 'Hé, Dex, dist ele, con je sui traïe! Je quidoie bien faire vostre service, mais n'avés cure ke je le face en tel maniere.' La dame plora tendrement. Et li mesiaus ki fu defors li dist: 'Feme, ne pleure mie. Jhesucris vers cui nule cose n'est coverte pour ta grant merite et por la foi de ton signor vos est pardonés li pechiés de l'omecide ke vos feïstes; si vos doing .i. don pardurable: quiconques sera soufraiteus d'ostel, si die sa Patre Nostre por vos et por cels ke vostre sire ocist, et il ne faudra pas a bon ostel.'

[80] They Live Seven More Years. But One Night
Robbers Come to the Hostel, and One of Them Kills Julian
and His Wife Together in Bed With One Blow

Atant s'est li mesiaus departis d'illueques, et cil demeurent tuit esbahi. Juliens conmença premierement tout en plorant a parler: 'Dame, dist il, buer fuissiés vous nee, car par le grant bien ki en vous est sommes nous sauvé. Or nos doinst Dex par son plaisir ke nos le puissons servir tous-

jors, et faire sa volenté.' Et si firent il si con je quit, car il servirent ensi
.vii. ans; mais par envie et par covoitise ki sont maistre de cest siecle, cil ki
ne sorent lor estre ne lor covine quidoient ke il fuissent molt riche. Et vindrent larron dou païs si se misent .i. soir en l'ostel. Et Dex les consenti a
ocirre en tel maniere con son pere et sa mere ocist, car uns lerres les ocist
ambesdeus a .i. colp. Et toutes lor coses remua, mais il n'i trouva riens fors
vitaille.

[81] *Their Relics Are At Brioude. Invocation*

Grans miracles avinrent souvent en la place u il gisoient, tant que il plot a
Dame Dieu ke l'en les portast a Brides. Illueques les mist on en une fiertre
d'argent. Encore i sont li os ensamble. Or prions Dame Deu omnipotent
ke il, par sa pitié et par sa misericorde, si vraiement con il fu mis en crois
por pecheors raiembre des [218d] paines d'infer, nos gart des mains a
diable, et ait de nous merchi, et nos pardoinst nos pechiés et nos face
avoec lui en sa gloire vivre, ki vit et regne et regnera *in secula seculorum
Amen.*

NOTES TO THE PROSE LIFE TEXT

1   *N'ama onques nules richeces* or *richetés.* Both words are attested, and Gothic *c*
   and *t* are often indistinguishable in any case. We have written *richetés* in 9 ('a
   lessié toutes terrienes richetés') because of its possible meaning of 'nobility.'
   Et encontre avient should certainly read *Et encore.*
   Et l'a merité, while not impossible, is not as satisfying as Tobler's conjectural
   emendation *par la merite.*
2   *Fist toz les provoires revestir.* 'Gave all the priests new clothes'; this is a possibility, despite Tobler ('f. t. les povres revestir').
   Au Mans ou ele estoit. Julian's father, the Count of Anjou, is also Count of Maine.
   There were no independent Counts of Anjou after 1205, but that fact does not
   help us date the poem, for such archaic appelations are quite common.
   Et cela son songe. cela is of course a form of *celer:* 'kept secret.'
4   *Au plus tost: plus tolt.* Ms., an easy error in the days of long *s.* The same confusion may have caused the readings *des mers et de sa terre* in 2 (*la terre?*) and
   se seigna in 6 (the Pope may bless Julian instead of making the sign of the Cross
   upon himself).
   Tendi son arc. 'Strung' and not 'drew' his bow.
   La beste besser, i.e. *berser*, 'shoot.'
   Conme il volt traire a li, ele conmença: et ele c. Ms.
   Si detint sa saiete ... et entesa sa saiete: detint and *entesa* are rather vague here;
   'eased,' then 'drew' again, but probably without removing the arrow from the
   bow.
   Et dit autel conme ele avoit ... 'and said the same thing as before.' The *heuses*
   Julian throws away may be leggings, trousers, or boots.

5 *Vous estes posteïs de totes choses fors de moi rendre mon fil* is probably not a denial of God's omnipotence but an elliptical statement (present in B.N. 6447 and 17229 also): 'you can do anything, but you won't give back my son.'
   Ele vestoit et pessoit les mesiaux et les contrez ... et levoit et couchoit. Pessoit 'fed'; *les contrez* 'the maimed'; *levoit* is probably a form of *laver* rather than the opposite of *coucher*.

6 *Si atornez qu'an ne connoüst quil le veïst.* 'No one who saw him thus would have recognized him'; as occasionally happens, the weakening of the final *l* in monosyllables has caused some confusion among forms. The *l* of *quil* is purely graphic, and that pronoun is to be read as relative *qui* (here and elsewhere, e.g. in 32, 'home quil le conneüst'). Also, the negative *ne* should presumably be understood as having lost the normal enclitic pronoun which appears in the standard form *nel.* Other such confusions will be noted in appropriate places.
   Sa char devint tote noire et perse de l'angoisse des froiz. B.N. Fr. 6447 has the variant discussed in Chapter Seven, page 74.
   Qui filz il estoit. 'Whose son he was'; *qui* is a graphy of dative *cui.*

7 *Le vit si engrant.* 'Saw how eager he was'; a later hand has written something presently illegible between the lines here.
   Ne m'alez mie delaient. Delaient is a present participle: 'don't hold me back.'

9 *Terrienes richetés.* Perhaps *terriennes*: the scribe's titulus is often similar to the accent used with *i.*
   Il le fesoit purement pour Dieu. Purement written twice, Ms. *Il se met engrant d'orer.* The Ms. may possibly have *d'oreter*; but it is not clear, and B.N. Fr. 6447 and 17229 both have the *lectio facilior.*

10 *Il n'en avoit cure.* The scribe first wrote *n'avoit cure*, then added *n'en* interlinearly, without correcting his *n'avoit: n'ennavoit.*

11 The reference to the Templars is not a useful indication of date, since the Order was in existence from 1118 to 1308.
   Cil passerent Julien. The Ms. apparently reads *il cil passerent*, a natural sequence; the scribe simply forgot to expunge *il.*

12 *Cil s'en ala avant touz ceus*, i.e. *touz seus*, 'alone.'
   Si en iront. I.e., of course, *si en iroit.*

13 *Ne trova quil le herbarjast. Quil* is, as in 6 above, relative *qui.*
   Il avroit tost forstrete la fille son oste. 'He would make short work of seducing his host's daughter.'

14 *Je sui vostre povre homs* has its origins in an almost certain misreading of *uns* as the abbreviation *vre* 'vostre'; both B.N. Fr. 6447 and Fr. 17229 have *uns povres h.*

15 *Il apela devant lui.* The pronoun is not noted: *il l'apela.*
   [*si*] and *a*[*i*] *nsint* are emendations made necessary by damage to the manuscript.

16 *Ainsit ala Juliens concher.* This graphic or phonetic confusion of *con-* and *cou-* is quite common, much like that of *monstier* and *moustier.*

17 *Si vous conment que vous soiez ... conment* is, in this case, a form of *commander.*

18 *A l'avaler qui firent.* Probably *qu'il firent*, the opposite of the graphy noted in para. 6; or we may read *qu'i firent.*

19 *Chevax qui gisoient si en parfont* appears to be incomplete; cf. *gisoient el fanc* ['*mire*'] *si en parfont* B.N. Fr. 17229. There is a confusion (again no doubt caused by the presence of long *s*) between *sanc* 'blood' and *fanc* in several mss. here; it is difficult to know which might have been the original reading.

20 *Ne se prist mie garde qu'il estoit. Qu'il* may be either a contraction or an example of personal *que.*

25 *Il ne trueve li ou esprover.* *Li* is *lieu,* 'occasion.'

27 *Noz genz sont si lassees qui ne se pueent mes aidier.* Here *l* of *qu'il* is obviously not noted.

28 *Atant e vous le seignor.* *E* or *es* is *ecce:* 'And then up came Julian's lord ...'

29 *Bon cheval en destre vous doine* is an interesting use of the adverbial phrase *en destre,* which normally occurs in the phrase *mené en destre* 'led with the right hand' (as the *destrier* was – whence its name, of course). Here the phrase does not fit the context perfectly; one suspects a figurative misuse of *en destre* as an adjective phrase, thus *cheval en destre* 'a good horse, fit to be led with one's right hand, a good *destrier.*' The usage is not attested in Godefroy or Tobler-Lommatzsch (but see other figurative uses, TL, II, 1798).

31 *Nous ont lessié li François et autre preudome de hors.* The *François* are men from the Ile de France (the countess's land being somewhere between Saint-Gilles and Spain), and are apparently mercenary soldiers, as are the other warriors 'from outside.'
De sa largesse ne parot nus, i.e., *ne parolt nus,* as in B.N. Fr. 17229: 'no one speaks ill of his generosity.'

34 *Lor liz fu apareilliez et saigniez,* i.e., *signez,* 'blessed.'

38 *N'i vaut riens desanester* is obscure and appears to be an error: B.N. Fr. 6447 and 17229 have *n'i vaut riens desamonester,* 'there is no point in discouraging me.'
De quoi vous voulez entremetre. Entremetrete. Ms. is an evident error.

40-41 *Riens fe[re].'* – *'[Dou] ce dame ... la con[tesse], di[tes] ... [bel] home.* The manuscript is damaged here. B.N. Fr. 17229 has 'nus ne li ose riens forfere.' – 'Douce dame, fet la contesse, dites moi ....'

42 *Si ne vit onques.* Probably *si ne vi,* 'I never saw ....'
Si a les elz [vairs]. *Vairs* is the inevitable cliché here; the Ms. apparently has *vaus.*
N'amoit nul deduit tant conme de chiens. This is hardly the same thing as an obsession with bloodshed (see our discussion above, pp. 90-92).

43 *Vost sa ravoier. Sa* is a graphy for *çà:* 'God has brought us back into the right path' (*vouloir* with the name of the Deity is a common periphrase for the simple verb).
Maint home ainment forest et deduit de chiens et d'oisiaus plus que d'autres. Julian's trait is therefore obviously quite normal. It probably serves, as much as anything else, as one of the elements of recognition by which his parents know him (42).
Et se l'en nous demande riens: se nen nous demande. Ms.

44 *Je vous pri que vous revaigniez par tens. Par tens* here as in 28 means 'soon' and not 'on time' ('je vous ferai chevalier mult par tens').

45 *Sa fame il vendra ele.* Here the weakening of final *l* has brought about confusion between the pronoun *il* and the adverb which we write *y.*

46 *Et .ii. [chevaliers] o li.* Omitted word supplied from B.N. Fr. 17229.

47 *Il fu alez eu bois.* *Alez* is written twice, Ms.

51 *La dame c'est alee esbatre.* Yet another misleading graphy: *s'est alee.*

52 *Et quant ce vint vers midi. Et* written twice, Ms. *Que il sot venuz* 'until he had come'; the scribe probably took the subjunctive *soit* (in other Mss.) for a dialect form of the past definite of *savoir.*

53 *Il terdoit s'espee.* 'He was wiping his sword'; this striking detail is shared with the Rouen and Chartres windows.

54 *Si renie Dieu, et vos, et foi, et charité, et pelerinage.* This passage has caused the scribes difficulties in more than one manuscript. *Renie* should probably be a

preterite or imperfect, according to the other manuscripts (perhaps the phonetic graphy *renié*).

Je le tornai tot a fable. Tot affable: Ms., is a common doubling of an initial consonant, a bit misleading here, perhaps.

55 *La dame qui au lit ala descouvrir le cors* is a fragment. *Descouvri* is the verb in B.N. Fr. 17229. The graphic singular of *le cors* is not unusual, although it rarely appears in this text.

56 *Juliens se dreça. Se deça*: Ms.

Por moi les avez ocis; pour moi avez Dieu perdu. Pour has here its sense of 'because of.'

57 *Je les connui* is the reading of B.N. Fr. 17229; Al. 27 has *conraii*, which does not yield a satisfactory sense.

61 *Granz [cris] demenoient.* Missing word supplied from B.N. Fr. 17229.

62 *Me demanderent se li quans ... chacier grant piece avoit.* The text in brackets in this passage is again that of B.N. Fr. 17229; the Alençon scribe has committed an obvious haplography.

64 *Que vous l'aiez espeneï.* 'So that you may expiate it.'

65 *Nule mie n'en estooient.* 'They kept, saved, not a crumb'; the verb is *estoier.*

66 *Il sont venu a Gardon. Gardon* is probably misunderstood; in modern French, at least, the common noun *gardon* designates no single river but any of a group of streams in the Cévennes, two of which (the *gardon d'Alès* and the *gardon d'Anduze*) come together to form the Gard. Our redactor is sure it is a particular river ('une eue de Provence'); he may be thinking of one of the *gardons* or of the Gard itself. It should be added that, although the medieval author may not have been aware of it, the Old French noun *gardon* is a variant spelling of *guerredon* 'reward'; the analogy would certainly have appealed to a thirteenth century rhetorician.

67 *Lessiez vostre truande.* I.e., leave her as your *gage.*

Vous n'estes mie si enyvrez! has no context; probably 'You're not that crazy'; *enyvré* used figuratively may mean 'bewitched' or 'seduced,' but none of its meanings (including 'drunk') fits very well here.

Si deüssiez vos neuz escorre. An ambiguous phrase; *escorre* may mean 'shake' or 'pull, rip, pull out'; the latter is the more likely sense here, given the figurative use of *neuz* 'knots' to designate the purse (which was tied shut with a knotted cord; see Tobler-Lommatzsch, VI, 668). 'You'd better get your money out fast.' We are indebted to M. Perrot for this suggestion.

Ta[nt nel] sevent lesdengier. The brackets enclose emendations made necessary by damage. *Lesdengier* is *laidengier*, 'taunt, insult.'

70 *Si en fu mult dolent. Mult* written twice, Ms.

78 *Couchiés moi tost en mon lit*, i.e., *en vostre lit.*

80 *Buer fussiés vous nee* can not be handily translated: 'you are of fortunate birth, you were born in a good hour.'

81 *Brides* is Brioude; our Julian is being confused with Saint Julian of Brioude, as he was earlier identified with Julian of Le Mans. The adventitious association of our hero with Brioude has influenced some secondary work on the Prose Life, but was of course unknown to Lecointre-Dupont, for his manuscript breaks off much earlier.

LECOINTRE-DUPONT'S ADAPTATION
OF THE PROSE LIFE

Lorsqu'aux grands jours de fête le château du moyen-âge ne retentissait point des chants profanes de guerre et d'amour, que la harpe du barde restait muette, et que le dictié du trouvère, le fabliau du jongleur étaient proscrits par la solennité du jour, de pieux récits, de saintes légendes charmaient les loisirs du manoir féodal.

Les exercices ascétiques, les pénitences et les macérations des saints, leur charité ardente, leur abnégation héroïque, n'auraient point captivé seuls un auditoire vain et léger, qui ne respirait que batailles, amour, blasons, tournois et aventures; aussi la vérité historique ne présidait pas toujours à ces contes dévots, et la pieuse fraude du narrateur, pour donner quelque attrait aux utiles vérités qu'il voulait faire entendre, imaginait en l'honneur des saints une haute généalogie, de périlleux voyages, de brillants faits d'armes au milieu des combats ou de grands coups d'épée à l'encontre des diables, et mille fictions merveilleuses qui ne le céderaient point aux gestes les plus poétiques des demi-dieux de la fable, si elles avaient été chantées par un Homère, un Virgile, un Hésiode ou un Sophocle.[1]

A l'Œdipe de l'antiquité la mythologie du moyen-âge peut opposer son saint Julien le Pauvre.[2] Vincent de Beauvais, Jacques de Voragine, Thomas Friard, les Bollandistes et nombre d'autres écrivains moins connus, qui ont dit la merveilleuse histoire de Julien, ont ignoré l'origine de ce saint. Mais un frère prêcheur, qui en savait sur son compte beaucoup plus long que les hagiographes que j'ai cités,[3] en donnant sa vie dans un manuscrit malheureusement incomplet de la bibliothèque d'Alençon,[4] place son berceau dans nos provinces de l'Ouest. C'est donc à l'imagination de nos pères qu'est due sans doute cette poétique légende; c'est dans nos vieux châteaux qu'elle fut d'abord contée; et, maintenant qu'elle est presque oubliée, sur la foi d'un *auteur respectable* qui promet grand plaisir à tous ceux qui voudront bien l'entendre (1), je me hasarde à vous la répéter.[5] Puisse-t-elle avoir pour beaucoup d'entre vous l'agrément de la nouveauté, pour les autres le charme d'un souvenir, ne vous rappelât-elle que la complainte autrefois populaire:

---

1 *Uns preudon raconte la vie monseignor saint Julien que il a tranlatée de latin en romanz, et dit que cil qui l'escoùteront volentiers i auront mult granz deliz.* Commencement de la vie de saint Julien dans le manuscrit d'Alençon.

Considérez la pénitence
Et la grande persévérance
Du bon Julien l'hospitalier.
Son histoire est très-véritable;
Adonc il était allié
A des gens très-considérables.[6]

Ces gens très-considérables étaient, selon notre manuscrit, Geoffroi et Emma, comte et comtesse d'Anjou et du Maine. Emma était au Mans (2) quand elle conçut Julien, et elle vit en songe[7] sortir de son corps un monstre à forme humaine qui la dévorait elle et son mari.

La naissance d'un fils donna grande joie au comte qui n'avait point d'enfants. Il y eut grandes fêtes et grands tournois dans toute la terre d'Anjou; tous les pauvres obtinrent largesse, toutes les prisons s'ouvrirent, et l'enfant reçut au baptême le nom de Julien, nom qui signifie *joyeux*, d'après l'étymologie trouvée par Jacques de Voragine (3).[8]

Julien en grandissant justifiait cet heureux nom; les grâces et la force se développaient en lui; de blonds cheveux ombrageaient son front; sa taille était élancée: on admirait sa mâle beauté, son maintien gracieux; et sa mère l'aimait tant qu'elle mit tout son cœur à l'aimer, et quant il lui souvenait du songe elle se prenait à pleurer.[9]

Après qu'il eut atteint sept ans, il fut, comme on est à cet âge, amateur passionné de déduits de chasse, de chiens et d'oiseaux. Rien ne lui plaisait tant que courir les forêts; et, passait-il un jour loin des bois, l'ennui déjà le prenait. Un soir, il avait lassé ses chiens, et ses compagnons fatigués l'invitaient au retour: *Allez-vous-en*, leur dit-il, *moi je ne vais point encore quitter ce bois, je veux y chercher aventure.*[10] Et prenant son arc il s'enfonce dans la forêt et se dérobe à ceux de ses compagnons qui persistent à le suivre. Bientôt il apercoit un cerf couché dans le fourré; il tend son arc, et va frapper la bête,[11] quand elle se retourne et se met à crier: *Enfant, ne me tue pas, je vais te dire ta destinée; tu dois tuer d'un seul coup ton père et ta mère.* L'enfant interdit a retenu sa flèche; cependant il l'ajuste de nouveau, et le cerf répète: *Enfant, ne me frappe point, toi qui tueras d'un seul coup ton père et ta mère.* Julien recule d'étonnement et d'épouvante, puis derechef il vise à la bête, et la bête recommence à crier: *Enfant, pourquoi vouloir me frapper quand je te dis la verité? Tu dois tuer d'un seul coup ton père et ta mère. C'est là ta destinée: tu l'auras. Dieu seul pourrait t'en préserver.*[12]

2 Deux paroisses du diocèse du Mans sont sous le vocable de saint Julien le Pauvre, et au Mans même une rue porte son nom.
3 *Julianus à voce jubilans.* Jacobi de Voragine Leg. aurea, sub die XXVIJ januarii.

Tu en as menti, vilain animal, s'écrie l'enfant. *Jamais n'irai en lieu où soient mes père et mère.* Et, éperdu, atterré, suant d'angoisse, il brise son arc et ses flèches, jette sa chevelure au vent, arrache ses éperons, déchire ses brodequins, et fuit nuit et jour dans l'épaisseur des bois.[13]

Longtemps il erra par sauvages terres nu-pieds et en pauvre habit. Comme un humble mendiant, il allait querant au hasard le toit et le pain de l'hospitalité. Souvent il eut mauvais lit et mauvais gîte, maintes fois même pas d'abri. Les pluies et les vents, la fatigue et la souffrance l'avaient rendu méconnaissable. Enfin, après bien long voyage, il parvint jusqu'à Rome.[14]

Le pape recevait alors les pèlerins de Jérusalem, et Julien vint avec eux se jeter à ses pieds.[15] Il lui conta d'où il venait, quels étaient ses parents, et tout ce que le cerf lui avait prédit. A ces étranges paroles, le pape se signa, et relevant Julien: *C'est un fantôme qui t'a trompé*, dit-il; *n'en doute point, tu n'as rien vu, rien entendu: va, je te le commande de par Dieu, retourne vers tes parents qui seront bien joyeux de te revoir. Repens-toi de les avoir ainsi quittés, et prie-les qu'ils te pardonnent tous les chagrins qu'ils auront eus pour toi.*[16]

Oh non, Seigneur, répondit l'enfant, *non jamais ne retournerai en la contrée qu'habitent mes père et mère. Au nom de Dieu, mettez-moi la croix pour celui qui en croix fut mis. J'irai le servir de tout cœur aux lieux où il vécut, où il est mort; j'irai croisé ou non croisé.* Et s'agenouillant aux pieds du Saint Père, il pleurait et le conjurait doucement de lui donner la croix.

Emu par une résolution si ferme, le père des fidèles prit une attache de son manteau, la mit en croix, la bénit et la donna à l'enfant, en lui enseignant à bien vivre et à éviter le péché.[17]

Je ne vous dirai point comment Julien passa en terre sainte et visita Jérusalem et tous les lieux où on lui dit qu'on devait faire pèlerinage, et point ne vous conterai les larmes et les prières qu'il versa sur le sépulcre du Seigneur, implorant la mort, plutôt que de faire le parricide que le cerf avait prédit. Sept années durant, vêtu seulement d'une peau de bête, il servit les lépreux sans vouloir nul salaire, car tout ce qu'il faisait, il le faisait pour Dieu; et pendant sept années il resta inconnu à tous, étranger à tous, et on ne s'enquit point d'où il venait ni qui il était, car, à le voir si pauvre, on ne pouvait soupçonner qu'il était fils d'un comte.[18]

Ce temps passé, désir lui vint d'aller devers Saint-Jacques. Il pourrait, songeait-il, voir, chemin faisant, quelques pèlerins de son pays. Il saurait si le comte et la comtesse d'Anjou vivaient encore tous deux; et, si l'un ou l'autre n'était plus, lui il irait sans crainte consoler le survivant, il pourrait revoir son doux pays d'Anjou, ses forêts si connues, certain dès lors que le cerf aurait menti.[19]

Il laissa donc les lépreux, prit nef à Saint-Jean-d'Acre avec les templiers qui le passèrent pour Dieu, et vint débarquer à Saint-Gilles où il trouva bonne compagnie qui cheminait vers Saint-Jacques.[20]

Cependant Geoffroi avait longtemps cherché dans tout le pays s'il retrouverait Julien, et sans cesse Emma priait Dieu de lui rendre son fils. *O Seigneur*, disait-elle, *vous m'avez ôté toute joie et enlevé tout réconfort que j'avais en ce monde. Rien ne saurait consoler mes douleurs, parce que je n'ai plus mon fils. Que puis-je faire, ô mon Dieu, pauvre et chétive que je suis? Mais vous qui pouvez tout, oh! rendez-moi mon enfant; et, si j'ai péché contre vous, prenez vengeance sur moi-même, ne la prenez pas sur mon fils innocent.* Et chaque jour elle répétait sa prière, et elle faisait messes chanter, et elle habillait les pauvres, et nourrissait les mésiaux, et faisait aumône aux pèlerins.[21] Mais ses larmes, ses prières et ses dons se répandaient en vain, et douze ans étaient passés sans que le comte et la comtesse eussent reçu quelque nouvelle de leur fils.[22]

Comme leur tristesse allait toujours croissant, il vint en la pensée au comte d'aller nu-pieds à Saint-Gilles, et il s'apprêta en secret à partir; mais il ne put le faire si à la dérobée que la comtesse ne devinât son dessein. Et un matin l'appelant à l'écart: *Sire*, fait-elle, *vous vous appareillez à aller en pèlerinage ouir bonnes nouvelles de notre fils. Si irai-je avec vous, car je l'avais moi aussi en pensée.—Dame*, répond le comte, *ne savez mie de quoi voulez vous entremettre. Jamais ne pourriez aller ainsi deschause comme il convient de faire, et ne feriez que m'arrêter. – Oh! Sire*, dit-elle, *plus que de ma peine ai souci de la vôtre. Il s'agit de revoir notre fils, rien ne me peut détourner. Je sais que Dieu nous rendra notre enfant, et il me tarde de partir. Une pucelle sans plus menerai pour mon service, et vous ne serez pas pour moi d'un seul jour retardé.*[23]

Le lendemain ils s'acheminèrent en silence, et Emma s'efforçait à marcher, et semblait n'en sentir nulle fatigue, parce qu'elle le faisait pour son fils (4). A tous les pauvres qu'ils rencontraient sur leur route ils donnaient une aumône, et ils honoraient les saints des villes où ils passaient. Ainsi baisèrent-ils le pas imprimé par Jésus-Christ lui-même dans la cellule de Radégonde, et ils se prosternèrent devant les restes vénérés de l'apôtre de l'Aquitaine.[24] Ils avaient bientôt atteint le but de leur pèlerinage, lorsqu'un soir ils virent un fier châtel, au donjon élancé, aux tours crénelées, dont les nombreux ponts baissés, dont les abords sans gardes annonçaient que le nom redouté du maître suffisait seul à le garder. Tout autour de

---

4   Li quens apareilla isnelement son harnois et la contesse le sien. Entor Pentecoste se sont esmeu en tapinage. La dame s'efforça mult d'aler. Et ne li greva riens, ce li semble, parce que ele le faisoit por son filz. Et à tous les poures qu'il encontrèrent donnèrent de lor argent et cuiderent bien lor fil trové par les ausmones qu'il font. (Manuscrit d'Alençon.)

belles moissons couvraient au loin la plaine, de nombreux troupeaux ani-
maient la prairie, et sous le château une jolie ville respirait l'aisance, la paix
et le bonheur.

Il est tard, dit le comte, *et il fait bon ici. Arrêtons-nous en ces lieux.*
Sans doute quelque saint les protége, et nous le prierons pour notre fils.
Cela dit, ils s'hébergèrent chez une veuve, et après le souper ils allèrent de-
viser au frais dans un préau où leur hôtesse les conduisit. *Dame*, fit Emma,
quel est le sire de céans? Il doit être brave et sage. Son châtel est le plus
beau, sa terre la mieux tenue que j'aie vus sur ma route.[25]

« C'est une merveilleuse histoire que vous allez entendre, si Dieu m'aide
à vous la raconter, lui repartit l'hôtesse. La fortune conseille ceux qu'elle
veut; elle abaisse les uns, elle élève les autres. D'un pauvre pèlerin, qui qué-
tait dans nos rues le pain et l'hospitalité, elle a fait le puissant comte de ces
lieux.[26]

» Il y a cinq ans passés, la guerre désolait nos contrées, le fer et la
flamme ravageaient ces campagnes aujourd'hui si brillantes, l'ennemi occu-
pait la plaine, la ville était remplie de guerriers, de laboureurs et de troupeaux, et nul étranger ne pouvait s'héberger ni continuer sa route, parce
que les ponts étaient brisés.[27]

» Alors un pauvre pénitent, nommé Julien, qui allait à Saint-Jacques,
implorait en vain un gîte pour sa nuit; chacun le repoussait comme un tru-
and, et partout la porte et le pain lui étaient refusés. Comme il suppliait
Dieu de lui donner hôtel, un chevalier entendit sa prière, et l'appelant à
lui: *Tu es grand et fort*, dit-il, *ne saurais-tu porter une lance ou une épée?*
Allons, viens avec moi, je te fais mon homme d'armes; et si Dieu veut te
donner vaillance, grand bien promptement t'en adviendra. Comme il parlait ainsi, le cri de guerre retentit; l'ennemi était aux portes, il enlevait le
butin, il l'entraînait par force. Chacun s'arme, le comte du château s'élance
le premier au combat, et ses chevaliers le suivent. Plus faible en nombre,
mais plus forte en courage, la gent du comte balaye la colline et accule
l'ennemi sur un gué. Alors l'action devient terrible, et des deux parts de
nombreux guerriers mordent la poussière.[28]

» Armé seulement de son bâton, le pèlerin avait suivi le chevalier; il
fend la presse avec audace, renverse un ennemi, prend son cheval et son
armure, et vole aux côtés du chevalier.[29] Celui-ci, qui combat au premier
rang, a son cheval tué dans la mêlée; Julien le remonte sur le coursier qu'il
a conquis. Il s'attaque aux plus vaillants guerriers, il n'adresse aucun coup
sans renverser son adversaire, et, franchissant le gué, il disperse le reste des
ennemis.

» Tous les guerriers avaient admiré la vaillance du pèlerin, il avait sur-
passé les plus braves, Il eut tout l'honneur du combat. Aussi, un dimanche
ensuivant, le comte l'arma chevalier en grande pompe et lui donna les plus

beaux coursiers et la plus belle armure. Jamais Julien ne voulait de repos, toujours il avait les armes en main et bien il savait s'en aider, plus de cent chevaliers tombèrent sous sa lance, et toute périlleuse entreprise il la menait à fin.[30]

» Une journée me suffirait à peine pour vous conter la moitié de ses exploits. Longtemps sa vaillance donna la victoire à nos armes. Mais, un jour de fête, le comte sortit désarmé de son château, et ses ennemis le surprirent et le tuèrent. Nos guerriers pleurèrent longtemps sa perte, car du jour de sa mort ils furent bien fréquemment vaincus, parce qu'ils n'avaient plus de chef qui pût leur commander. Aussi les ennemis reprirent courage, et ils refusaient toutes trèves et toute paix.[31]

» Seule, affligée, sans secours, sans alliés, la comtesse, malgré tout son mérite, ne pouvait soutenir la guerre. Elle n'avait mie vingt ans, et chaque jour elle voyait du haut de ses remparts sa terre dévastée par l'ennemi, ses campagnes en cendres, ses défenseurs vaincus. Chaque jour sa gent s'amenuisait dans les combats, nul allié ne venait à son aide, elle n'espérait de secours de nulle part et n'avait personne à qui pouvoir se fier.[32]

» Comme elle ne voyait rien dont elle ne fût dolente, les hauts hommes du pays s'assemblèrent, et venant à elle: *Madame, dirent-ils, vos ennemis ne cessent point leurs attaques, et, depuis que notre sire est mort, ceux qui nous combattent ont toujours triomphé. Vos alliés vous ont abandonnée, vos défenseurs ont été pris ou tués, et vos forteresses vous seront bientôt enlevées si vous n'écoutez promptement nos conseils. Au nom du ciel, donnez-vous un époux qui défende vos biens et votre honneur, à nous un capitaine qui nous guide aux combats. Vous avez en votre terre le plus beau et le plus vaillant chevalier qui existe, prenez-le pour seigneur. Julien saura protéger vos domaines quand ils seront les siens.*

» *Seigneurs*, répondit doucement la comtesse, *vous me l'offrez, je le prends volontiers; que Dieu me donne en lui et profit et honneur.*[33]

» Aussitôt les cris de joie retentirent, toute la ville fut en fête. Les seigneurs allèrent chercher Julien, et le conduisirent en grande pompe à la comtesse; et, quand le prêtre eut béni leur union, il y eut grandes joutes et grands tournois et belles appertises d'armes, et tous les chevaliers firent l'hommage et le guet au nouveau comte. Puis ils sortirent avec lui dans la plaine, et fondirent sur l'ennemi qui ne put résister à leur audace. Chaque jour chevaliers et sergents accouraient sous sa bannière, jaloux de combattre sous un chef si redouté. Aussi les ennemis aux abois vinrent bientôt implorer sa clémence et déposer à ses pieds les clefs de leurs châteaux.[34]

» Depuis ce temps le pays est en paix sous les lois de Julien. Il rend à ses sujets prompte et bonne justice, et, entouré de brillants écuyers, il prend chaque jour dans nos forêts les plus nobles loisirs.[35]

Suspendus à la bouche de leur hôtesse, le comte et la comtesse d'Anjou avaient écouté son récit avec un mélange d'inquiétude et d'espérance. Quand elle l'eut terminé, *Douce dame*, dit Geoffroi, *quel âge a votre comte, quel est son air, et quel est son pays? – Sire*, fit-elle, *il n'a pas trente ans, et c'est le plus bel homme que j'aie vu de ma vie; ses cheveux sont blonds, son front élevé, sa taille haute et majestueuse; mais de sa naissance et de son pays il ne veut rien en dire, et nul étranger n'est venu dans ces lieux qui ait pu le connaître.*[36]

Emma pleurait de joie, elle remerciait dans son cœur sainte Marie et saint Gilles du bon succès qui paraissait promis à son pèlerinage; et, comme la nuit fut venue, elle se retira avec Geoffroi dans une chambre bien close. Ils s'entretenaient ensemble comment ils pourraient voir le châtelain et s'assurer s'il était bien leur fils, et ainsi devisèrent-ils jusqu'au jour et point ne s'endormirent de la nuit.[37]

Dès que l'aube fut levée ils montèrent au château, entrèrent jusques à la chapelle, et ils se tenaient humblement en prière à la porte, attendant si le comte paraîtrait, mais déjà il était parti pour prendre ses ébats dans la forêt. Après qu'ils eurent longtemps prié, le chapelain arriva, et Geoffroi allant à lui, *Nous sommes des pèlerins*, dit-il, *qui aurions grand désir de messe entendre, et voudrions voir le comte dont on dit si grand bien. – Le comte est déjà à la chasse*, répond le chapelain; *mais je vais chanter la messe à la comtesse, qui, pour rien au monde, ne manquerait à l'entendre un seul jour.*[38]

La comtesse vint donc à la chapelle et fit longues oraisons. Elle s'appelait Basilisse (5); elle était pleine de vertu et de piété, et, telle parmi les autres dames que la rose est au milieu des fleurs, elle était la plus belle et la plus accomplie des femmes de son siècle.[39]

Plus d'une fois, aux premiers jours de son hymen, alors que d'habitude l'amour ne tait rien à l'amour, Basilisse, prenant son époux dans ses bras: *Julien*, lui disait-elle, *puisque vous m'avez à femme, ne pourriez-vous me dire quel nom ont vos parents et quelle terre ils habitent?* Et Julien lui répondait: *Mon père si a nom Geoffroi et ma mère Emma, et sont comte*

---

5   Le manuscrit d'Alençon ne donne point le nom de la femme de saint Julien; mais comme il paraît avoir emprunté quelques particularités à la vie de saint Julien l'Hospitalier, martyr d'Antioche, pour les donner à saint Julien le Pauvre, j'ai cru pouvoir, sans plus de scrupule, donner aussi à ce dernier la femme du premier. Quant à l'éloge de la dame, je suis exactement le manuscrit: *Or vous dirai de la contesse. ... Ele n'avoit mie XX anz. Mes diex ne fist onques fame de sa valor. Et ce fu puis chose bien esprovée. Car, ausint come la rose seurmonte toutes autres flors en biauté, ausint étoit-ele plus bele et plus sage des autres dames du pays et onques en son tens ne fu fame se plaine de bontez ne de si ferme joy.*

et comtesse du pays où ils sont nés; mais point n'en saurez davantage. Elle avait bien retenu ces noms en sa mémoire, et souvent elle priait le ciel de lui donner de connaître les parents de Julien.[40] Lors donc qu'elle sortit de la chapelle, Emma l'aborda, et lui dit: *Dame, je suis Emma, comtesse d'Anjou, et voici le comte Geoffroi, mon mari. Nous allons nu-pieds à Saint-Gilles, nous allons querre notre fils Julien, qui s'est desvié à la chasse il y a tantôt douze ans. Partout nous l'avons fait chercher, sans de nulle part en avoir de nouvelles; mais nous avons fiance que Dieu nous le rendra. – Chers parents,* répondit la châtelaine, *remercions Dieu, vous avez retrouvé votre fils. Votre Julien est mon époux. Maintenant il est à chasser dans les bois, mais il reviendra ce soir et vous le reverrez. Venez, venez en l'attendant vous reposer. Oh! combien vous êtes fatigués d'avoir supporté tel voyage, moi je sais bien que j'en mourrais.[41]* – Cela dit, la châtelaine les conduisit au château, puis, dit la complainte,

> Les fit dîner, coucher ensuite
> Dans son lit très-honnêtement
> Ces gens de si bonne conduite (6).

Et après les avoir entourés d'epaisses et moelleuses courtines, elle se retira avec ses femmes dans une autre partie du château, de peur de troubler leur repos; et bientôt un doux sommeil endormit dans les bras l'un de l'autre les vieux époux enivrés de bonheur.[42]

Julien cependant avait fait chasse heureuse et avait quitté les bois plus tôt que de coutume. Il arrive, impatient de revoir Basilisse, il vole droit à sa chambre, et, à la clarté douteuse de la porte entr'ouverte, il entrevoit dans son lit deux personnes endormies. Sa femme est adultère, songe-t-il, et il frappe. ... L'oracle est accompli.[43]

L'âme égarée et le cœur plein d'une joie féroce pour la triste vengeance qu'il croyait faite à son honneur, Julien contemplait avec des yeux hagards le lit ensanglanté. Au moment même, la chaste Basilisse, rayonnante de bonheur, accourait vers lui en lui tendant les bras: *Oh! Julien,* disait-elle,

6 Voyez, je vous prie, femmes, et apprenez de celle-ci le respect que vous devez à vos beau-père et belle-mère. Cette bonne dame s'estant informée de ces bonnes gens qui ils estoient et ceux qu'ils demandoient, reconnut que c'estoit vrayment le père et la mère de son mary: et les receut avec une grande affection, les caressant et les traittant comme s'ils eussent esté les siens propres: après quoy l'heure de se reposer estant venue elle les invita de prendre repos. C'estoit à la vérité une femme bien nourrie et qui scavoit bien en quoy consistoit le point d'honneur: car encore qu'il y eust beaucoup de lits beaux et honnestes en d'autres chambres où elle pouvoit librement et honnestement les accomoder; toutefois pour un plus grand respect elle leur quite et cède le sien: tesmoignage certes de l'affection qu'elle avoit envers son mary. – Thomas Friard, Vie des Saints, p. 292.

soyez en grande joie. J'ai là tels hôtes qui bien vous surprendront, Geoffroi le comte d'Anjou et la comtesse Emma. Ah! sire, pourquoi me cachiez-vous qu'ils étaient vos parents? Ces bons parents, ils vont, pour vous chercher, tout nu-pieds à Saint-Gilles et sont bien travaillés. Voyez-les, je les ai mis coucher en notre lit.[44]

A ces mots, comme frappé de la foudre, Julien tombe renversé; et, quand longtemps après il revint à lui-même: *Misérable*, dit-il, *pour quoi ai-je tant vécu! Pèlerin de Saint-Jacques, j'ai oublié ma foi et mon pèlerinage, j'ai suivi le démon et l'orgueil; aussi j'ai tué mes bons parents, j'ai accompli la prédiction du cerf. Adieu donc, trop aimée sœur, adieu; adieu, pauvre je vins en cette terre, pauvre je la fuis pour toujours. Adieu dès maintenant, car il ne sera plus de repos pour moi avant que je sache que Dieu agrée ma pénitence. – Non, bon frère, non, tu ne me quitteras point,* répondit Basilisse, *avec toi je fuirai, comme toi je livrerai mon corps à la souffrance. J'ai été la compagne de tes joies, je partagerai tes peines et ton exil, et nous aurons ensemble tout le mal et le bien que Dieu nous donnera* (7).[45]

A l'instant ils revêtent les haillons de la misère,[46] et, muets, se frappant la poitrine, ils fuient les murs témoins du parricide. Sans argent et sans guide, ils errent à l'aventure au milieu des forêts, chargés de leurs sombres pensées. Les glands et les faînes des bois, et le pain noir que leur jette la pitié des bûcherons, font leur seule nourriture, et les antres sauvages font leur seul abri. Nulle voix ne saurait dire leurs tourments.[47]

Après qu'ils eurent longtemps promené leurs souffrances et leur misère, ils parvinrent sur les bords du Gardon.[48] Le courant était profond et rapide, et il n'y avait point de gué où l'on pût le traverser. Deux nautoniers passaient les voyageurs dans un bac, et chacun qu'ils passaient, tant pauvre et mésaisé fût-il, leur donnait deux deniers, et s'il ne pouvait payer, ils le jetaient à l'eau. En vain Julien les pria-t-il de le passer pour Dieu lui et sa femme, pour ce qu'ils n'avaient point d'argent; ils le repoussèrent avec menaces et blasphèmes, et éloignèrent leur barque du rivage.[49]

Assis tristement sur la rive, Julien et sa femme pourpensaient en eux-mêmes comment ils pourraient passer outre: *Sire*, dit Basilisse, *restons toujours sur ce rivage et travaillons à avoir un bateau. Jamais nul homme souffreteux ne viendra, sans que nous le passions pour Dieu.*[50]

7   Heu, inquit, impletum est verbum cervi, quia ego meos parentes occidi. Jam nunc vale, dulcissima soror, quia jam de cætero non quiescam, donec acceptaverit Dominus penitentiam meam. Cui illa: Absit, inquit, dulcissime frater, ut sine me discedas, et, quæ fui particeps gaudii, non sim et particeps doloris. Mecum ergò sustine quicquid sufferre decreveris. – Vincent de Beauvais, Miroir historial, liv. ix, c. 115.

Ce projet leur plut fort, et de suite ils se mirent à l'ouvrage, travaillant moult et gagnant peu, tant qu'ils purent acheter une barque et se bâtir sur la rive une cabane pour héberger les malheureux qui en avaient *mestier* et le demandaient pour Dieu. Depuis huit ans ils n'avaient point cessé de servir les pèlerins et les pauvres, et, au moyen de ce qu'ils avaient reçu, ils avaient pu élever un hospice où ils prodiguaient tous leurs soins aux voyageurs qu'ils passaient dans leur barque, donnant pour Dieu tout ce qu'on leur donnait, sans rien garder pour eux. Le renom de leur charité s'était au loin répandu; tous les mendiants du pays connaissaient bien leur hôtel et y venaient souvent, et chaque jour leur amenait des hôtes.[51] Un soir cependant il se fit une horrible tempête, qui dura sans cesser tout le jour et la nuit, et personne n'osait quitter l'abri qui le couvrait. Basilisse se tenait constamment à sa porte où elle attendait des hôtes, et elle s'affligeait de n'en pas voir venir, car elle craignait que Dieu ne l'eût abandonnée: *Seigneur*, disait-elle, *donnez-moi de grâce tels hôtes que vous voudrez, et bien les servirai du mieux que je pourrai.*[52] Le jour passa et la nuit vint, et point ne se calma l'orage et point n'arriva d'hôte. De plus en plus inquiète et troublée dans son cœur, Basilisse ne pouvait s'endormir. Assise sur son lit, l'oreille en attente, elle se plaignait de la pluie et des vents qui lui ôtaient ses hôtes; et les sourds grondements de la foudre, et les mugissements des flots, et les combats des vents répondaient seuls à sa plainte. *Dame*, lui disait Julien, *reposez-vous tranquille. Quel homme eût pu, par cet orage, s'aventurer dehors; et si Dieu ne nous donne pas tout ce que nous voulons, devons-nous penser de là qu'il soit irrité contre nous?* Et, cela dit, lui-même commençait à dormir, lorsque le vent apporta à la chambre ce cri plaintif poussé delà les eaux: *Ah! Julien, pour Dieu passez-moi.* – *Levez-vous au plus tôt*, lui cria Basilisse, *il me semble que j'ai entendu une voix qui vient delà le fleuve. C'est quelque pauvre qui vous attend: vite allez le chercher, ou bien je l'irai querre, si vous n'avez assez cure du bien que Dieu consent à vous donner.* – Et au même instant le cri revint plus lamentable: *Ah! Julien, pour Dieu passez-moi, je suis plein de mésaise.*[53]

L'orage augmentait sans cesse; la nuit était sans étoiles; gonflé par les pluies, le torrent se précipitait en épais bouillons avec un bruit effrayant qui allait se répétant de cascade en cascade et d'écho en écho tout le long du rivage.[54] A la lueur vacillante d'un brasier que Basilisse a allumé sur le bord du fleuve, Julien pousse sa nacelle au large, les vents le rejettent à la rive; il lutte et il avance; le courant l'entraîne, et la tempête couvre sa barque de flots et d'éclairs. Il ne perd point courage; il prie Dieu de lui donner de sauver le malheureux qui l'appelle; fort de sa charité, il méprise les dangers, et redoublant d'efforts il atteint enfin la rive opposée. Quand il fut descendu de la barque: *Où êtes-vous*, s'écria-t-il, *vous qui m'avez appelé? Confiez-vous vite à ma conduite; tant pauvre et souffreteux soyez-*

vous, vous n'en serez pas moins bien reçu. Il parlait encore, quant à ses pieds la foudre éclaira d'un sillon blafard la hideuse figure d'un lépreux demi-mort. *Seigneur,* dit le pauvre d'une voix éteinte, *hébergez-moi pour cette nuit seulement; je suis un malheureux mesiaux tout rempli de souffrances, si faible que je ne puis marcher. Au nom de Dieu, portez-moi dans vos bras, et le Seigneur vous rende tout le bien que vous voudrez me faire.*[55]

Julien le prit sur ses bras, l'appuya contre sa poitrine, et le front rongé d'ulcères du lépreux retomba sur le front de son hôte, et le sang livide des plaies du pauvre roula sur les joues et sur la bouche de Julian, qui le souffrit avec joie, car il le faisait pour Dieu, et il avait toujours en souvenance la passion de Jésus-Christ qui le réconfortait. Il le porta ainsi jusqu'à la nef, traversa le fleuve, et, aidé de Basilisse, il déposa le lépreux dans sa maison, sur le coussin le plus moelleux qu'il put trouver. Les deux époux eurent bientôt allumé un brasier ardent; et ils commencèrent à laver les plaies du pauvre, et à couvrir de chauds vêtements ses membres transis, et ils l'efforçaient de manger, car il était encore à jeun: mais rien ne pouvait échauffer son corps plus froid que neige; et plus le feu était vif, plus le lépreux refroidissait.[56]

En vain Julien et Basilisse ont redoublé leurs soins hospitaliers et multiplié leurs efforts.[57]

La glace de la mort gagne déjà le cœur du pauvre; sa voix est tout-à-fait éteinte, et déjà ses yeux obscurcis ne voient plus la lumière. Il va donc mourir? ... Non. La courageuse charité de ses hôtes n'a point encore été poussée à son comble; ils n'ont point encore assez bravé pour Dieu le danger de la plus affreuse existence; ils n'ont point encore assez vaincu tous les dégoûts de la nature. Maintenant les saints époux étendent entre eux, dans leur lit, le corps glacé du pauvre, leurs membres couvrent ses plaies hideuses, pressent ses chairs en lambeaux, et enfin, ranimée par leur chaleur, la vie recommence à circuler peu à peu dans les veines du lépreux.

Tenant ainsi entre eux le lépreux réchauffé, et heureux du succès de leur héroïque dévoûment, Julien et Basilisse avaient céde à la fatigue de la nuit et s'étaient endormis tous les deux; ou plutôt, sans doute, une main divine avait appesanti leurs sens et avait fermé leurs yeux. Tout-à-coup les sons d'un concert angélique remplissent la chambre où reposent les saints époux, les parfums du ciel mille fois plus délicieux que le lis et la rose embaument l'air qu'ils respirent, et une douce clarté répandue autour de leur lit éclaire un dôme d'un azur diaphane. Le lépreux avait disparu; mais, rayonnant de lumière et de gloire, le Sauveur des hommes s'élevait majestueusement vers les cieux et bénissait ses hôtes: *Julien,* disait-il, *j'ai agréé ta pénitence en faveur de ta grande charité; bientôt tu en auras la récompense, et vous reposerez tous les deux pour toujours dans le sein de celui que vous avez reçu.*[58]

Peu de jours après, en effet, Julien et Basilisse avaient quitté la terre. Aucuns disent qu'ils confessèrent la foi de Jésus-Christ, et qu'ils ajoutèrent aux mérites de leurs bonnes œuvres la couronne du martyre.[59] Selon d'autres hagiographes, ils s'endormirent doucement dans le Seigneur, et leurs âmes, portées sur les ailes des chérubins, dans un cercle d'étoiles, s'envolèrent au bienheureux séjour que leur hôte leur avait préparé (8).[60] De là elles protégent encore les pèlerins et les pauvres qui errent ici-bas. Aussi, quand le voyageur, égaré dans sa route, cherche vainement un gîte pour sa nuit, s'il se recommande avec confiance à la vertu des saints époux, s'il dit une *pate-nôtre* en leur honneur, son humble prière lui obtient toujours de trouver un abri (9).[61]

Le manuscrit d'Alençon est de format petit in-folio, écrit sur deux colonnes et relié entre deux ais. Après avoir fait partie de la bibliothèque de l'hôtel de Castellane, il était passé dans le chartrier de l'abbaye de Saint-Evroult. C'est ce que nous apprennent ces deux mentions écrites sur le premier feuillet: *Ex bibliothecâ Castellanâ. – Ex mōrio Sti Ebrulphi, congregatioīs Sti Mauri*, 1711. Il contient deux ouvrages bien distincts, d'abord une espèce de catéchisme ou de traité dogmatique sur les péchés capitaux, figurés *par les sept chefs de la beste que saint Jehan vit*, sur le symbole, les commandements, les vertus, la manière de bien mourir et les dons du Saint-Esprit; puis, les vies des apôtres, des évangélistes et des martyrs (10), enrichies de tous les merveilleux détails dont les a chargées l'imagination des légendaires. Malheureusement il présente beaucoup de lacunes et de transpositions. Ainsi, après avoir trouvé un feuillet de la vie de mon saint au milieu des sept têtes de la bête de l'Apocalypse, j'ai vainement cherché la page qui devait contenir le récit de la vision et du martyre de Julien; ainsi la vie de saint Pierre manque totalement, et *la conversion monseigneur seint Pol li beneoiz apostres nostre Seigneur Jhū-Crist, si comme il fu convertiz et li-meesmes converti plusieurs*, est en tête de ce qui nous reste du second des deux ouvrages.[62]

A la fin du traité sur les dons du Saint-Esprit, est écrite cette note: *Ce livre compila et fist 1 frère del ordre des prescheurs à la requeste dou roy de France Phelippe: en l'an de l'incarnacion nostre Seigneur Jhu-Crist* MIL CCLXXIX.

Je n'hésite pas à attribuer au même auteur les Vies des saints. J'y retrouve les mêmes expressions, les mêmes tournures de phrases, et quelque-

---

8 Voir le panneau supérieur du vitrail de la cathédrale de Rouen.

9 Et encontre avient que quant aucuns est destroiz d'ostel, si doit-il dire la pat'nostre en honor de lui et de sa fame, et pour l'âme de son père et de sa mère, et Diex le conseille d'ostel. – Manuscrit d'Alençon. Vincent de Beauvais intitule ainsi le chapitre où il parle de notre saint: *De alio Juliano pro quo dicitur oratio dominica.*

10 Saint Julien le Pauvre est classé au nombre des martyrs.

fois le même fonds de pensées. Dans l'un comme dans l'autre ouvrage, le style paraît modelé sur la chronique de Villehardouin.[63]

Malheureusement ce n'est point un original que possède la bibliothèque d'Alençon, c'est une copie assez incorrecte, qui me paraît dater de la seconde moitié du quatorzième siècle, et qui n'offre d'autres ornements que des initiales assez mal colorées en carmin et en azur.[64]

Tel n'était pas sans doute le manuscrit qui fut offert au fils et au successeur de saint Louis. Nous eussions vu sur ses marges la mise en action de son texte; ses précieuses vignettes eussent déroulé à nos yeux et le cerf fatidique, et les splendeurs de Rome, et les austères images des lieux saints, puis les combats et les tournois du moyen-âge, et Julien sur son trône recevant l'hommage des vassaux qui l'ont élu pour comte. Peut-être eussions-nous retrouvé aux pieds du tombeau de Radégonde le comte et la comtesse d'Anjou,[65] priant Dieu pour leur fils. Mais bientôt le peintre eût assombri ses couleurs; il nous aurait montré le parricide, puis Julien sous son crime fuyant avec Basilisse à travers les forêts, et sa barque chancelante au milieu des éléments bouleversés; puis enfin, animant de flots d'or les tons les plus suaves de laque et d'azur, il eût fait descendre sur la terre les tentes éternelles, les chœurs des séraphins, et le Roi dont la beauté toujours nouvelle fait le bonheur des élus.

Ces miniatures ont existé sans doute,[66] et sans doute comme tant d'autres elles ont péri pour toujours. Mais il est encore des monuments debout sur lesquels l'*imagier* du moyen-âge a transcrit les infortunes et le triomphe de notre saint. En Belgique, vous retrouverez fréquemment son image: c'est un jeune chevalier qui porte sur sa main une petite nacelle avec un cerf à ses côtés (11). Dans la cathédrale de Rouen, le vitrail de l'aile gauche qui fait face à la quatrième arcade du chœur nous offre dans ses nombreux panneaux les scènes diverses de sa vie (12). Dans la cathédrale de Séez, les verrières de la première chapelle à gauche, au-dessus du transept, nous le montrent encore. Ici, la couronne en tête, il est assis sur le trône où l'ont placé sa vaillance et la main de Basilisse; là il frappe de sa hache les auteurs de ses jours. La tête du comte d'Anjou a déjà roulé à terre, et l'arme est de nouveau levée pour un second parricide. (Pl. VII.)[67]

11 Voir dans les Bollandistes, *Acta Sanctorum januarii*, tom. 2, pag. 974.
12 Voir l'Essai sur la peinture sur verre, par Hiacynthe Langlois; et le procès-verbal de la Société libre d'émulation de Rouen, année 1823, pag. 46 et pl. 1re.

NOTES TO LECOINTRE-DUPONT ADAPTATION

1 These first paragraphs are a curious mixture of anachronism, cultural imperialism, naiveté, and rhetorical trifling. We have discussed this curious (but typically Romantic) understanding of medieval literature on pp. 41-42.

2 This appellation for Julian Hospitator was not uncommon in the medieval period. For the confusions around 'Saint Julian,' see pp. 23-24.

3 We discuss the list of hagiographers above, p. 41. We have also noted that the 'frère prêcheur' has no connection with the Julian story (see footnote 63 to this Appendix, p. 166).

4 Although Lecointre-Dupont states here quite clearly that his manuscript is incomplete, he nowhere indicates the precise point at which his manuscript ends. For reasons we discuss on pp. 47-48, he ceases following Alençon 27 even before its incomplete end in favor of covertly imitating Langlois. Necessarily, he masks this infidelity so as to appear throughout to be reporting the material of Alençon 27. We believe Flaubert was as completely deceived by this, as most of our predecessors appear to have been.

5 In thus drawing attention to this indication of Julian's birthplace, Lecointre-Dupont is perhaps tacitly contrasting his manuscript with the study by Langlois, who had noted (p. 170) that Julian's birthplace was unknown. The Alençon manuscript is thus proved to be more complete, as Lecointre-Dupont had claimed.

    While it is possible that the association of Julian with Le Mans may be as meaningful as Lecointre-Dupont here claims, that is much less than sure; and, whatever the facts, such an association would not prove that Julian's tale was written or first copied in the west of France (and we do not know whether it was commonly read aloud). Saint Julian of Le Mans is, in the eyes of Jacobus da Varagine at least, another saint entirely; yet we may not discount the possibility that the existence of his homonymic fellow saint is the reason why Julian's mother will shortly be said to have conceived him in Le Mans. Saint Julian of Brioude is yet another personage, in reality; but the author of the Prose Life will claim that Julian Hospitator's relics were located in Brioude.

6 Jasinski (see our Bibliography, No. 21) gives a slightly different text for this *Complainte*, which he cites in its entirety.

7 We discuss on p. 13 the role of the premonitory dream in the development of the Julian legend. It also appears – though in a different form – in the Julian Windows at Chartres and Rouen (see Appendix C).

8 In Flaubert's *Légende*, there are such *grandes fêtes* at just this moment (p. 80). There are no verbal similarities between the two passages, which agrees with our thesis that the influence of Lecointre-Dupont does not make itself felt until considerably later in the redaction of the *Légende*. See our discussions, pp. 52-53 and 56-58. Further notes here will draw attention to the passages relevant to this question. Most will prove – as here – to involve the sort of events drawn from daily life which we have posited as tending to recur in any telling of a given hagiographical legend.

    Significantly, the word *fêtes*, and the tourneys, are Lecointre-Dupont's additions (and his only additions) to this paragraph: such motifs are eminently consonant with the Romantic concept of the Middle Ages. The *largesse* Lecointre-Dupont borrowed from the account of the mother's penitence; and *prisons* is apparently a misunderstanding of the false cognate *prison* in paragraph 2 of the

Prose Life: in fact it means *prisonniers*. Jacobus's etymology, quoted in Lecointre-Dupont's Note 4 is, of course, pure fantasy.

9 We have treated this paragraph above, pp. 41-42. It is an excellent example of Lecointre-Dupont's substitution of typically formal Romantic phrasing for the simple prose of the original: the reader will notice many others like it. One clause here, the next-to-the-last, is as nearly as possible a direct quotation from the manuscript (its archaic redundancy no doubt having appealed to Lecointre-Dupont) and the last clause is a paraphrase of the original (see paragraph 3).

10 In this paragraph (often very close to Flaubert's *Légende*, because the material is all commonplace), Lecointre-Dupont's hand is visible in several ways. 'Comme on est à cet âge' may be a misreading of 'fu mult granz de son aage,' in 3, but seems more likely to have been Lecointre-Dupont's own touch, with only an accidental reminiscence of the original. For some reason, the translated phrase 'il avait lassé ses chiens' is preceded by an erroneous 'Un soir' (the Old French has *un jor*). Flaubert's hunt begins in the early morning and lasts until sundown or just thereafter. The rest of the paragraph through these italicized words is a rough paraphrase of the original, with no major error. We discuss other features of this material on pp. 49 and 70.

11 The Prose Life never uses any specific term for the animal Julian hears, only the generic *beste*. Later in the Prose Life (para. 60), a talking animal tells Julian's retainers of the slaughter of the parents; this beast is specifically called a 'chevreuil.' Lecointre-Dupont omits this later episode.

12 The animal's first warning Lecointre-Dupont renders accurately, except for one error which he makes consistently, that of translating *enfes*, 'young man,' by *enfant*. The second time the animal speaks, however, we may note Lecointre-Dupont's practice of expanding and explicitating, of which we have spoken in our discussions (p. 42). Instead of contenting himself with following his manuscript, which reports only that 'the animal said the same thing it had said before' (4), Lecointre-Dupont clearly feels it more appropriate to put down a specific warning. A medieval redactor might well have concurred, obviously; but he would probably not have inserted, as Lecointre-Dupont did here, the text of the warning appearing in the *Legenda aurea*, in words strikingly similar to those used by Langlois. See our Chapter Five for further uses to which Lecointre-Dupont put Langlois.

The last statement attributed to the animal contains a minor error: 'C'est ta destinée: tu l'auras' is not the reading of the original, but may result from the fact that in the manuscript the phrase *ia cele part niras* ('wherever you go') is not distinct enough to be easily read.

13 The Romantic 'épaisseur du bois' is Lecointre-Dupont's addition; he also abridges Julian's reply to the animal and appears to have deliberately suppressed the *je* from its second sentence: the subject does occur in the original. Its omission could, of course, be a printer's error. Finally, Lecointre-Dupont has modified and consolidated the list of Julian's gestures as he begins his flight.

Like Lecointre-Dupont's Julian, Flaubert's, too, will be overcome after hearing the prediction. We believe that this *rencontre* is coincidence only (see Note 8, above). Flaubert elects to have his Julian kill the stag – a psychological necessity for the *Légende* – and return, albeit briefly, to his family.

14 This paragraph is part translation, part imitation, part résumé. In the second sentence, *mendiant* is not a good match for the Old French *peneanz*, 'penitent.' 'Après bien long voyage' has no parallel in the original.

We discuss on page 56 the important fact that Flaubert does perhaps appear to make use of this passage, but that he does so in relating, not Julian's first flight as here, but Julian's second flight. In Flaubert, Julian's first flight leads to a series of brilliant successes. Hence none of this tone can appear; rather it is all transferred to the second flight. As we have noted, we believe Flaubert did read (or reread) Lecointre-Dupont at a slightly later moment in his redaction. Relevant passages from Flaubert's account of Julian's *second* flight are: 'Il s'en alla mendiant sa vie par le monde. Il tendit sa main aux cavaliers sur les routes, avec des génuflexions s'approchait des moissonneurs, ou restait immobile devant la barrière des cours; – et son visage était si triste que jamais on ne lui refusait l'aumône. Par esprit d'humilité ...' It is similarity of tone more than verbal similarities to which we would draw attention. See also Note 8, above, and the end of Note 29, below.

At this point in the *Légende*, Flaubert writes, 'Le vent tanna sa peau,' which resembles Lecointre-Dupont's notation, itself in turn based on a statement in the Prose Life. On pp. 73-74, we discuss why we do not believe Flaubert's sentence derives from his predecessors.

Julian now sets out for Rome and the Near East. Flaubert's plan for his story makes no provision for such a trip: hence he could make no direct use of such materials as Lecointre-Dupont here offered him, even if he did know Lecointre-Dupont's account at this time.

15 There are no 'pèlerins de Jérusalem' in the Prose Life; Julian comes alone to the Pope.

16 For the most part the Pope's words here represent a rearranged translation of the Old French. Such facile, and somewhat misleading, Romantic terms as *chagrins* serve here to abridge longer notations in the original. Part of the Prose Life is in indirect discourse (up to 'je te le commande. ...'). Lecointre-Dupont elects to omit the Pope's explanation that animals are not reasoning beings, and that Faith and Scripture are opposed to the notion that an animal could speak; did it embarrass him? Perhaps for similar reasons, he also omits Julian's fainting at this moment. 'N'en doute point, tu n'as rien vu, rien entendu' (besides being transposed from its original position) is a curiously aberrant translation of *ne doutes riens que tu as oïe ne veüe*: 'do not be afraid of anything you have seen or heard.' Perhaps Lecointre-Dupont was sensitive to the contradiction he had introduced into the Pope's words: the animal, although a *fantosme* or spirit, has real existence in the Prose Life, but Lecointre-Dupont's term *fantosme* probably implied, to him, an imagining or dream.

17 The outline of this paragraph is that of the action in the Life; but *le père des fidèles* is Lecointre-Dupont's rhetoric, and Old French *enseigner* is a further false cognate: the Pope in fact 'gives Julian instructions' in the original.

18 As the reader will have sensed, this paragraph marks a considerable departure from the Prose Life (paras. 7-9). 'Je ne vous dirai point' is, of course, Lecointre-Dupont's formula, not that of the medieval redactor, who does in fact tell Julian's adventures *outremer* in detail. The narration accompanied by dialogue of paragraphs 8 and 9 is reduced, in this adaptation, to a few selected details.

Flaubert's Julian will ferry his passengers across the river without demanding pay. As this is a cliché of hagiography, we see no reason to invoke this passage as a specific source (see Note 8). The same notation recurs two paragraphs below.

19 Noteworthy in this paragraph are the archaisms Lecointre-Dupont introduces into the first sentence ('désir lui vint' replaces normal order, and *devers* stands for the medieval *à*). The rest of the paragraph is transcribed or imitated from the

original, with the signal exception of the phrase 'son doux pays d'Anjou' (the original has only *son pais*, and does not mention forests).

20 Despite Duckworth's Note 99, this paragraph is surely the 'source' for the mention of the Templars in Flaubert, if any source be needed (which we doubt). We believe Flaubert had probably not turned to Maury, and hence Lecointre-Dupont, until a page or so beyond his mention of the Templars (p. 98). Lecointre-Dupont does misrepresent the original in at least one detail: the *bone conpaignie* of the Prose Life is a reference to the fact that the rich among the pilgrims have promised to aid the poor during their voyage. For argument against seeing this cliché as a source for Flaubert, see Note 18.

21 The entire paragraph up to this point is transposed from its original position as paragraph 5, where it follows immediately upon Julian's flight and thus interrupts the sequence of Julian's adventures. Lecointre-Dupont seems unwilling to accept the normal medieval narrative technique of abrupt change of protagonist, preferring instead unity of action. Flaubert's treatment of Julian's response to the prediction is sufficiently different so that this transposition could have no effect on his Tale.

The mother's lament is largely authentic (although a confusing original text is replaced by 'Mais vous qui pouvez tout, oh! rendez-moi mon enfant. ...').

22 The transition ('ses larmes, ses prières') is Lecointre-Dupont's invention, necessitated by his rearrangement of the order (see Note 21). The rest of this paragraph is a patchwork of authentic details, but from paragraphs 37-38, from which point the narrative goes forward.

23 This garbled paragraph has no parallel in Flaubert, who does not dwell on the parents' decision to seek their son; thus the details of Lecointre-Dupont's errors and inventions need not detain us. The source for the next few paragraphs after this one is the episode contained in paragraphs 38-41 of the original, with the changes needed to adapt it to its new place in the sequence of events.

24 As with the material of Note 18 above, these clichés of medieval hagiography recur in Flaubert's account of Julian's wanderings after the murders. Similarly, Flaubert has Julian's parents feel all their trials and fatigues were worth it to find their son.

The entire remainder of the paragraph is Lecointre-Dupont's invention. It is entertaining that he should thus slyly interpolate a reference to the Poitevin Saints Radegund and Hilary ('l'apôtre de l'Aquitaine'). His fellow members of the *Société des Antiquaires de l'Ouest*, in whose Bulletin he published his article, would have recognized them at once, for the seat of the Society was Poitiers, where Lecointre-Dupont himself was living at this time. Hence he had personal knowledge of these relics. Saint Hilary's are in the church dedicated to him, and the footprint left by Christ in the cell of Saint Radegund is still venerated in her church there. Lecointre-Dupont returns to this interpolation later: see our Note 65.

25 The count's remark at the beginning of this paragraph is Lecointre-Dupont's invention, as are the phrases 'Il doit être brave et sage,' and 'sa terre la mieux tenue ...' attributed to the mother.

26 This transitional paragraph contains Lecointre-Dupont's usual mixture of authentic and created detail. In 41-42, a 'bourgeoise' does give a very rapid account of Julian's arrival in the land of which he is now lord. Lecointre-Dupont's decision to let her recital stand for the greater part of the Old French narrative to this point (he has her narrate paragraphs 12-37) prevents him from giving any account at all of Julian's moral struggle and decision to abandon his pilgrimage, as we shall see.

The first two sentences are for the most part accurate representations of what the hostess says, except for *conseille*, which is a misunderstanding of the Old French verb, whose sense was ordinarily 'aid,' 'help.' *Pèlerin* is a further misunderstanding: the original has *peneanz*, 'penitent' (see Note 14, above). Everything following *le pain* in the last sentence is Lecointre-Dupont's clarification, necessitated by the new context he gives to these remarks.

27 This short paragraph is an attempt at adapting 12 to the new context created by the attribution of vital narrative material to the hostess.

28 This paragraph is a key one, for it contains the first really serious departure Lecointre-Dupont makes from the text he claims to be transmitting. The first sentence comes approximately from 13, and Julian meets the knight as in 14; but their entire discussion with its important references to Julian's *paresse*, and the long night of rationalization during which Julian decides to become a warrior again, are both missing. Instead, we have a largely invented and relatively simplistic invitation attributed to the knight, and then, immediately thereafter, the battle which is to be Julian's first, and which does not occur in the Prose Life until paragraph 18, everything between disappearing in Lecointre-Dupont's adaptation.

There are a few errors: *plus faible en nombre* results no doubt from a misreading of Ms. *meudre*, 'meilleur,' as *mendre*, 'moindre.' Also, Lecointre-Dupont has not understood the topography of the land upon which the battle takes place: in the original, the count's men do not 'sweep the hillside,' but charge down it, and they do not hem the enemy in at the ford, but drive him across it, whence one or two adjustments Lecointre-Dupont was obliged to make in the ensuing account. In addition, he seems unable to accept the medieval tendency to give impossibly large, suggestive figures rather than precise counts or approximations as we do: he replaces the unlikely *en chaïrent plus de cent* by 'de nombreux guerriers mordent la poussière.'

Finally, the opening of the paragraph foreshadows clearly Julian's actions in Flaubert's *Légende* at the opening of Part III. See above, Note 14.

29 For no discernable reason, Lecointre-Dupont has Julian kill a knight in order to have the necessary equipment for the battle. The original offers simply a logical and traditional motif: Julian picks up his gear from the ground, and frees a mired horse, as it was all too easy to do in an area where the medieval mêlée had passed.

The other aspects of Julian's prowess, which are standard fare in medieval narratives, do appear in Julian's combats at the start of Flaubert's Part II. We find such recurrences inevitable and not evidence that Flaubert already knew Lecointre-Dupont. The contact becomes a certainty a few pages later, as we have noted. See our discussion of similar material in the Prose Life as source for Flaubert, above, pp. 68-69.

30 Again, an important indicator of the medieval Julian's character – his impatience between battles – has disappeared from Lecointre-Dupont's account, as have certain steps in Julian's rise to eminence, by the omission of paragraphs 23-28 of the original. Lecointre-Dupont has excised in its entirety the second battle, in which Julian wins the good graces of the count himself by a display of unthinking lust for combat. Similarly, only a phrase or two ('plus de cent chevaliers tombèrent sous sa lance') must do for all of paragraphs 29 and 30, describing Julian's entry into the count's service and his exploits afterwards. Finally, the rest of the paragraph, archaisms and all, is Lecointre-Dupont's invention.

The word *chevaliers* occurring in the last sentence corresponds, we believe, to a similar passage in the Prose Life, which Duckworth wished to see as a source for

Flaubert (see our discussion, pp. 68-69). We find neither Lecointre-Dupont nor
the Prose Life necessary as a 'source': the material is a cliché only, in our view.
See our Note 8, above.

31 Perhaps the most noteworthy change in this paragraph is the attribution to the
hostess of a narrator's intervention from 30; 'une journée me suffirait à peine. ...'
is copied from the second sentence of that Prose Life paragraph, where, of course,
the *bourgeoise* is not speaking. Paragraph 30 is fairly well presented here, in résumé;
the Prose Life does say specifically that the count was killed in the period of the
Feast of Saint John (presumably the midsummer feast); and the explanatory
clause, 'parce qu'ils n'avaient plus de chef ...' is Lecointre-Dupont's.

32 This paragraph summarizes paragraph 31 of the Prose Life. However, Lecointre-
Dupont transferred some elements of the latter to the description of the countess
which he gives somewhat later (see Note 39). 'Elle n'avait mie vingt ans' is a transcription of the original. The mention of the ramparts turns the figurative *voyait* of
the original into a literal act of seeing: there is a trace of the figurative original in
Lecointre-Dupont's next paragraph, however.

33 Again Lecointre-Dupont abridges and transposes, with serious consequences for
the reader's understanding of the story. Lecointre-Dupont translates the propo-
sition which the assembled lords make to the countess, with approximate accuracy
and only minor compressions and omissions. But for some reason, he entirely sup-
presses the lady's crucial reaction. In the Prose Life she does not acquiesce immediately with gentle mien. On the contrary, her concern for her rank (she is 'parante
la roïne de France') leads her to express displeasure at the idea of marrying a beggar, mighty though he is. Only the barons' persistence leads her to accept Julian,
for she dares not refuse her retainers' request in her difficult circumstances. Yet
she prays that she may not thereby tarnish her bloodline. This, then, is the real
context of her remark: 'que Dieu me donne en lui profit et honneur.' Its signifi-
cance, the reader will see, changes singularly in Lecointre-Dupont's transposition.

    The countess's concern for status is to have vital consequences; for the Prose
Life makes clear that her questioning of Julian, as they lie in their marriage bed,
stems from her desire to know whether her new husband is of noble birth. He
never tells her where his father's lands are, but, at her insistence, he does give her
his parents' surnames, which allows his wife to recognize them when they appear
at the castle, and thus to put them into her bed. There is, obviously, nothing similar in Flaubert (see our discussion, p. 8, note 10).

34 This paragraph is a very much abridged representation of paragraphs 33-36 in the
Prose Life, with many embellishments typical of Lecointre-Dupont (e.g., 'il y eut
grandes joutes et grands tournois et belles appertises d'armes,' details absent from
the Prose Life). One of Lecointre-Dupont's additions foreshadows Flaubert: 'jaloux
de combattre sous un chef si redouté' is similar to Julian's success as a leader during
his first flight in Flaubert's *Légende*. Flaubert's sentence reads: 'Des esclaves en
fuite, des manants révoltés, des bâtards sans fortune, toutes sortes d'intrépides
affluèrent sous son drapeau. ...' (p. 98). Again, and despite the resemblance of
drapeau and *bannière*, we find here no more than clichés recurring quite naturally,
as we have frequently suggested.

    On the other hand, although Lecointre-Dupont does invoke Julian's clemency in
the banal formulation of the final sentence, he does not state it as directly as does
the Prose Life. It is, of course, another common motif. Paragraphs 34-35, omitted
here, Lecointre-Dupont inserts later, but with the changes he needs to bring them
into line with his edulcorated version of the countess's attitude toward her husband
(see Note 33).

Although we believe Flaubert had already read Lecointre-Dupont when he wrote of Julian's marrying the daughter of the Emperor of Occitania, we have suggested that his plans for his Tale were too far advanced to permit of his adopting this mode for Julian's marriage, even had he wished to do so.

35 This transition is, of course, Lecointre-Dupont's way of attaching to its new context the material he earlier displaced from its original order. The preceding paragraph brought the account up to the end of 36; 38-41 he had already recounted as an introduction to the story the hostess tells (see Notes 23-26). The purpose of the transition, which borrows from 37, is therefore to bring the story back to 42. An invented character (and not the narrator) gives the description of Julian's new life, as we have remarked (Note 26). That fact suffices to explain the absence of any equivalent for the Prose Life's essential statement that Julian 'has returned to his nature,' in 37.

In Flaubert's *Légende*, too, the countryside is at peace after Julian's marriage; but there this serves only to heighten Julian's ennui, for (unlike Lecointre-Dupont's Julian or the Prose Life's) Flaubert's hero at first refuses to hunt.

36 With this paragraph, based on 42 but bearing the marks of Lecointre-Dupont's style and prejudices, we return to the order of events occurring in the original. Thus Lecointre-Dupont has given us the action of the Prose Life in the following order: first, the equivalent of paragraphs 1-4, then 6-11 (abridged), then 5, then an invented transition; then 38-41 (with one detail from 37) followed by a considerably abridged version of 13 (with some details based on 12), 14, and 15; then 18, 19, 20, and the beginning of 21; then a few details from 29, followed by an abridged version of 30-33; then 36 and a detail or two from 37, and finally the necessary transition to bring us back to the account of the parents' meeting with Julian's wife. The adaptation will now follow the sequence of the Prose Life more or less accurately, except for the insertion of a modified résumé of 34-35 on pages 147-48.

The first sentence of this transitional paragraph ('suspendus à la bouche ...') is Lecointre-Dupont's and the psychology in it is his invention. He also attributes a speech of Emma's to her husband. Why Lecointre-Dupont has Geoffroi ask Julian's *pays* is a mystery, for the hostess has just explained that he came from nowhere. Thus the original has the hostess give Julian's name here for the first time, and Lecointre-Dupont has instead her explanation that he has never revealed his origins to anyone. Finally, the important detail of his enjoyment of the chase, and the parents' reaction to that revelation, in 42, is not present in Lecointre-Dupont's adaptation, although it is referred to at the end of the previous paragraph. Other changes are minor.

37 This paragraph is a patchwork of authentic details from 42 and 43, but in a different order, with omissions made to bring the episode into line with the modifications discussed in the preceding note.

38 Again Lecointre-Dupont makes changes which reveal his principal biases. He omits the change of protagonist represented by 44 and no more than hints at Julian's absence on the hunt. We do not know why the redactor of the Prose Life insists on the preparation of the baths, which is virtually the only detail he does report concerning the second hunt; but in any case, Lecointre-Dupont does not repeat that detail. Geoffroi's speech at the end of this paragraph, although italicized, is transposed from 43; the original states that both parents, not only the father, spoke, but it reports no direct discourse here. Finally, Lecointre-Dupont rewrites and abridges the response of the chaplain.

We discuss above, pp. 13-14, the various reasons different redactors found to ensure Julian's absence from his castle at the moment when his parents arrived. His being away hunting is one of the two explanations offered (the other was war). Hunting is the reason provided, not only in the Prose Life (and hence in Lecointre-Dupont) but also very widely among other redactors. Hence we believe Flaubert could readily have invented it himself. On the other hand, if he knew Lecointre-Dupont's work in 1856, it may have been what suggested this reason for the absence to him. We discuss above, pp. 52-54, why we believe it is not possible to say definitively whether or not Flaubert read Lecointre-Dupont as early as 1856.

39 The countess's name is never given in the original. As we have suggested (p. 43 n4), the notion of calling her Basilisse may have come to Lecointre-Dupont from a misleading remark of Langlois's. The confusions present in Lecointre-Dupont's Note 5 concerning various medieval Julians, we discuss on p. 23. In Lecointre-Dupont's note, his transcription from 31 contains a few copy errors. The description of the countess comes, as we have noted, from 31 (see our Note 32).

40 Paragraphs 34-35 having for some reason been omitted from their correct place, we now find them here, at the very last point at which they may occur, since they explain how Julian's wife is able to recognize his parents. Lecointre-Dupont continues to suppress all mention of the countess's curiosity concerning her husband's origins, a theme which is essential in the Prose Life (see our Note 33). Instead, he revises the episode in a Romantic vein: the flowery first clauses are his entirely; he modifies the dialogue between Julian and his wife to remove any hints of her insistent concern to know Julian's birth, the names of his parents, and his place of origin. Finally, her prayer to heaven is an invention which effectively hides her less wise motivation as the original showed it.

41 When the countess leaves the chapel, we return to 46. Lecointre-Dupont abridges the dialogue and modifies it to fit the changes he has already made and to which he must now conform. For example, in the Prose Life, Julian's mother specifically refers here to his love for the hunt; but since Lecointre-Dupont skipped this detail when recounting the material of 42, he must now suppress it here. For once, however, Lecointre-Dupont is trapped: in the original, the parents have already been to Saint-Gilles (as had Julian) by the time they reach their son's castle, and they are following the route to Saint James of Compostella, exactly as he had been. Lecointre-Dupont reports Julian's having been to Saint-Gilles, where he met the pilgrims in whose company he entered the land of which he is now lord. But for reasons which we cannot now fathom, Lecointre-Dupont does not have the parents follow the same route. Hence he considers them as being on their way to Saint-Gilles, and must contradict his manuscript here, for its logic requires that they be en route for Saint James of Compostella as their son was, and that is what they say when the countess meets them.

Also the mother's phrase, 'nous avons fiance que Dieu nous le rendra,' replaces a reference to the name of the new lord, which Lecointre-Dupont must omit, since he had revised the scene in which the parents had learned it (see Note 36).

Finally, and more importantly, Lecointre-Dupont follows his earlier decision to hide the countess's burning curiosity about Julian's origin: he compresses this scene, in which the countess is motivated to ask the parents' names, because they do not volunteer them in the Prose Life: 'now she will know the things her husband has hidden from her.'

'Il reviendra ce soir' is a minor contradiction both of the manuscript and possibly of Lecointre-Dupont's own later version as well. Finally, the naive declaration of the countess, 'moi je sais bien que j'en mourrais,' is not Lecointre-Dupont's invention, but an authentic part of the Prose Life (49). Flaubert, too, will note how fatigued Julian's parents are on their arrival at Julian's castle; we have, however, suggested on p. 36 that we believe he originally took this idea from Mlle Langlois's drawing of the Rouen window. Perhaps that original impetus found reinforcement here.

42 Of course the baths, present in the Prose Life, are omitted here, since Lecointre-Dupont had already omitted mention of them earlier. The paragraph is otherwise much abridged by comparison with 50-51 (for example, the redactor of the Prose Life gives some explanation of why the arrival of Julian's parents is kept secret from the household). The *courtines*, curiously, are those which surround the bathtubs in the original, and have no connection with the bed: they could only obscure Julian's view of the latter when he arrives. We discuss above (pp. 75-76) the practical necessity for the narrative to include and explain that Julian's parents are sleeping in partial but not complete darkness. We do not, therefore, find this or any similar passage a 'source' for Flaubert (see also Note 43). 'Avec ses femmes' is Lecointre-Dupont's idea, as is the emotional tone of the last clause.

Lecointre-Dupont is unique among the sources available to Flaubert in so clearly keeping 'Basilisse' inside the castle. See our discussion above, pp. 54-55, suggesting that this passage may perhaps have been what led Flaubert to adopt the same plan for his Tale.

43 This rapid paragraph further exemplifies Lecointre-Dupont's increasing tendency, as he nears the end of his version, to give his work psychological and emotional overtones characteristic of his age and not present in the original. Here, his Julian flies impatiently into his room, as he specifically does not in the original: Flaubert's Julian will be similarly exasperated. On the other hand, Lecointre-Dupont does not report the role of the Devil in Julian's passionate crime ('li anemis le deçut d'ire et d'angoisse, si sacha s'espee conme home desvez').

We treat the details of the paragraph in Note 13 to Chapter Seven. In Flaubert's first drafts for the second hunt, he envisaged making it a successful one, like Lecointre-Dupont's; he may have been led to this by this passage. It will be recalled that the final form of the *Légende* makes this second hunt hideously unsuccessful. The Prose Life, unlike Lecointre-Dupont, has no indication of how the hunt went. 'Plus tôt que de coutume' is Lecointre-Dupont's explanatory invention: the original is indeed unclear about the reasons for the wife's absence from the area of her room at noon, even though she expected Julian back at 'tierce ou ançois.'

44 The style of the paragraph departs considerably from that of the relatively sober Prose Life. The first sentence, with its *joie féroce* and its *lit ensanglanté* is entirely Lecointre-Dupont's invention. Flaubert will make much of the blood spilled in the murders, quite possibly because of this indication. He also emphasizes Julian's ferocity, but this is not necessarily because he read this passage: it was inevitable in his understanding of Julian. Hence he had been preparing the reader for Julian's response at this moment from very early in the Tale.

The Prose Life has the typical medieval dialogue between the fainting Julian and his wife, in which they make explicit their reactions to the tragedy, and their intentions; but the Life gives no description of the scene, nor does the narrator intervene to discuss the psychology, save the single phrase, 'Mult fu liez de ce qu'il les avoit endeus ocis' (53).

Again Lecointre-Dupont omits any reference to the wife's pride of status ('nul ne devroit tel prince celer'). 'Ces bons parents' is Lecointre-Dupont's moralizing phrase, and the archaizing 'et sont bien travaillés' and 'je les ai mis coucher' are likewise his inventions. Note the reference to Saint-Gilles, corresponding to the earlier changes (see our Note 41).

45 In contradistinction to all his sources, Flaubert has Julian leave alone. We discuss this matter in Note 16, p. 36. In his Note 7, Lecointre-Dupont cites Vincent of Beauvais. The same ideas but with slightly different phrasings appear in the *Legenda aurea* (quoted on p. 102). Lecointre-Dupont conflates the passage from Vincent with the parallel lament in the Prose Life, to create this paragraph: thus he continues to write passages which are not in his sources, but with acknowledgement this time. On the other hand, he omits all the long dialogue in 54-56, including Julian's apparent statement that the Devil is more powerful than God.

46 This cliché is suggested in Flaubert's *Légende* as well, as Julian leaves on his second exile (see Note 13, above).

47 Lecointre-Dupont passes over the various laments of 54-58 and here offers a résumé of 59, to which he adds rhetorical touches of his own creation ('se frappant la poitrine' has no parallel at all in the original, nor does 'leurs sombres pensées'). We do not know where the woodcutters and their black bread or the caves in which the couple take shelter may have come from. Paragraph 60, the account of how the parents are discovered and buried, Lecointre-Dupont omits entirely. Imitating the Prose Life, he also notes that Julian and his wife ate 'glands.' We discuss on page 73 the possible relevance of this word to indicate a source; we doubt that it is one, either here or in the Prose Life.

48 Our predecessors have felt it at least possible that the 'Gardon' is a confusion on the part of the redactor of the Prose Life, here echoed by Lecointre-Dupont; they propose that the 'Gard' is what was intended. That river's course is such that Julian and his wife might most readily have settled upon its banks. Further to the north, it is true, the Gard is formed by the junction of two of the streams called 'gardons,' and either of the two could also be meant, despite their greater distance from Saint-Gilles and the presumptive area where Julian and his wife now find themselves. See Huet, p. 47, Note 1, and cf. our note to the Prose Life, paragraph 66. We find no compelling evidence which would settle the matter one way or the other. Nor is there any way to tell whether the Life was or was not written by someone familiar with the South of France.

49 This paragraph parallels 66 and summarizes the double exchange of 67. The couple's pilgrimages and their visit to Rome, where the Pope advises them, disappear (63-64). 65 is swallowed up in the first sentence. The other changes are relatively minor.

Some of Julian's passengers will treat him, in Flaubert's text, as these churlish boatmen here treat Julian and his wife.

50 This brief paragraph represents material from 67 combined with a translation of the wife's speech from the beginning of 68.

51 Again, Lecointre-Dupont chooses to omit all mention of an important aspect of his model. He allows the wife to suggest that a hostel be built, as she does at greater length in the original; but he does not dwell on her sacrifices in the service of the poor, as the Prose Life does (to the exclusion of any Julian may make). Thus the moralizing tone of the medieval text is largely lost.

The figure of eight years' service combines information in 68 and 69. Flaubert's

Julian, too, will give all he earns to the poor; but this is, again, a cliché and we do not point to Lecointre-Dupont as a necessary source.

52 This much of the paragraph is a fairly accurate résumé of material in 69, except that 'elle craignait que Dieu ne l'eût abandonnée' comes from 70. Immediately after this point, Lecointre-Dupont begins to depart seriously from his original (see Notes 56 *et seq.*).

53 This passage is rather thoroughly revised. Its elements occur in a different order in the Prose Life, and it is somewhat abridged, as is Lecointre-Dupont's usual practice; but more important, it has additions which show clearly Lecointre-Dupont's tendency to depart from his text. Besides an occasional adjective (*plaintif*) and the un-medieval 'Ah!' preceding each of the leper's cries, the entire storm clause treated in Chapter Five ('les sourds grondements de la foudre,' etc.) is Lecointre-Dupont's work.

Lecointre-Dupont has made, on the other hand, further important omissions. The wife's reaction to the sound of the leper's voice (71) and Julian's initial refusal to go after the nocturnal traveller (72) are passed over; the result is a version which greatly reduces the role of Julian's wife – as has been Lecointre-Dupont's practice all along.

54 For the first time, Lecointre-Dupont has succumbed to the temptation to write the story himself, with little or no guidance from the original, except on the general plane of order of events. The description of the storm in the first sentence is entirely Lecointre-Dupont's: see our discussion of the filiation from Langlois to Lecointre-Dupont and on to Flaubert, pp. 44-45.

55 As before, see our discussion on pp. 44-45 for the relationship of this text to Langlois and to Flaubert. Lecointre-Dupont continues to write without important attention to his original. The detail of the wife's tending a fire is in the Prose Life, but receives very different treatment there. Julian's struggle to cross the river is pure invention (in Flaubert, it will be an easy crossing; he does appear to have used some of this material in describing the difficult return journey). Julian's prayer, and the ensuing efforts, are not in the laconic Prose Life account. The sentences in Julian's speech after his landing are out of order. The lightning which dramatically reveals the leper's state to Julian is Romantic and not medieval. And the dialogue between Julian and his passenger, in which the Prose redactor gradually reveals the leper's pitiful state, is reduced to a single long sentence here. We discuss the relation of this passage concerning the leper to Flaubert's *Légende* on pp. 46-47.

56 Lecointre-Dupont's changes in this paragraph include the addition of the grotesque details of the first sentence (which Flaubert will adapt to his own purposes): in the Prose Life, the leper's breath is in Julian's face, but there is no mention of blood or sores. Further, Lecointre-Dupont inserts here a detail from the first crossing of the river in the Prose Life: 'il avait toujours en souvenance la passion de Jésus-Christ. ...' Flaubert will make use of this suggestion for his own, and difficult, second crossing.

The rest of the paragraph is a scrambled representation of 74-76 (it is Lecointre-Dupont's last attempt to adapt his manuscript to his needs: see the following note), with a much abridged version of the second crossing, and with added details of his own invention (the *coussin* is 'moelleux,' and they wash the leper's sores, which are not referred to in the original).

57 With this transitional sentence, Lecointre-Dupont abandons even the sequence of events offered to him by the Prose Life, and begins, without warning, to write the

ending which is unique to his work (though influenced by Langlois) and which in turn influenced Flaubert in the ways discussed in Chapter Five. The rest of the adaptation bears no resemblance to the Prose Life, except for the reference made later to the prayer which is part of Julian's cult (the Prose Life refers to it in paragraph 1), and perhaps the word *glace* at the start of the paragraph which follows immediately. The word occurs in 76, which Lecointre-Dupont used for the end of the immediately preceding paragraph; but there he substituted *neige*. Flaubert's leper will report that 'C'est comme de la glace dans mes os!'

As we have noted, Lecointre-Dupont's source manuscript does not end with this scene. He had available to him all of the material in 77, none of which he reports, for the reasons we suggest in Chapter Five (notably the fairly explicit sexual references; see our pp. 47-49). It is not possible to detect the departure from the manuscript here without access to one of the medieval copies of the Prose Life. That fact is, we believe, essential to the impression Lecointre-Dupont's remaining paragraphs made on Flaubert. Lacking any evidence to the contrary, Flaubert felt as much authorized to use this material as he did to use anything else in Lecointre-Dupont. We have already drawn attention (pp. 58-59) to the striking fact that Flaubert's heaviest borrowings are from these final pages in Lecointre-Dupont. We may even suggest that almost all the earlier passages which parallel Lecointre-Dupont could be explained as common clichés used by Flaubert, perhaps without his even realizing they also occurred in Lecointre-Dupont.

58 Lecointre-Dupont is here paraphrasing and extending the *Legenda aurea* (or one of its several analogues): 'Juliane, dominus misit me ad te, mandans tibi, quod tuam poenitentiam acceptavit et ambo post modicum in domino quiescitis.' It is unlike the angel's words (addressed to Julian's wife) in the Prose Life (see paragraph 79 as transcribed from B.N. Fr. 6447).

59 As we noted above, p. 14, it is never made entirely clear in Julian's *vita* precisely how he is a *martyred* saint. When Lecointre-Dupont indicates in the next sentence that 'other hagiographers' have another version, he is suggesting more than the facts appear to warrant. He knows Langlois and the drawing included in his book, as we noted on p. 50; he also knows the *Legenda aurea* and other texts of this tradition; but he shows no awareness of any 'other' traditions (e.g., those noted by Oberziner or Gaiffier, or the Prose Life from a second manuscript).

60 Lecointre-Dupont's footnote refers his reader to the 'panneau supérieur du vitrail de la cathédrale de Rouen': in fact, he means the panel immediately below that one. As his text carried a line-drawing based upon that prepared by Mlle Langlois, no important confusion resulted.

61 The transcription of his manuscript provided in Lecointre-Dupont's footnote is accurate.

62 The displaced folio is now No. 5. The dogmatic treatise is, as we have noted on p. 106, the *Somme le roi*, an allegorical work written in the thirteenth century by a certain Friar Laurent. The second *ouvrage* is, of course, a standard *légendier*, although incomplete, as Lecointre-Dupont notes. Lecointre-Dupont's phrasing concerning the lost folios of his manuscript is, once again, vague at best. It may even be a deliberate inaccuracy intended to mask the fact that he did not transcribe even the end of the material he did have (see our discussion above, pp. 47-49 and Note 57). Such a suppression of the wife's heroic and saintly role – she has agreed to go to bed with the leper at the very end of Alençon 27 – is consonant with much of the rest of Lecointre-Dupont's treatment of Basilisse. In similar fashion, he does not even admit that she might have been 'martyred' along with her husband!

Despite Lecointre-Dupont's explicit statement that the end of his source text was missing, none of our predecessors seem to have noticed the fact, not even the editor of B.N. Fr. 6447, Rudolf Tobler (see *Archiv*, 106 [1901], 303).

63 Of course, the *frère del ordre des prescheurs* is the author of the *Somme le roi.* There is every reason to think he had nothing whatsoever to do with the writing of the *légendier* or of the Prose Life. The use of similar syntax and expressions is – the point is hardly new – the rule among authors of a given period, even great ones like Flaubert, and is particularly marked among the insignificant. The style of the *Prose Life* does not resemble Villehardouin's any more than it resembles that of any other thirteenth-century prose.

64 The Alençon manuscript is indeed, as nearly all preserved medieval manuscripts are, a copy of another manuscript, and Lecointre-Dupont is right to say it is not a particularly clean copy, although it is not markedly incoherent either. The dating of plain fourteenth-century manuscripts is difficult at best; we will not attempt here to go any further than our predecessors, who all agree the Alençon manuscript belongs to that century (although it is not obvious which half).

65 Lecointre-Dupont returns here to his sly interpolation concerning the Poitevin saints: see above, Note 24.

66 The existence of an entire cycle of miniatures illustrating Julian's life is not likely. In any case, the notion that the Prose Life was written for presentation to Philip III depends on the mistaken presumption that it was written by Friar Laurent; it could easily be more than a quarter of a century older than the beginning of Philip's reign (1270). The only manuscript iconographical tradition for Julian, to our knowledge, is that of showing him in the act of beheading his parents, in a single miniature at the beginning of the Prose Life text, as in B.N. Fr. 6447. There are historiated initials in B.N. Fr. 17229, which would repay examination; at the time we consulted that manuscript, however, our concerns were exclusively textual, and we may have overlooked something of interest.

67 Lecointre-Dupont is grotesquely wrong in his interpretation of this window. His error was not, however, suspected for over a century until Professor Jean Lafond re-examined the window, only to discover that it tells, not the story of Julian, but the story of Saint Nicholas! Lecointre-Dupont managed to mistake the butcher of the Nicholas legend for Julian, but then compounded his misinterpretation by seeing Julian once again in the wife of the butcher. See Jean Lafond, 'Les Vitraux de la cathédrale de Sées,' in *Congrès archéologique de France*, CXI[e] Session (1953) (Paris and Orléans: 1954).

The Julian Legend in the Rouen Window

Flaubert's initial impetus to write the *Légende de Saint Julien l'Hospitalier* came from the Julian window at Rouen, filtered through the eyes of his friend Langlois, who was typical of his period in his Romantic vision. Langlois was also typical (and has remained so) in being unable to decipher many of the panels in his window, whole sequences in fact at times. Moreover, he was frequently mistaken in the interpretations he offered. The meaning of the panels can, however, be deduced by an extremely close study of each and by constant comparisons with the Julian window at Chartres, to which the Rouen one is closely related. We give below what we believe to be the valid interpretation of the Rouen window, leaving to another study the reasoning which leads to it.[1] We use the numbering of Mlle Langlois's drawing, which is reproduced as our frontispiece.

Figures 1, 2, and 3. Donors: the fishmongers.
Figure 4. Julian, his mother, and his father walk from their castle to a neighboring one, where Julian will begin his service as a page. His mother and father each carry one of the younger children.
Figure 5. Julian greets the lord and lady whom he will serve.
Figure 6. Julian pledges to serve his new lord faithfully, while his father expresses his gratitude to the lord.
Figure 7. Julian, who is now older, is given a baton as the mark of enlarged responsibility, perhaps a military command. The baton, which is actually there in the window, Mlle Langlois was not able to see and hence did not record.

---

1   The data and deductions to support the arguments are very lengthy and will form part of a separate study, currently in preparation by Bart, who assumes responsibility for what is here offered, though he has had the counsel of Cook in reaching these conclusions.

Figure 8. Julian serves his lord and lady at table.[2]
Figure 9. Julian's new lord lies dying and is given Extreme Unction.
Figure 12. Julian's new lord lies dead, mourned by the widow and by Julian.
Figure 11. Julian and the widow are married. The 'turban' on the head of the priest is a misreading by Mlle Langlois.[3]
Figure 10. Julian and one of his knights ride off to war, presumably in defense of his new bride. He was victorious.[4]
Figure 13. That night, asleep in his tent, Julian dreams that his wife is committing adultery.[5]
Figure 14. Meanwhile, his parents, who have set out to find him, reach his castle. They are exhausted by their journey.[6]
Figure 15. They are greeted by Julian's wife.
Figure 16. Driven by jealousy, Julian returns to his castle, unaware of the arrival of his parents.
Figure 17. As a gesture honoring them, Julian's wife has placed his parents in the bed normally occupied by herself and Julian. Predisposed by his evil dream, Julian believes the two sleeping figures are his wife and her lover. He kills them.
Figure 18. His wife, who was away from the castle at the moment of his arrival, returns just as Julian leaves the castle, still wiping the blood from his sword. His wife is appalled: the full explanation on both sides will come in a moment.
Figure 19. Imposing a penance of exile upon themselves, Julian and his wife set out upon their journey.
Figure 20. Establishing a hospice by the side of a river, Julian and his wife care for sick travellers.

2 Langlois was unable to decipher any of the panels up to this point and contented himself with recording that Julian's parents 'l'élevèrent dans les exercices convenables à son rang.' This authorized Flaubert to develop his own childhood for Julian.

3 Flaubert felt free to alter his version to have Julian marry the daughter of the Emperor of Occitania.

4 Langlois did not understand this panel, for it marks a deviation from the *Legenda aurea*; hence he skipped it. Since Langlois then follows the *Legenda aurea* in giving no reason for Julian's absence from his castle at the moment of his parents' arrival, Flaubert was forced to motivate it otherwise than by having Julian away fighting. He may have been moved to have Julian off on a hunt by having read Lecointre-Dupont. See above, pp. 13-14, and p. 161.

5 As Langlois was unable to interpret this panel, he omitted it. Hence there was no occasion for it to influence Flaubert.

6 The fatigue shown by both parents in this panel is the obvious source for Flaubert's notation in his first plan of 1875 for the Tale: 'Deux vieux appuyés sur des bâtons viennent demander l'hospitalité' (B.N., N.A.F. 23663, fol. 493 recto).

Figure 21. Julian ferries travellers across the river.

Figure 24. One night Julian and his wife are awakened by a voice calling from the far side of the river. Julian hastily completes dressing.

Figure 23. Julian crosses the river to fetch the traveller; it is probably a stormy night.[7]

Figure 22. Reaching the far bank, Julian discovers that the traveller is Christ.

Figure 25. On the way back, the saint (note his halo) is blessed by Christ, who forgives him his sin of parricide.

Figure 26. His wife, on the shore before the hospice, holds a torch to guide her husband.

Figure 27. Once within the hospice, Christ blesses the saintly pair.

Figure 30. After Christ's departure and again at night, a voice calls; this time it is the Devil, in a development parallel to the earlier visit of Christ.[8]

Figure 29. Julian ferries the Devil across the river.

Figure 28. That night as the holy couple chastely sleep fully clothed, the Devil appears in their dream, about to carry off the hospice. (Mlle Langlois was unable adequately to make out this panel. It is high in the window and ill-lit. Hence she turns what is actually the hospice into the odd, flag-shaped objects behind the Devil.)

Figure 31. The holy couple die at the same moment and angels escort their souls to heaven, while two further huge censing angels stand on either side and Christ awaits them in heaven, holding the orb and blessing.[9]

---

7 Whether the panel indeed represents a stormy night is a matter of conjecture: Langlois, however, was sure of it. His account is the initial basis for the storm scene in Flaubert.

8 Langlois omits this sequence of three panels, because he does not understand them. Hence they had no effect on Flaubert.

9 Professor James W. McCrady analyzes the window in his 'The Saint Julian Window at Rouen as a Source for Flaubert's *Légende de Saint Julien L'Hospitalier,*' *Romance Notes*, 10 (1969), 268-76. The present interpretation differs from his at a number of points, a matter which will have to be justified in the study mentioned in Note 1. One point should, however, be considered here. McCrady finds that his reading of the window breaks naturally into three successive 'main groups,' which correspond to the three parts of Flaubert's Tale: 'Flaubert has employed the structure of the window exactly as it would have struck his eye. ...' It may be so. However, the tripartite division of the story first appears in the plan made in Brittany, when Flaubert no longer had the window or Mlle Langlois's drawing before him. In 1856, when he had them both, he divided his story into five parts (see above, pp. 83-86).

Langlois on the Julian Window at Rouen

We present below the relevant pages from Eustache-Hyacinthe Langlois's *Essai historique et descriptif sur la peinture sur verre ancienne et moderne* (Rouen: Edouard Frère, 1832, pp. 32-9). They were a prime source for both Lecointre-Dupont and Flaubert. For the history of the filiation of these texts, see pages 40-51. The footnote references appear in the text of Langlois. We have renumbered them, however.

Revenons maintenant à la vitre consacrée à saint Julien-l'Hospitalier, et donnons, dans un sommaire de la vie de ce bienheureux, l'explication des sujets compris dans les compartimens de cette curieuse verrière.

Ce saint, sur les lieux de la naissance et de la mort duquel les légendaires ont gardé le silence, sortait de parens illustres qui l'élevèrent dans les exercices convenables à sa condition relevée; aimant, dans sa jeunesse, passionnément la chasse, un jour qu'il poursuivait un cerf qu'il était près d'atteindre et de mettre à mort, l'animal, se tournant vers son persécuteur, lui cria d'une voix terrible: *Tu me poursuis, toi qui tueras ton père et ta mère.*[1] Frappé d'horreur, et voulant éviter l'accomplissement de cette épouvantable prophétie, le chasseur, à l'instant même, se bannit pour jamais du manoir paternel, et se retire en secret dans une contrée lointaine, vers un certain prince (*fig.* 7) qui, bientôt appréciant ses grandes qualités, lui confie le commandement de sa gendarmerie (*fig.* 10) et lui fait obtenir la main d'une jeune veuve châtelaine de la plus haute extraction (*fig.* 11).

Dans ces entrefaites, le père et la mère de Julien, inconsolables de sa perte, entreprennent sa recherche (*fig.* 14), et le sort, après beaucoup de

---

1 La représentation de cette miraculeuse aventure que, dans un siècle sinon plus ami du merveilleux, au moins plus croyant que le nôtre, le peintre-verrier n'a très-probablement pas omise, devait faire partie des vitraux historiés de quelque fenêtre voisine, avec lesquels elle aura disparu.

peines et de fatigues, les conduit, à leur insu, dans le château de ce fils bien-aimé, absent alors. Cependant la châtelaine (*fig.* 15) reçoit avec bienveillance ces vénérables voyageurs, s'informe de leur condition, et, les reconnaissant à leurs discours pour les parens de son mari, joint aux plus tendres égards la respectueuse attention de les faire reposer dans son propre lit. Ramené par sa fatale étoile, Julien revient chez lui vers le point du jour (*fig.* 18); sans s'informer de ce qui s'y était passé pendant son absence, il monte dans son appartement pour embrasser son épouse, et s'approche doucement de la couche nuptiale à peine éclairée par la lueur incertaine du crépuscule. ... O douleur! ô cruelle méprise! il se croit trahi par un criminel adultère. Transporté de fureur, il ne délibère pas, tire sa funeste épée et fait, sans rompre le silence,[2] passer de leur paisible sommeil à celui de l'éternité les déplorables auteurs de ses jours. Aussitôt, désespéré, l'âme égarée, il s'enfuit avec horreur de sa propre demeure, dont à peine il a franchi le seuil, que sa chaste et douce épouse, revenant de la messe de l'aurore, se présente devant lui la sérénité sur le front (*fig.* 16). A cette apparition inattendue, les yeux de Julien sont dessillés; dans son trouble, dans son affreuse inquiétude, il demande, en frissonnant, le nom de ceux qu'il a surpris dans son lit, et la réponse qu'il reçoit achève de lui déchirer le cœur:

Dieu tout puissant, s'écrie-t-il, mes affreux destins sont donc accomplis! Adieu, ma chère soeur,[3] ajoute-t-il en embrassant tendrement son épouse après l'avoir instruite de son malheur, adieu, vivez heureuse, oubliez un misérable qui va dans le fond d'un désert s'imposer une pénitence dont il ne pourra proportionner la rigueur à l'énormité de son crime, mais qui, peut-être, lui en obtiendra le pardon de la miséricorde infinie. Ah! mon frère, répond la châtelaine fondant en larmes, pouvez-vous méconnaître à ce point le coeur de votre épouse, pouvez-vous le croire capable de vous abandonner lâchement sous le poids de vos maux? Oh! non, non, jamais! Eh bien, renoncez au monde, partez si vous le voulez; mais, après avoir partagé vos plaisirs, je m'attache à vos pas pour partager vos peines.[4]

Voilà donc les tristes époux en route (*fig.* 19). Au bout de quelques jours, ils atteignirent un lieu sauvage où coule une grande rivière célèbre par le nombre des victimes de son onde perfide. C'est là que Julien se consacre, en qualité de simple passager, à la sûreté des voyageurs et des pélerins;

---

2 *Silenter, extracto gladio, ambos pariter interemit.* Legenda aurea.
3 Façon de parler fort commune autrefois entre les époux de toutes les conditions.
4 Ce dialogue pathétique est traduit presque mot pour mot des légendaires.

c'est là que bientôt s'élève sur le rivage un petit hôpital où, nuit et jour, le charitable couple prodigue les plus tendres soins à l'humanité souffrante (*fig.* 20).

Au bout de quelques années écoulées de la sorte, dans le fort d'un rigoureux hiver et vers le milieu de la nuit, les deux époux entendirent la voix lamentable d'un homme qui, de la rive opposée, les appelait en gémissant (*fig.* 22). Dans cet instant, une effroyable tempête semblait confondre les élémens, et les vents furieux bouleversaient les flots du fleuve qui rugissait au sein des plus noires ténèbres. Que fera Julien? doit-il s'exposer pour un inconnu, pour un brigand, peut-être, à une mort presque certaine? Il ne balance point cependant, et sa femme elle-même approuvant son généreux dévoûment, le saint batelier se couvre à la hâte de ses vêtemens (*fig.* 24), s'élance dans sa barque, et, luttant avec succès contre les vents et les vagues, guidé par le fanal que tient son épouse restée sur le rivage (*fig.* 26), il accueille et conduit chez lui le pauvre étranger (*fig.* 25).[5] De quel pénible spectacle est témoin alors le couple hospitalier! L'inconnu, hideux rebut de la nature et de la société, est couvert d'une lèpre vive qui révolte horriblement l'odorat et la vue, et les membres glacés de ce malheureux ne peuvent recouvrer, par l'impression du feu le plus ardent, le mouvement et la vie; déjà son coeur ne bat plus; c'en est fait, il va mourir ...... O sainte, ô ingénieuse pitié! Que font les deux époux? S'aveuglant sur le terrible danger auquel ils s'exposent, ils étendent au milieu d'eux, dans leur propre lit, leur affreux hôte, et se pressent à ses côtés pour lui communiquer leur chaleur naturelle; enfin ils le voient avec transport revenir à la vie, et bientôt le sommeil et la paix planent sur la couche vénérable. Généreux martyrs de la charité, quel beau jour va luire sur vos têtes! Déjà ses premiers rayons pénètrent dans votre sainte et secourable demeure, et, vous éveillant l'un et l'autre, vous cherchez, saisis d'étonnement et de crainte, à reconnaître le misérable malade dans l'être surnaturel qui, resplendissant de lumière et de majesté, se montre à vos yeux éblouis. Mortels bienfaisans, n'en doutez point, vous le voyez encore cet objet de votre héroïque pitié,

---

5 Les nombreux individus qui composaient autrefois le corps de la *Ménestrandie*, prirent saint Julien-l'Hospitalier pour protecteur, probablement à cause des dangers auxquels les exposait, sur les chemins sans police des tems reculés de la monarchie, l'existence vagabonde attachée à leurs divers emplois. Ayant, en 1330, fait à Paris plusieurs fondations pieuses sous l'invocation de ce saint et celle de saint Genest, comédien, patron particulier des jongleurs, ils firent fabriquer un sceau de cuivre sur lequel on voyait Jésus-Christ, sous l'apparence d'un malade, dans un bateau dont une extrémité était occupée par saint Julien, faisant agir deux avirons, et l'autre par sa femme, tenant un aviron et une lanterne. Cette composition est beaucoup plus d'accord avec notre vitrail que Vincent de Beauvais et quelques hagiographes qui, d'après cet écrivain, peut-être, substituent, dans cette aventure nocturne, un ange à Jésus-Christ.

mais dans Jésus lui-même, dont la voix vous console, dont la main vous bénit (*fig.* 27). C'est ton Sauveur, ô Julien, qui, touché de tes longues douleurs, vient essuyer tes larmes, t'apporter le pardon de ton crime, et t'annoncer que tu dois, ainsi que ta vertueuse épouse, embrasser, dans le séjour de la gloire éternelle, tes bons et malheureux parens.

Aussitôt le divin fils de Marie disparut, et, peu de tems après, ses vertueux hôtes s'endormant de la mort des justes furent chercher dans son sein le bonheur dont ses paroles leur avaient donné l'assurance (*fig.* 31).[6]

Saint Julien-l'Hospitalier est un des bienheureux auxquels furent consacrées jadis les chapelles de la cathédrale, et l'examen des figures représentées dans les n°s. 1, 2 et 3 de cette verrière, nous la fait, ainsi que le poisson placé dans l'angle de la bordure, regarder comme un don fait à cette église, dans le XIIIe. siècle, par les bateliers-pêcheurs ou les marchands-poissonniers de Rouen. Nous hésitons d'autant moins à faire cet honneur à l'une ou à l'autre de ces corporations, dont les attributs nous paraissent clairement exprimés, que dans les cartouches inférieurs de la vitre voisine, représentant la vie de Joseph, on remarque des tondeurs de draps tenant leurs forces à la main, et une grande figure de cet instrument, emblême irrécusable de la profession des donateurs.

6 Nous n'avons pu nous rendre compte de plusieurs sujets de ce vitrail, notamment des deux scènes diaboliques comprises sous les n°s. 29 et 30, qui, sans doute, appartiennent à quelque légende qui nous est inconnue; mais elles ne pourraient apparemment rien ajouter à la physionomie dramatique de la vie de saint Julien, dont le peuple chante encore la complainte avec autant d'intérêt que de plaisir.

Au surplus, il serait possible de donner une description beaucoup plus complète de ces divers médaillons, au moyen de quelques recherches nouvelles; et surtout en recourant à la vie de saint Julien et de sa femme, sainte Basilisse, dans les *Acta Sanctorum, aut. Joann. Bollando*, tom. 1, p. 570-87. Nous nous bornerons à dire ici que le Diable, monté sur le lit des deux époux, n°. 28, semble exprimer les combats qu'ils eurent à soutenir contre le démon de la chair. C'est ce que témoigne clairement, par le passage suivant, lc légendaire précité: '*Beata vero Basilissa exultans in Domino dixit; gratias tibi Domine Jesu-Christe, qui pugnas carnales ita devicisti in nobis   insulto tibi serpens libidinis* (Metaph. *serpentis voluptas) quia vasa Deo dicata nullis artibus abdicasti. ... tu solus tuâ confusione uterè* (DIABOLO), p. 578, col. 2, n°. 14, h.l.'

The LaVallée Version of the Legend

Among the numerous works on hunting which Flaubert read and anno-
tated in preparation for writing his description of the young Julian's hunting was *La Chasse à tir* by Joseph LaVallée.[1] The book is a careful account
of this form of hunting, interspersed with a number of brief anecdotes intended to relieve the otherwise monotonous tone. One of these reports is
an otherwise unknown version of the Julian legend, which LaVallée, who
knew Spain well, heard there and recounted in his book as being of interest
to hunters. LaVallée's text bears certain resemblances to standard versions,
which is hardly surprising; but it departs from them in other and striking
ways. In addition, it contains a number of close parallels to Flaubert's own
account. Flaubert read LaVallée in early November, 1875, just before he
undertook to write his paragraphs on hunting; he had finished the entire
text of his story by 18 February, 1876, only three months later. Hence it
must have been clearly in his memory as he wrote. We give the text below,
with annotations to draw attention to the parallels.

Julien, fils d'un riche seigneur de la Calabre, préférait la chasse à tout autre
plaisir. Un jour qu'il avait lancé un cerf, et que déjà il le poursuivait depuis
longtemps, il vit tout à coup l'animal s'arrêter, se retourner vers lui, et il
l'entendit prononcer ces paroles: 'Julien! Julien! pourquoi me persécuter,
toi qui dois être le meurtrier de ton père et de ta mère?' Le jeune homme,
éffrayé, laissa fuir le cerf sans songer à le suivre davantage, puis, réfléchis-
sant à cette sinistre prédiction, il forma le projet de se soustraire par la
fuite au malheur dont il était menacé. Il quitta l'Italie sans instruire ses
parents du lieu où il se rendait. 'Ne prenez pas ma fuite pour un acte d'in-
gratitude, leur écrivait-il; il faut que je vous quitte, le ciel le veut; ne cherchez donc pas à découvrir ma retraite, car vos démarches seraient vaines.'

---

1   Joseph LaVallée, *La Chasse à tir*, 5th ed. (Paris: Hachette, 1873), pp. 254-7.

Il passa en Espagne, s'attacha à la fortune d'un prince de ce pays, et combattit pour la cause qu'il avait embrassée avec autant de vaillance que de bonheur: aussi bientôt eut-il mérité la faveur et l'amitié de celui qu'il servait. Parmi les dames de la cour se trouvait une cousine du prince, remarquable par ses grâces et ses vertus; Julien ne tarda pas à en devenir ardemment épris.[2] Il demanda, obtint sa main, et reçut pour dot un castel entouré de giboyeuses propriétés.[3] Il avait ainsi une femme jolie; il en était aimé, la chérissait, et en était même fort jaloux.[4] Il avait avec cela des terres fertiles; cependant il ne se serait pas tenu pour parfaitement heureux, s'il eût fallu qu'il renonçât à poursuivre le gibier dont ses domaines abondaient. Il passait quelquefois plusieurs jours et même plusieurs nuits de suite à la chasse. Un matin qu'il revenait avant le point du jour,[5] en entrant dans sa chambre, sur un meuble, près du lit, il aperçoit des vêtements d'homme;[6] il s'approche, et, sur l'oreiller, voit reposer deux têtes que les reflets mourants d'une lumière éloignée n'éclairaient qu'à peine;[7] alors, plein de furie,[8] et persuadé qu'un adultère a souillé sa couche, il frappe et donne à la fois deux morts.[9] Ensuite il veut fuir; mais, au moment où il allait sortir de sa maison,[10] il rencontre sa femme qui, radieuse, accourait au-devant de lui: 'Arrière! arrière! s'écriait-il en la voyant, âme en peine! ne m'approche pas, je te ferai dire des messes! ... *Retro, retro, Satanas!!*' Et il faisait le signe de la croix.

2 This is the only version with which we are familiar to give such strong emphasis to Julian's affection for his wife. It recurs in Flaubert, added to the story only after his return to Paris and his reading of LaVallée. Contrast B.N., N.A.F., 23,663, fol. 493 recto, which contains all the material written on the wife while Flaubert was still in Brittany: 'sa femme d'humeur gaie et enfantine,' and 'vains efforts de sa femme gentille [pour le consoler].'

3 Here, too, to our knowledge LaVallée is alone in suggesting this. It recurs in Flaubert, but in material which cannot be positively dated as before or after his return to Paris.

4 Jealousy is a fairly common note in other versions and may even occasion the parricide. See above, p. 13 and Appendix D, p. 171.

5 Flaubert will use the same moment.

6 Cf. Flaubert: 'Julien se prit les pieds dans des vêtements par terre. ...' (p. 110).

7 Like all the other versions, this one, too, must emphasize the dim light. Cf. our arguments in Chapter Seven, p. 75.

8 Cf. Flaubert of Julian at this moment: 'Eclatant d'une colère démesurée ...' (p. 111). The same note occurs in Brunet, Langlois, and Lecointre-Dupont: cf. Appendix A, p. 103, Appendix B, p. 148, and Appendix D, p. 171.

9 The single blow for the two murders is fairly common in other versions. See above, p. 25.

10 Here, as in the Rouen and Chartres windows, and in the *Legenda aurea* and Langlois, Julian's wife is away from the castle at the time of the murder. Only Lecointre-Dupont appears not to have her absent.

Mais elle, en lui jetant autour du cou ses jolis bras et en le couvrant de baisers, lui disait: 'Mon cher Julien, que tu vas être heureux! ton père, ta mère t'ont longtemps cherché, mais ils sont ici; je les ai reconnus tout d'abord; ton père te ressemble tant![11] J'ai voulu leur faire honneur, ils reposent dans notre chambre, dans notre lit, pendant que moi j'ai été prier; je viens de la chapelle, je viens de remercier le Seigneur.

– Grand Dieu! grand Dieu! s'écria Julien; mon père, ma mère!!! ... la voilà donc réalisée, cette exécrable prédiction! ...'

Puis il conta sa fatale méprise. ... 'Adieu, répéta-t-il à sa femme, je vais te quitter, je veux quitter le monde; il n'y a plus pour moi que douleur et remords.'

Mais elle répondit: 'Je ne te quitterai pas: j'ai partagé tes joies et ton amour; je veux partager tes jours de souffrance et de deuil.

– Non, non, disait-il, je dois faire pénitence et prier.'

Mais elle répondit: 'Je ferai pénitence comme toi, je prierai comme toi. ... pour toi. ... avec toi. ...'

Tous deux, après avoir vendu leurs biens, allèrent s'établir au bord d'un fleuve rapide, y construirent un hospice et consacrèrent leur vie à donner asile aux malheureux ou à passer d'un bord à l'autre les voyageurs qui voulaient traverser le fleuve. Sans doute Julien obtint la rémission de sa faute, car l'Eglise l'a rangé au nombre des saints.

Dans les aldées[12] de la Catalogne, on conserve pour saint Julien un culte tout particulier. Souvent, pendant l'hiver, lorsqu'au soir on fait cercle autour du *brasero*, les vieillards content à leurs fils les malheurs de saint Julien. Les peuples de la Sicile et de la Calabre ont aussi pour lui une vénération traditionnelle. Presque toujours ils le représentent vêtu en chasseur; mais quelquefois aussi on le peint en habit de noble guerrier, tenant la main appuyée sur une nacelle et ayant un cerf à côté de lui. On célèbre sa fête, en Espagne, le 9 janvier, et, en France, le 29 du même mois; il est vénéré sous le nom de saint Julien l'Hospitalier. Quant à sa femme, si belle, si tendre, si dévouée, elle était sainte aussi; mais la mémoire des hommes n'a pas conservé son nom.

---

11 Cf., much later in the story (pp. 117-18), a possible reminiscence when Julian observes his own face in the well and thinks it is his father's. We note this only because there is proof that Flaubert read the story close to the time of the redaction.

12 'Aldées' is somewhat improperly used here. Littré defines it: 'Terme de géographie. Sert à désigner les bourgs et les villages des possessions européennes en Afrique et dans les Indes.' LaVallée is presumably transliterating the Spanish *aldea*, 'village,' 'hamlet.' He had travelled extensively in Northern Spain, where he apparently heard the legend he reports here.

We suppose that LaVallée himself heard this version under circumstances similar to those he describes. Despite certain wordings, the account he gives is uncontaminated by written sources which LaVallée could easily have consulted: witness his obvious ignorance of the ending of the legend. Its fundamental outline is close enough to the major versions to make us suspect it is a truncated rather than an undeveloped account.[13] The wording of the stag's curse is no more than a translation of the form in the *Legenda aurea*. Julian's letter to his parents is, we presume, a relatively later addition. The tone of the phrasings describing the wife's seductiveness may have been heightened by LaVallée in retelling the legend for a nineteenth-century French audience, accustomed to such passages in its lighter readings.

13 Other Spanish versions, similarly truncated, from Salamanca and particularly from Catalonia are reported by Bonifacio de Echegaray, 'La Leyenda de San Julián el Hospitalario en romances castellanos,' *Bulletin hispanique*, 53 (1951), 13-33, esp. pp. 22 f. and 30. They also concur in having Julian born in Italy.

BIBLIOGRAPHY AND HISTORY
OF THE QUESTION

Bibliography and History of the Question

The Bibliography is divided into two sections. In Section A we give an abbreviated historical summary of the question of Flaubert's use of legendary sources in his *Saint Julien*. It lists in numbered chronological sequence all the materials from ca. 1100 to the present which are referred to in the text and which relate directly to the question: stained glass (and descriptions of stained glass), manuscripts, catalogues of manuscripts and editions of manuscripts, and books and articles discussing the various forms of the Julian legend. The list begins with the most important medieval materials concerning Saint Julian and continues with the later publications of these materials and studies on them; in addition, after the publication of Flaubert's *Légende de Saint Julien* in 1877, the list also includes all items containing significant treatments of Flaubert's use of the legendary materials and, finally, works of scholarship discussing the various forms of the Julian legend.

Section B completes the Bibliography by listing alphabetically all other works cited.

SECTION A
A CRITICAL LIST OF MATERIALS RELATING TO
SAINT JULIAN AND FLAUBERT'S *LÉGENDE*

The Julian legend comes into existence in the twelfth century, or earlier, with the circulation of oral and perhaps unrecovered written materials of semi-literary character. The earliest known written materials, from late in the twelfth century, refer to the saint as intercessor for a night's lodging. After 1200 the developments of the legend which lead to Flaubert follow three paths, represented today by three related but distinguishable traditions: (1) the Rouen and Chartres windows; (2) the Old French Prose Life; and (3) the Latin *vita* and translations of it into French.

1 Probably during the first half of the thirteenth century, related but not identical windows at Notre-Dame de Chartres and at Notre-Dame de Rouen, both in the north deambulatories, recounting the life of Saint Julian. They display in their approximately common programs a version of the legend in some ways unique among those currently known (e.g., a premonitory dream rather than the stag's prediction; episodes from Julian's childhood and from the period after the ferrying of the 'guest'). The 'guest' is Christ; he appears not to be a leper.

2 The Old French Prose Life (undated; late twelfth or early thirteenth century).

A version of some twelve to fifteen folios (when copied, as it usually is, in double columns). There are many episodes; the 'guest' is Christ in most copies, but not in all. It is represented today by a number of known manuscripts, of which only two are of interest to the present study:

2a Bibliothèque Municipale of Alençon, Ms. 27 (fourteenth century?). The manuscript used as a source in the nineteenth century by Lecointre-Dupont for his retelling of the life of Saint Julian (No. 7). The manuscript lacks its final leaf, in which the identity of the 'guest' – Christ or an angel – would have been revealed. Flaubert knew Lecointre-Dupont's account of Julian's life based on this manuscript. In Appendix B we reproduce the text of the manuscript.

2b Paris, Bibliothèque Nationale, Ms. Fr. 6447 (fourteenth century?). Another copy, very similar to No. 2a, but complete. It has been seen as a direct source for Flaubert, a claim we doubt (See, below, Nos. 24, 26, 29, and 32, and above, Chapter Seven). It was reproduced by Rudolf Tobler in 1901 (No. 15). The 'guest' happens to be Christ.

There is also a similar but not identical version of the Life in octosyllabic verse, which we treat briefly in Appendix B but which does not concern us directly here.

3 The Latin *Vita.*

This much shorter version, in which the 'guest' is a messenger angel, occurs in several places, notably in Vincent of Beauvais (before 1248), Saint Antoninus, and the *Acta Sanctorum*, as well as in the *Legenda aurea*, the form specifically used by Flaubert, which we follow and which we reproduce in Appendix A.

3a Jacobus da Varagine. *Legenda aurea* (ca. 1260-1270). We cite the text of Graesse (2nd ed., Leipzig, 1850), generally held to be the most authoritative, as we know no way to determine what edition or editions may have been used by Langlois (No. 6) and Lecointre-Dupont

(No. 7); Flaubert owned and presumably used the French translation by Brunet (No. 10). Saint Julian appears under the date of January 27.

3b *Acta sanctorum* [ed. J. Bollandus, G. Henschenius, *et al.*] *januarii tomus secundus*. Antwerp: Joannes Meursium, 1643. [This ed. reached the end of October with its 59th vol. in 1884.]

The standard Latin life occurs, with a few variations, on page 974. It is styled *vita ex Sancto Antonino*, but the Bollandists also knew the versions given by the *Legenda aurea*, Vincent de Beauvais, and Petrus de Natalibus. The history of the *Acta sanctorum* is quite complex; the other principal editions are the eighteenth century one done in Venice, which reaches mid-September in 41 vols., and the Carnandet re-edition in the nineteenth (Paris: Palmé, 1863-1925, in 67 vols.).

4 Various eighteenth- and nineteenth-century catalogues of parts of the collection of French manuscripts in the Cabinet (Département) des Manuscrits of the Bibliothèque Nationale, Paris.

The manuscripts mentioned in Appendix B were in large part catalogued by Flaubert's time, although the catalogues which mention them are often no more than simple lists giving no details about the manuscript's content (Paulin Paris's *Manuscrits françois de la Bibliothèque du roi*, a printed description of most of the manuscripts through B.N. Fr. 993, formerly 7310, is a qualified exception) and are also inaccurate at times. The principal handwritten catalogue which Flaubert might have been advised to use is the so-called 'Catalogue Vert' of the *Ancien supplément français* (i.e. of those mss. now, as in Flaubert's time, numbered 6171-15369 of the Fonds Français), a somewhat confused and quite summary subject list presently classified as N.A. Fr. 5560-93. The standard catalogue of the Ancien Fonds Français (now Fr. 1-6170) had begun to appear in 1868, but was not finished until 1902 (*Catalogue des manuscrits français. Ancien fonds.* 5 vol. Paris: Firmin-Didot). Only the first volume was available to Flaubert, but it gives a very clear reference to the isolated Prose Life of Saint Julian in Fr. 1546, the only copy found outside the legendaries, on its page 247. Of course, Julian is called Saint Julian of Brioude in the reference, because the Prose Life contains that confusion.

Paulin Paris's *Manuscrits françois* (7 vol., Paris: Techener, 1836-48) gives a considerable amount of detail about many manuscripts of the Ancien Fonds, and although it slights the *légendiers* in general, it refers us to at least one which gives the Prose Life (the present Fr. 987, formerly 7306$^{3.3}$, which Paris lists under the number 7306^3 in his table of saints' names, volume 7). The whole situation is complicated by the multiplicity of names under which our saint was known in the Middle

Ages; but a diligent seeker surely could have found Fr. 987 at least, and possibly also Fr. 183 and 185 (then numbered respectively 6845 and 6843[4,4]), especially since the latter *légendiers* were mistakenly thought to be French translations of the *Legenda aurea*, a title which would surely have caught Flaubert's eye. We give in Chapter Seven our reasons for thinking that, even if he did come to be aware of one of the copies of the Prose Life in the Bibliothèque Nationale, Flaubert did not use it.

5 [Ginguené, Pierre-Louis.] 'Autres auteurs anonymes en prose et en vers.' *Histoire littéraire de la France*, 15. Paris: Didot; Treuttel et Wurtz, 1820; rpt. Paris: Palmé, 1865, pp. 483-5. The pagination is the same in both editions.

   Mentions and describes a manuscript seen apparently at the abbey of Marmoutiers before the Revolution (presumably Tours, Bibliothèque Municipale 1015, but ill-described) and transcribes the first sentences of the standard Prose Life from it, with a few remarks. Probably the earliest mention of the Prose Life, but a most unlikely source for Flaubert's (or Lecointre-Dupont's) knowledge of the Prose Life's existence: Ginguené names no Paris mss., only the one at Marmoutiers, and does not seem to know what had become even of that one.

6 Langlois, Eustache-Hyacinthe, *Essai historique et descriptif sur la peinture sur verre ancienne et moderne* ... Rouen: Edouard Frère, 1832.

   Written by an old friend of the Flaubert family, this volume includes an account of the Julian window at Rouen, enriched with many elements from the *Legenda aurea*. The 'guest' is Christ in Langlois as in the window. The drawing of the window by Langlois's daughter is the prime visual source for Flaubert. We reproduce Langlois's text in Appendix D, and Mlle Langlois's drawing as our frontispiece. The pages on the Julian Window had already appeared in Langlois's *Mémoire sur la peinture sur verre et sur quelque vitraux remarquables des églises de Rouen* (Rouen: F. Baudry, 1823).

7 Lecointre-Dupont, G.-F.-G. 'La Légende de Saint-Julien le Pauvre, d'après un manuscrit de la Bibliothèque d'Alençon.' *Mémoires de la Société des Antiquaires de l'Ouest*, 1838 (published at Poitiers, 1839); also published separately as a brochure of 24 pages (Poitiers: Saurin, 1839) with line-drawings taken from Langlois (No. 6).

   Referred to in a footnote in Maury's *Légendes pieuses du Moyen-Age* (No. 9), which is where Flaubert probably learned of this study. It provides a romanticized version of the Old French Prose Life based on the

Alençon manuscript (No. 2a). Lecointre-Dupont borrows from Langlois (No. 6) to complete the missing end of the manuscript. Thus, in
his version the 'guest' is Christ. We reproduce Lecointre-Dupont's text
and that of his manuscript in Appendix B.

8 Hugo, Victor. 'Légende du beau Pécopin et de la belle Bauldour.' *Le
Rhin: Lettres à un ami.* Paris: Imprimerie Nationale, Librairie Ollen-
dorff, 1906. Lettre XXI, pp. 185-228.

A fantastic tale (first published in 1842) whose hero, Pécopin,
accomplishes two symmetrical hunts, as Julian does. Flaubert refers to
a re-reading of this work in 1856, when he was working on his first
plan for the *Saint Julien.* See Chapter Seven, D: The Problem of Structure.

9 Maury, L.-F.-Alfred. *Essai sur les légendes pieuses du Moyen-Age.*
Paris: Ladrange, 1843.

Written by an old acquaintance of Flaubert's, this study contains a
footnote reference to Lecointre-Dupont (No. 7) on page 72, in connection with Maury's brief discussion of Saint Julian. Flaubert owned this
book and used it during the redaction of his Tale: See pp. 57-58.

10 Brunet, Gustave, translator: Jacques de Voragine, *Légende dorée*
(No. 3a). Paris: Gosselin, 1843.

Flaubert seems to have owned a copy of this work: see Appendix A.
We reproduce the section on Saint Julian in Appendix A.

11 LaVallée, Joseph. *La Chasse à tir.* 5th ed. Paris: Hachette, 1873.

Flaubert consulted this work as part of his documentation concerning hunting upon his return to Paris in November, 1875. See, e.g., B.N.
N.A.F. 23663, fol. 487 recto, where LaVallée's name occurs. This
book contains a brief report of an incomplete legend of Saint Julian
which the author heard in Spain. Flaubert appears to have used some
details from it. We reproduce it in Appendix E.

12 Flaubert, Gustave. 'La Légende de Saint Julien l'Hospitalier,' in *Trois
Contes.* Paris: Charpentier, 1877.

Flaubert began work on his Tale in 1856. Some, perhaps all, of the
notes he made on his readings at this time are in the Bibliothèque
Nationale in Paris: N.A.F. 23663. In the same volume are bound his
plans, scenarios, drafts, and autograph manuscript of the *Légende*, as
well as the copyist's manuscript and further notes from his readings, all
drafted in 1875-1876. Flaubert's autograph material may be distin-

guished as to date by the obvious change in the handwriting from 1856 to 1875. The Bibliothèque historique de la Ville de Paris possesses further notes Flaubert made on readings at this time (*Carnets de lecture de Flaubert*, No. 17; see p. 52, n1 for our dating these from 1875 and not 1874). These, and the notes at the Bibliothèque Nationale, are the only ones now known to exist: they are probably all, or nearly all, he actually made. There are no known notes concerning the history and the older forms of the Julian legend.

13 Schwob, Marcel. 'Préface' to *La Légende de Saint Julien l'Hospitalier.* Paris: Ferroud, 1895. Reprinted widely, e.g., in *Spicilège* (Paris: Mercure de France, 1896).

An account of the background of Saint Julian in folklore and legend.

14 Tobler, Adolf. 'Zur Legende vom heiligen Julianus.' *Archiv für das Studium der Neueren Sprachen* [*und Literaturen*].

In four parts: I, vol. 100 (1898), 293-310 (discusses the *Legenda aurea* and the Spanish *Animal profeta*); II and III, vol. 101 (N.S., vol. I, 1898), 99-110, 339-364 (discusses Flaubert and analyzes the Verse Life of Julian found in the Arsenal manuscript); IV, vol. 102 (1899), 109-178 (edits the Verse Life).

15 Tobler, Rudolf. 'Die Prosafassung der Legende vom heiligen Julianus.' *Archiv für das Studium der Neueren Sprachen* [*und Literaturen*], 106 (1901), 294-323, and 107 (1901), 79-102.

Edition of the Prose Life (No. 2) in diplomatic style (i.e., in this case, without punctuation, and with abbreviations indicated) according to Ms. B.N. Fr. 6447, but with occasional corrections from a few other manuscripts. This edition, which is rather difficult to read, was the only text apparently available to Smith (No. 24); thus the coincidence of Tobler's having used B.N. Fr. 6447 (which is probably not the best ms.) has led to an irrelevant insistence upon the importance of that particular copy.

16 Meyer, Paul. 'Légendes hagiographiques en français.' *Histoire littéraire de la France*, 33, Paris: Imprimerie Nationale, 1906, 328-458.

Still the standard study on the *légendiers* and the Lives in prose and verse which were copied into these collections. Mentions the life of Saint Julian Hospitator in particular on pp. 360, 379 (without justifying his opinion on the priority of the Verse Life), 387-88, 403, 405.

17 Gossez, A.-M. *Le Saint-Julien de Flaubert.* Lille: Le Beffroi, 1903.

A general study of the Tale, filled with carelessness in the use of data from all periods of Flaubert's life with no indications that some of the quoted material was written decades away from the redaction of the Tale and in quite other contexts. He gives the primacy as a source for the Tale to the Rouen window and to Mlle Langlois's drawing of it, but he is aware that Langlois's explanation of the scenes in the window leaves much to be desired. His own is, unfortunately, no less imaginative. In addition, though without offering any proofs, he states that 'Flaubert consulte tous les hagiographes,' but Gossez gives first place to the *Acta sanctorum* which Flaubert probably never used. He also notes a statue at Caudebec as a possible source (See Raitt, No. 32, for a discussion of the matter).

18 Descharmes, René. '*Saint-Julien l'Hospitalier* et *Pécopin.*' *Revue biblio-iconographique*, Troisième Série, 12 (1905), 1-7, 67-75.
  This study, rarely cited, points out an important source for the *Légende*, Hugo's 'Légende du beau Pécopin et de la belle Bauldour' (No. 8). We discuss the *Pécopin* in detail in Chapter VII, Section D; it may well have furnished Flaubert the notion of the symmetrical but dissimilar hunts, which Vinaver (Nos. 37-8) considers essential to the Tale, but which do not occur in the Prose Life.

19 Huet, Gédéon. 'Saint-Julien l'Hospitalier: Légendes et sources,' *Mercure de France*, No. 385, Tome 105 (1 Juillet 1913), 44-59.
  Studies the background in legend of the Julian story. Huet mistakenly believed that Flaubert knew the Old French Prose Life through the study of Langlois (No. 6), whom – again erroneously – Huet believed to have known it directly. See above, pp. 32-33, for a discussion of these errors. Huet gives a résumé of the Old French Prose Life following the versions published by the two Toblers (Nos. 14 and 15). He also studies other related legends and the general background of the Julian legend in fable and folklore: some of his conclusions seem exaggerated today. He also relates the themes and personages to the narrative tradition in France and proposes, no doubt correctly, that the legend developed around a saint invoked by travellers. Huet knew no versions prior to 1200. In general he shows a wise refusal to conclude in the presence of uncertain data, which would have earned him the gratitude of Flaubert, and gains him ours.

20 Giraud, Jean. 'La Genèse d'un chef-d'oeuvre: "La Légende de Saint-Julien l'Hospitalier,"' *Revue d'histoire littéraire de la France*, 26 (1919), 87-93.

Giraud points to Langlois (No. 6) and is the first to identify Lecointre-Dupont (No. 7) as an important source. He suggests that Flaubert could have come to know Lecointre-Dupont's work through Maury, who was an old friend. Maury could simply have told him of Lecointre-Dupont; or Flaubert could have found the appropriate reference in Maury's *Légendes pieuses du Moyen-Age* (No. 9). We suggest, pp. 57-58, why the latter seems to us the more probable.

21 Oberziner, Marcella. 'La Leggenda di S. Giuliano il parricida,' *Atti del Reale Istituto Veneto di Scienza, Lettere ed Arti*, 93, Part 2 (1933-34), 254-309.

A good review of the development of the legend, with particular emphasis on Italy. To be completed by Gaiffier (No. 25).

22 Jasinski, René. 'Sur le *Saint-Julien l'Hospitalier* de Flaubert,' *Revue d'histoire de la philosophie et d'histoire générale de la civilisation*, 3 (1935), 156-72.

Using Giraud (No. 20) as a starting point, Jasinski examines all possible parallel passages in Lecointre-Dupont. He is to be used here only with caution. And we are unconvinced that the *récit* he quotes, by 'lord Wigmore,' is indeed a source in any meaningful sense of the term. See p. 54, Note 6, for a discussion of the matter.

23 Pauphilet, Albert. *Flaubert et La Légende de Saint-Julien l'Hospitalier.* Cours de Sorbonne (Paris: Centre de Documentation, 1935).

An interesting contribution to the general study of the Tale, but which adds nothing new in the area of legendary sources; particularly it makes no mention of the Prose Life.

24 Smith, Sheila M. 'Les Sources de la *Légende de saint Julien l'Hospitalier* de Flaubert.' Unpublished MA thesis, University of Manchester, 1944.

Disregarding the hypotheses of Giraud and Jasinski (Nos. 20 and 22), Miss Smith compares Flaubert's Tale to the Old French prose version, and particularly B.N. Fr. 6447 (No. 2a), as printed by Tobler (No. 15), and comes to the conclusion that Flaubert must have read it, even misread it in certain places (see our Chapter Seven). She may well have learned of the existence of the Prose Life from an error of Huet's (No. 19). Her work is the source for Nos. 26 and 29, so far as we know, and thus it marks the beginning of the lengthy controversy over B.N. Fr. 6447 as a source for Flaubert.

25 de Gaiffier, *le père* Baudouin. 'La Légende de S. Julien l'Hospitalier,' *Analecta Bollandiana*, 63 (1945), 145-219.

The most comprehensive study of the legend of Saint Julian to have come to our attention. Completes and corrects Oberziner (No. 21).

26 Vinaver, Eugène. 'Flaubert and the Legend of Saint Julian,' *Bulletin of the John Rylands Library* [University of Manchester], 36 (1953-1954), 228-44.

Adopting the Smith thesis (No. 24), Vinaver urges B.N. Fr. 6447 as the crucial source for Flaubert. This was the first publication to bring Miss Smith's MA thesis to general attention, so far as we know. Vinaver rejects Lecointre-Dupont (No. 7) as a source and fails to mention Giraud (No. 20) and Jasinski (No. 22).

27 Burns, C.A. 'The Manuscripts of Flaubert's *Trois Contes*,' *French Studies*, 8 (1954), 297-325.

Though excellent in many regards, this study attempts in too hasty fashion to make sense out of the extremely jumbled drafts and plans for *Saint-Julien*. In particular Burns failed to realize that Flaubert prepared his fair copy as he went along in his redaction. Since Burns states that there does appear to be a fair copy made only after the redaction of the entire Tale, other scholars were led to infer that Flaubert had left Concarneau before he began the final redaction and hence could readily have consulted Lecointre-Dupont (No. 7) and B.N. Fr. 6447 (No. 2b) in time for them to affect the final form of the entire redaction. We suggest, pp. 55-56, why this is impossible.

28 Cigada, Sergio. 'L'Episodio del lebbroso in *Saint Julien L'Hospitalier*,' *Aevum*, 31 (1957), 465-91.

In the course of this excellent study of a particular episode, Cigada also took occasion to reject the Smith-Vinaver thesis (Nos. 24 and 26). This was, to our knowledge, the first time the thesis was challenged; it was, unfortunately, done only in passing.

29 Duckworth, Colin, editor: Flaubert, *Trois Contes.* London: Harrap, 1959.

A textbook intended for, and widely used by, students of French literature. This edition gave wide general currency to the Smith-Vinaver thesis (Nos. 24 and 26), for the Introduction and Notes assume Flaubert's contact with B.N. Fr. 6447 (No. 2a). See our Chapter Seven.

30 Baldick, Robert, translator: Flaubert, *Three Tales.* London: Penguin, 1961.

Baldick provides an Introduction, Notes, and Commentary based in part on the Smith-Vinaver thesis (Nos. 24 and 26) as articulated by Duckworth (No. 29). See our Chapter Seven.

31 Cigada, Sergio. Review of Colin Duckworth, editor: Flaubert, *Trois Contes* (No. 29) in *Studi francesi*, 22 (1964), 177.

Disputes the Smith-Vinaver thesis (Nos. 24 and 26) adopted by Duckworth, on the grounds that Flaubert lacked the skills requisite to reading B.N. Fr. 6447 (No. 2a).

32 Raitt, A.W. 'The Composition of Flaubert's *Saint Julien l'Hospitalier*,' *French Studies*, 19 (1965), 358-72.

A full, detailed, and careful examination and refutation of the Smith-Vinaver thesis (Nos. 24 and 26) as articulated by Duckworth (No. 29). Raitt proposes, soundly we believe, a return to Langlois (No. 6) and Lecointre-Dupont (No. 7) as the principal sources, to the exclusion of B.N. Fr. 6447 (No. 2a). Raitt suggests Flaubert read Lecointre-Dupont in 1856; we have indicated our position on pp. 52-59. He also points to Du Camp's account of Flaubert's first idea of writing the story at Caudebec and provides a careful examination of the data; he prefers to refer instead to a prior visit to Caudebec with Langlois, in 1835. Raitt, who had not personally examined the documents involved, was incorrectly informed that none of Flaubert's notes from 1856 survive: they are in the Bibliothèque Nationale and will be discussed in Bart's edition of the *Saint Julien*, currently in preparation (see also No. 12). Similarly, the notes he assigns to 1874 are in fact from 1875 (see above, p. 52, note 1). Finally, we doubt his hypothesis that Lecointre-Dupont is the source for the sadism in the Tale as told by Flaubert (see above, pp. 53-54).

33 Fletcher, John. *A Critical Commentary on Flaubert's 'Trois Contes.'* London: Macmillan, New York: St. Martin's Press, 1968.

Written after Raitt's refutation (No. 32) of Duckworth, but before Duckworth's reply (No. 34), this study accepts the former: 'A.W. Raitt's article, especially p. 360, probably settles an argument that Dr Duckworth conducts at some length in his edition. Flaubert did not consult a Bibliothèque Nationale manuscript of the medieval prose tale, but Lecointre-Dupont. ...' (p. 55, footnote 1).

34 Duckworth, Colin. 'Flaubert and the Legend of Saint Julian: A Non-exclusive View of the Sources,' *French Studies*, 22 (1968), 107-13.

An effort to meet Raitt's arguments against B.N. Fr. 6447 (No. 2a) as Flaubert's source (No. 32). Duckworth acknowledges the role of Lecointre-Dupont (No. 7) but suggests B.N. Fr. 6447 is still involved in a few specific cases. See our Chapter Seven, Section B.

35 Duckworth, Colin, editor: Flaubert, *Trois Contes.* London: Harrap, 1969.

A revision of Duckworth's earlier student edition of the Tale, of 1959 (No. 29). While taking some account of Raitt's arguments (No. 32) against the use of B.N. Fr. 6447 (No. 2a), this edition maintains the original stand for the most part, no doubt because of the great expense involved in changing so many of the notes.

36 McCrady, James W. 'The Saint Julian Window in Rouen as a Source for Flaubert's *Légende de Saint Julien l'Hospitalier*,' *Romance Notes*, 10 (1968-69), 268-76.

Correctly sees the window as an important source, but holds that Flaubert's structuring of the story is based upon it. We find the latter claim exaggerated. See our Appendix C, note 9.

37 Vinaver, Eugène. 'La Légende de saint Julien l'Hospitalier et le pro-blème du roman,' *Bulletin de l'Académie Royale de langue et littérature françaises* [Brussels], 48 (1970), 107-22. Reprinted Brussels: Palais des Academies, 1970, repaginated.

A paper read before the Academy in September, 1970. Repeats the Smith-Vinaver thesis (Nos. 24 and 26), rejects Raitt (No. 32) without reference to Duckworth (Nos. 34 and 35). Attempts to discuss the in-spiration Flaubert drew from B.N. Fr. 6447 (No. 2a). A very valuable study, despite our disagreements on this score. See our Chapter Seven.

38 - *The Rise of Romance.* New York and Oxford: Oxford University Press, 1971.

Presents the material of No. 37 in the context of a general discussion of the role of pure form, of 'poetic coherence,' in literary creation throughout the ages. One can only concur in the remark that Flaubert's Julian tale has narrative coherence thanks to the parallels between Jul-ian's first hunt and his second; it is rather more difficult to agree that psychology does not have equal importance in the creation of the Tale and its unfolding. And we repeat that we find the Old French Prose Life (No. 2a) irrelevant to the study of Flaubert, except to the extent that his known sources reflect it (see our Chapter Seven).

39 Daniels, Douglas J. 'A Structural Analysis of Three Narrative Works of Gustave Flaubert.' Unpublished doctoral dissertation, The University of Minnesota, 1972.

On pp. 169-99, Dr Daniels examines certain problems of the filiation from the *Legenda aurea* to Langlois and Lecointre-Dupont and on to

Flaubert. Daniels uses a structuralist approach and has other interests than ours. Nevertheless, his conclusions concerning the filiation concord with ours.

40 Dakyns, Janine R. *The Middle Ages in French Literature, 1851-1900.* Oxford University Press, 1973.
   This Oxford doctoral thesis, for which A.W. Raitt was an examiner and which appears in the Oxford Modern Languages and Literatures Monograph series of which Raitt is an editor, repeats Raitt's rejection of the Prose Life hypothesis (No. 32). We note also that Dakyns sees autobiographical tendencies in Julian's character: 'Julian is clearly Flaubert, ... in a large measure ... his suffering is unmistakably Flaubertian' (cf. our Chapter Two). She is also aware of the desire for particularized detail as a Romantic trait, and mentions both *Pécopin* and *Notre-Dame de Paris* as precursors of Flaubert's work. See esp. pp. 186-91, 179.

41 Flaubert, Gustave. *La Première Education sentimentale et les Carnets de lecture.* Paris: Club de l'Honnête Homme, 1973.
   Reprints (pp. 401-06) the pages of Carnet 17 (Bibliothèque historique de la Ville de Paris) containing some of Flaubert's notes on his readings for the *Saint Julien.* The transcriptions are in general accurate, though omissions are not always indicated. Bart hopes to reprint these more fully in his forthcoming edition of the *Légende.*

42 Swan, Carolyn T. 'The Old French Prose Legend of Saint Julian the Hospitaller.' Unpublished doctoral dissertation, Northwestern University, 1973.
   After submission of our manuscript, but before going to press, this 112-page dissertation (done under the direction of Professor Vinaver) became available, and we were able to consult it on microfilm. It is an edition of the Prose Life based on the Alençon manuscript, but with numerous editorial changes, including additional material from manuscripts Lecointre-Dupont (No. 7) did not know. A brief introduction covers the history of the legend. Unlike Dr Swan, we think Julian Hospitator was always distinct from homonymic saints such as Julian of Antioch or Julian of Brioude, with whose legends his does not seem to share any important features. Swan's reading of the thirteenth-century windows does not match ours. Postulation of a single verse source for the Prose and Verse Lives, while ingenious, does not seem to us to resolve the problem of their relationship beyond any possible doubt.

43 Flaubert, Gustave. *La Tentation de saint Antoine. Trois Contes.* Paris: Club de l'Honnête Homme, 1974.

Gives the standard text and appropriate introductory material on the redaction of the Legend. On pp. 472-78, this edition provides selections from the plans, scenarios, and drafts. The transcriptions, though sometimes incomplete, are in general accurate. 'Scenarios' and 'drafts' are perhaps not so clearly distinguishable as this edition suggests. On pp. 609-10, the editors report briefly on Flaubert's notes on his readings preserved at the B.N. (N.A.F. 23663): see our No. 12. The transcriptions do not take account of the change in handwriting and hence do not note the dates at which the notes were taken.

44 Bart, Benjamin F., and Robert Francis Cook, '*D'où vient Saint Julien?*' in *Colloque de Londres, Canada (1973). (The Department of French, The University of Western Ontario). Langages de Flaubert.* Paris: Minard, 1977, pp. 77-94.
   A presentation of our central thesis.

45 - 'Flaubert's *Légende de Saint Julien l'Hospitalier: Légende* or *Conte?*' *University of South Carolina French Literature Series, II: The French Short Story*, pp. 189-94. Columbia, S.C.: University of South Carolina, 1975.
   Examines, in the terms used in the present work, the ways in which the re-telling of a legend may and may not be thought of as generically related to the *conte.*

46 Bart, Benjamin F., 'Flaubert and Hunting: *La Légende de St-Julien L'Hospitalier,*' *Nineteenth-Century French Studies*, 4 (1975-76), 31-52.
   In the course of an examination of the hunting sources Flaubert used, this article incidentally provides some of the evidence that Flaubert read (or reread) all the books he used for the Tale in the winter of 1875-76.

SECTION B
LIST OF ADDITIONAL WORKS CITED

Arnoldi, Francesco Negri. 'Elisabetta d'Ungheria, langravia di Turingia.' *Bibliotheca Sanctorum*. Rome: Istituto Giov. XXIII della Pontif. Univ. Lateranense, 1964. IV, cols. 1110-23.
Baring-Gould, S. *The Lives of the Saints.* 2d rev. ed. Edinburgh: John Grant, 1914.
Bart, Benjamin F. *Flaubert.* Syracuse, NY: Syracuse University Press, 1967.
- 'Flaubert's Concept of the Novel.' *PMLA*, 80 (1965), 84-9.
- 'Psyche into Myth: Humanity and Animality in Flaubert's *Saint-Julien.*' *Kentucky Romance Quarterly*, 20 (1973), 317-42.

Cigada, Sergio. 'L'Episodio del lebbroso in *Saint-Julien l'Hospitalier* di Flaubert.' *Aevum*, 31 (1957), 465-91.

– 'La "Leggenda aurea" di Jacopo da Varagine e le "Tentation de Saint Antoine" di Flaubert.' *Contributi del Seminario di Filologia moderna*, I, 278-95, in *Pubblicazioni dell'Università cattolica di Sacro Cuore*, Nuova Serie, Vol. LXXII (Milan: Società editrice 'Vita e Pensiero,' n.d.).

Cook, Robert Francis, and Larry Stuart Crist. *Le Deuxième Cycle de la Croisade*. Geneva: Droz, 1972.

Crist, Larry S. 'The Legendary Crucifixion of Jehan Tristan.' *Romania*, 86 (1965), 289-306.

Delaporte, Yves. *Les Vitraux de la Cathédrale de Chartres*. Chartres: Houvet, 1926.

Delehaye, Hippolyte. *Les Légendes hagiographiques*. 4th ed. Brussels: Société des Bollandistes, 1955.

Delisle, Léopold. *Le Cabinet des Manuscrits de la Bibliothèque Impériale [Nationale]*. 4 vol. Paris: Imprimerie Impériale [Nationale], 1868-81.

Dickson, Arthur. *Valentine and Orson: A Study in Late Medieval Romance*. New York: Columbia University Press, 1929.

Durry, Marie-Jeanne. *Flaubert et ses projets inédits*. Paris: Nizet, [1950].

Flutre, L.-F. *Table des noms propres ... dans les romans du Moyen Age*. Poitiers: C.E.S.C.M., 1962.

– 'La Partie d'échecs de *Dieudonné de Hongrie*.' *Mélanges offerts à Rita Lejeune*. Gembloux: Duculot, 1969. II, 757-68.

Frappier, Jean. *Les Chansons de geste du Cycle de Guillaume d'Orange*. 2 vol. Paris: S.E.D.E.S., 1955-65.

Goncourt, Jules and Edmond. *Journal*. Ed. Robert Ricatte. Monaco: Imprimerie Nationale, 1956.

Hélin, Maurice. *A History of Medieval Latin Literature*. Tr. Jean Chapman Snow. New York: William Salloch, 1949.

Hollister, C. Warren. 'The Strange Death of William Rufus.' *Speculum*, 48 (1973), 637-53.

Jaufré, ed. Clovis Brunel. Paris: S.A.T.F., 1943.

Karr, Alphonse. *Contes et Nouvelles*. Paris: Lecour, 1852.

Langlois, Ernest. *Table des noms propres ... dans les chansons de geste*. Paris: E. Bouillon, 1904.

Loisel, Armand. *La Cathédrale de Rouen*. 'Petites Monographies des grande édifices de la France.' Paris: Laurens, [1913].

McCrady, James W. 'The Saint Julien Window at Rouen as a Source for Flaubert's *Légende de Saint Julien l'Hospitalier*.' *Romance Notes*, 10 (1968-69), 268-76.

Nagy, Maria von, and N. Cristoph de Nagy. *Die Legenda aurea und ihr Verfasser Jacobus de Voragine*. Berlin, Munich: Francke, 1971.

Omont, Henri. *Bibliothèque Nationale: Catalogue général des Mss. français. Nouvelles Acquisitions françaises.* Vol. II (nos. 3061-6500). Paris: Ernest Leroux, 1900.

—*Catalogue général des Mss. des bibliothèques publiques de France. Départements.* Vol. II. Paris: Plon, 1888.

Propp, Vladimir. *Morphologie du Conte.* Trans. by Marguerite Derrida, Tsvetan Todorov, and Claude Kahn. Paris: Poétique/Seuil, 1970.

Renart, Jean. *Le Roman de la Rose ou de Guillaume de Dôle.* Ed. Félix Lecoy. Paris: Champion, 1969.

Wyzéwa, Téodor de, tr. Jacques de Voragine: *La Légende dorée.* Paris: Albin Michel, 1929.

Index

The reader is referred to the Bibliography and History of the Question (pp. 181-95) for the names of scholars who have treated the history of the Legend of Saint Julian, together with their contributions to the subject, in chronological order.

UNIVERSITY OF TORONTO ROMANCE SERIES